REKINDLING DEVELOPMENT

MULTINATIONAL MANAGERS AND
DEVELOPING COUNTRY CONCERNS

Lee A. Tavis, series editor

*Multinational Managers and Host
Government Interactions,* 1988

*Multinational Managers and Poverty
in the Third World,* 1982

ϒ

Rekindling Development:

Multinational Firms and World Debt

Lee A. Tavis, Editor

University of Notre Dame Press
Notre Dame, Indiana

Library of Congress Cataloging-in-Publication Data

Rekindling development.

(Multinational managers and developing
country concerns)
Papers from a symposium at the University
of Notre Dame held in Sept. 1986.
1. International business enterprises—
Developing countries—Congresses. 2. Debts,
External—Developing countries—Congresses.
3. Economic development—Congresses.
4. International economic relations—
Congresses. I. Tavis, Lee A. II. Series.
HD2932.R45 1988   338.8'881724   87-40619
ISBN 0-268-01634-8

TO THERESE AND TAMI

Contents

Foreword

This volume presents the issue of what to do about the immense debt overhang in the Third World and the stalled development of those countries in a proper ethical and equity context. As a foreword, let me share my ideas on Third World debt here as I shared them with the seminar participants at the beginning of their discussion.

The question of Third World debt is everyone's concern. It is not just our problem, it is not just their problem, it is a world problem. The solution is not going to come without coordinated effort from many sides. At the moment, the innocent populations of Third World countries are paying an immense price to satisfy the IMF and the banks, but there is a limit to the austerity they can endure. This is a moral issue. We have the responsibility to relieve their burden. In the process, the banks will have to accept a loss. Bankers do not do business from altruistic motivations. They loaned the money at high rates to cover the risk, and their goal was profit. Now, the time has come when they must say, "We made a mistake and we are going to have to pay. Our profits will be less; we will have to accept a longer payback period; and we are going to have to lower the limit to something like four percent and keep it there, no matter what happens."

The international financial community will have to back these banks. Their financial security must be assured so they do not have to go bankrupt. But in return for that financial security, the banks must shoulder a part of the debt burden as did the people who have been put on austerity programs.

Dealing with the debt overhang is only the beginning. New development capital must flow—and it must be even more than the tremendous amount of the debt. This capital is required if these countries are to again pick up their own economic development and regain lost developmental momentum.

The situation requires major surgery. The present tentative ways of handling the debt so that the banks get paid their interest this year are, as Felix Rohatyn said, "A bridge to nowhere." It is a bridge of sorts, but unless firm ground is established on the other side of that bridge, the ground of development, future loan repayments will not be possible. If people have made financial mistakes through poor loan analysis, as I think many banks have, then they should not emerge fat and happy, but be accordingly lean. Perhaps they will learn a lesson by extricating those people who are now their victims. If some are doing better than others financially, they should give more financially of what they have gained. The great purveyors of capital, such as the Japanese, must be encouraged to put their funds into world development, particularly in that part of the world that is suffering so deeply and so thoroughly.

Unless this is done, the loans are not going to be paid—one cannot expect blood from a turnip. Austerity can be pushed only so far before people revolt. In that case the banks will lose everything, not just interest payments, and the world will be one disastrous mess economically.

If everyone were to take a little share of the blame, if people who are enormously successful would put a little more back into the system that has treated them so well, if the interest payments were cut in half or more and there were the necessary infusion of capital for development, if we could admit that austerity beyond a certain point is asking for social revolution, and if the United States were to throw its full power behind these programs, then maybe we would have a future as a human race. If not, the debt crisis will intensify all our global problems to the inestimable harm of the human family.

Rev. Theodore M. Hesburgh, C. S. C.
The University of Notre Dame

Acknowledgments

As with the first two volumes in this series, the credit for the insight reported in the following pages goes to the seminar participants. They have given of their time and talent and, most importantly, been remarkably open with their ideas in the presence of others who may be very critical of their world-views. This takes a great deal of confidence and commitment. The participants are listed in the appendix of the book.

Six women have been the backbone of this operation. Jule Poirier has been the program's administrative assistant for seven years. She coordinates the workshops, serves as the program secretary, and has typed and retyped this manuscript as well as shared in the editing process. Carole Roos, the assistant editor for Notre Dame Press, is responsible for the editorial flow of what was originally many different writing styles. I have learned a great deal about banking, at the grass roots, from sharing the experience of the bankers in the Tavis family—Tami Lange, Therese Beckwith, and Gloria Trevino. I want to express a deep appreciation to my wife Sparky who has demonstrated heroic patience through the long hours of putting the program on "Multinational Managers and Third World Development" together as it has grown in size and complexity over the last decade.

Funding for our study of global debt has been provided by a major grant from the Rockefeller Foundation and supporting monies from sixteen multinational corporations:

Aluminum Company of America
Caron International, Inc.
Castle & Cooke, Inc.
Caterpillar Tractor Company
The Coca-Cola Company
CPC International Inc.
General Mills, Inc.
W. R. Grace and Company
H. J. Heinz Company

Johnson & Johnson
Mobil Oil Corporation
Mine Safety Appliances
   Company

Pfizer Inc.
Ralston Purina Company
SmithKline Beckman
   Corporation
Texaco, Inc.

The Rockefeller Foundation and the supporting firms are of course not responsible for the wide range of views expressed in this volume. Any errors in representing accurately the ideas and judgments of the various participants are mine.

Introduction

Third World debt has dramatically increased the interdependence of developed and less-developed countries. The loans, so effectively cycled through the financial system of the First World, fueled a hectic expansion in the developing countries during the 1970s. The Third World proved to be vulnerable to the availability of these credits: Unfortunately, most of the funds were used to pay for the soaring cost of imported products (especially oil) and distressingly little was used for truly productive investments. As a result, the ability of most countries to service those debts has not grown apace with the growth in the levels of the debts. The debts became due but unpayable in the 1980s.

After August 12, 1982, when the Mexican default triggered the present phase, and up to the Brazilian stand-off in 1987, extensive rescheduling of debt avoided major debtor-creditor confrontations (leaving aside the Peruvian case because of the somewhat smaller amount of debt involved). The international financial system has demonstrated remarkable resilience throughout this period. The austerity associated with this rescheduling, however, has slowed or even stopped development in much of the Third World.

So far, the banks have fared surprisingly well. Although they have experienced decreased returns on the initial loans through the rescheduling process (cutting interest rates spreads, dropping administrative fees, and extending maturities significantly), the debt has been serviced. Bankers are still taking money out of the debtor countries on a net basis. They have also built a cushion in their capital accounts against future debt servicing shortfalls. Moreover, secondary markets are developing that will allow further decreases in exposure, although at a high cost.

1

On the debtor's side, the opposite is true. After almost six years of severe adjustment, the economic outlook for these countries remains clouded. Following a particularly difficult year in 1983, debtor countries have found it impossible to resume sustained economic growth. The ten largest debtor countries, for example, after a drop of 3.3 percent in gross domestic product in 1983, struggled to a positive 3 percent in 1985, only to fall back to a 2.7 percent increase in 1986. These averages mask greater swings in countries such as Mexico and Brazil. It is estimated that, for Latin American countries, the pre-debt crisis levels of growth in gross domestic product will not be achieved until sometime in the 1990s. For sub-Saharan African debtors, the delay will be far longer.

The present economic *cum* political cusp of Third World debtors will surely plumb the capability of the international financial system. We in the First World must not be misled by the apparent success of our system in handling the crisis thus far. The remarkable organization and cooperation of rescheduling is effective only on one side of these negotiations, that of the banks and the International Monetary Fund. The creditors' success is increasingly viewed by Third World peoples as the debtors' failure. There are great political implications associated with these views. While observers may disagree over the extent of the likely challenges and the ability of the system to respond, few would claim that the most difficult time of the crisis is behind us. The international financial system is at risk, more now than at any point since 1982. The vulnerability of the Third World becomes the vulnerability for our own First World financial system.

To argue that the Third World did not need to borrow the funds in the first place, or that the 1982 crisis was brought on by investing the borrowed monies in consumption or nonproductive public enterprises, while having a strong element of truth, is to miss the point. Most of the countries are trying desperately to service the debt, but the servicing resources are becoming slim. Many analysts, including myself, are amazed at the commitment of Third World governments to meet their debt obligations in light of the crushing economic and political consequences. As Bill Hank said at the initiation of the seminar,

"We must start from where we stand."

Through it all, however, there is one stark reality. The cost of dealing with the debt overhang is being borne in the developing debtor countries by the peoples who can least afford it. Just as incomes in the Third World are highly skewed, so is the burden of debt repayment. The upper classes have access to hedging mechanisms against the repayment-induced recessions. They can enter international transactions with the associated opportunity to move their funds to safer havens. Members of the upper and middle classes who moved their money out during the period of capital flight are now the creditors, not the debtors. Most of these same people also have the means to hedge internally against recession, especially the wealthy. The group which did not gain from the credit-induced growth, but which is being called upon to bear the heaviest repayment burden, is the poor. They have less chance of hedging against the debt-related depression in their countries and in many cases have had to seek refuge in the informal sector. The depressed state of the economies translates to the collapse of their support systems for education, health, and nutrition.

In this milieu, there are three issues that stand out.

1. The most important issue is an ethical one. Since 1982 the poor who can least afford the cost are bearing a heavy burden of servicing the debt. Those poor who were not involved in the creation of the problem and who gained the least as the credit accumulated, are paying the most. This is unethical.
2. Rekindling development is of equal importance to the First as well as to the Third World countries. Ties between the developed and the developing countries are strong, interrelationships have been tightened by the debt problem. To this point, all efforts have been targeted to keeping the debt current (if not repaid) with little attention—indeed, with severe damage—to debtor country development. It is absolutely essential that the short-term focus of debt servicing be subjected to the longer-term goal of renewed development for the benefit of both the First and Third Worlds.
3. The international financial system is at risk. Lurching from

one crisis to the next, it has yet to be tested by a major country's repudiation of its debt.

What do these issues mean for the managers of multinational firms—of multinational banks and of multinational corporations such as agribusiness, manufacturers, resource corporations, and service companies? These firms are inextricably involved in the crisis. Banks are under great pressure at home to deal with the opportunities and competitive threats of deregulation, problems with non-performing agricultural, real estate, and energy loans, and competition from foreign banks in their U.S. markets. The pull of opportunities and problems in the United States reinforces the push to reduce Third World exposure.

Multinational corporations are as involved in the Third World as are banks. The debt crisis has had a chilling effect on their activity in these countries, with decreases in the promise of return and a perception of increasing risk. The depressing effect of austerity on local markets, the associated possibility of political instability, the loss of import protection and pressure for exports, the lack of new credits, (indeed, the "decapitalization" of the private sector in the poor countries of Africa, Asia, and Latin America)—all enter as negative coefficients in multinational decision models.

Still, multinational corporations must protect their existing investments with new, or reinvested capital, just as the banks are trying to reschedule debt to stave off default. Many multinational corporations have their future tied to the Third World, and once they get out, it is more difficult to get back in than in the case with multinational banks. Multinational corporations also have greater flexibility to explore Third World opportunities than do multinational banks.

This volume addresses the above issues from the multinational manager's point of view. As with all business decisions, it is incumbent upon the manager to understand how his or her firm's environment is changing. With the Third World debt problem, environmental monitoring is a challenge. The effects of the debt are so pervasive and the issues so often clouded by the technical aspects of international finance and economic development, it is difficult to keep in touch with the basic issues.

In the materials that follow, we attempt to provide an environmental overview in non-technical terms. We will address the situation as it is unfolding and the principles that must be addressed, whatever tradeoffs are made or technical solutions sought. We trace the tentacles of the debt problem beginning in Part 1 with the poor in the Third World, through the response of debtor developing country governments in Part 2, to the condition of the international financial system and the role of commercial banks in Part 3. In Part 4, we turn directly to the meaning of the debt crisis for multinational corporations and their potential role in rekindling development. Part 5 summarizes the issues of the volume in terms of the strategies that might be followed by multinational banks and corporations.

Part 1 sets firmly the basis of our ethical concern—the impact on the poor of the Third World. The debt crisis exerts its effect on them in two ways. The crisis itself has stopped development in many of those countries, the development that it was hoped would eventually improve conditions for the poor. Second, the way that the crisis has been handled exacts a particularly high price on these poor.

The first paper traces the ties between externally imposed conditions and the standard of living for the poor, although data on the marginalized members of society is never very good. Bolivia and Zambia are presented as case histories. The respondents in this first section stress the political ramifications of the adjustment-induced recessions and the need for an emphasis on long-term economic growth and human development.

The response of Third World governments is considered in Part 2. Coping strategies are outlined for three geographic areas: Latin America, Asia, and sub-Saharan Africa. Through the pre-crisis growth and the post-crisis adjustment, each country has learned a great deal from its experience, experience that will be reflected in developmental strategies. For Latin America, the stress is placed on the unique national developmental positions, the learning that has taken place, and the importance of allowing flexibility for countries to pursue their own policies. In Asia, Korea is set as an example of how a concise, coordinated governmental response countered the external shocks that triggered the crisis for so many countries. Unlike the progress of Asia, and the uncertain promise of Latin America, most of sub-Saharan Africa is clearly trapped in debt and economic stagnation.

Four participants respond to the analyses of Latin America, Africa, and Asia. They call for creativity in approaching the debt problem and, in the discussion, demonstrate their own. A summary of the seminar discussion completes this second section.

Against this background of what is happening in the Third World and what developing country coping strategies are available, we turn to the international financial system in Part 3. This session was the most difficult of the seminar in that we had trouble judging the condition of the international financial system. On the one hand, as noted above, the banking component of the system has significantly reduced its exposure to Third World debt. On the other hand, the possibility of economic collapse and/or political upheaval in the debtor countries will surely pose significant challenges in the future.

The initial paper in this session traces the debt problem from its pre-crisis roots in the 1960s to the most recent data, analyzing the conditions necessary to resolve the problem. The respondents assess the paper from two viewpoints, that of a U.S. commercial banker and of a Third World central banker. Four observers then comment on specific aspects of the system: the role of the international financial institutions, the vulnerability of U.S. commercial banks, strategies available to these commercial banks, and the ritualistic aspects of rescheduling. A range of participant views are covered in the discussion summary.

Part 4 turns to the implications for the multinational corporations. The debt crisis has changed the relationship between multinationals and host governments. The power of multinationals relative to Third World countries has increased dramatically as the developing countries need the financial, technical, managerial, and material resources of the multinationals now more than ever. These firms are in a position to enhance local productivity and to provide access to international markets, characteristics coveted by the newly export-oriented host governments. At the same time, Third World internal markets as sources of demand for multinational output are not growing. While the rate of investment has dropped during the debt crisis, multinationals cannot abandon the Third World. Resource firms must obtain materials there; agribusiness must stay although many are getting out of the production phase to concentrate on processing and distribution; U.S. producers of durable goods are being pushed to lower-cost, foreign localities.

The question addressed in Part 4 is, "If development is to be rekindled, how can and should multinationals contribute to this new environment?" Two authors propose the market conditions and forms within which this contribution can take place. The respondents to these papers reflect the breadth of views on the possible and proper role of multinational corporations in development. Participant reaction is captured in the discussion summary.

The last section, Part 5, summarizes much of the volume in terms of the strategies employed by the various groups involved in the debt problem. The needs for correcting the economic and ethical misallocation associated with rescheduling are discussed—changes in the International Monetary Fund policies and the initiation of a dialogue to modify the international financial system. Based on the situation as outlined in Parts 1–4 and the concept presented in the previous volumes of this series, strategies for the management of multinational banks and corporations are recommended.

The materials in this volume are drawn from a seminar held at the University of Notre Dame in September 1986. The deliberations offered an opportunity for an unusually diverse group of observers to struggle together with the complexities of the debt problem. We are executives from multinational corporations and banks, past governmental officials and central bankers from developing countries, local Third World entrepreneurs, missionaries, and academics from theology, law, economics, and political science as well as business administration at Notre Dame and other universities. These participants are listed in the appendix. With this diverse group, no views went unexplored. Each seminar paper was followed by a panel of respondents or open discussion to ensure that all aspects of the problem were aired.[1]

This is the third volume published in the series on "Multinational Managers and Developing Country Concerns." The first two are also reports on Notre Dame seminars, and this volume builds upon the conceptual foundation addressed in them. In the initial volume, *Multinational Managers and Poverty in the Third World,* the many nuanced views of the proper role of the multinational corporation in less-developed countries was explored. This study group analyzed the different levels of conflict and analysis from the individual firm interacting with its local community, to multinationals as a group channeling resources and pressures as components of the international economic system.

The title of the second volume is *Multinational Managers and Host Government Interactions.* Given that the host government bears the final responsibility for development in its country, and that multinationals can be a critical component of that process, this study group explored the dimensions of the relationship between corporate managers and governmental officials, as they interact with each other and with other groups in the society, to work out the role of the firm. The existence of the debt crisis is an important component of this analysis in that it has fundamentally changed the power relationships between multinational firms and host governments.

Building upon this previous work, the present volume confronts the central economic problem of our time—the debt crisis.

NOTE

1. Two of the papers were presented at meetings other than the seminar. The paper by Michael Curtin, "The Role of International Institutions in the Debt Crisis," was given to a research seminar at Notre Dame on November 13, 1986. Henry Terrell's paper, "The Vulnerability of Multinational

Banks to an International Shock,'' was presented at a session of the Financial Management Association annual meeting on October 16, 1986. In each case the paper was followed by discussion.

PART 1

Vulnerability in the Third World

Our entry point for discussing the present debt problem in the Third World is the peoples in Africa, Asia, and Latin America who are leading lives of increasing deprivation due to the austerity associated with the various attempts to deal with the crisis. The poor and destitute in these countries are not directly a part of the crisis. They are enduring, slipping a little each day. They are unaware of the increasing volatility of the international financial system. These people had no complicity in the events that caused the crisis. Moreover, they benefited little from the credit-spurred economic growth of the 1970s. Now, they are paying far more than their share of the price exacted to repay the debt.

In the first section, Peter Henriot, S. J., and Kenneth Jameson explore the effects of the present attempts to work out of the debt crisis and their impact on the poor. They focus on the issue of equity, asking, "Which society and who in society should bear the brunt of debt adjustment?" Bolivia and Zambia are presented as examples of how national austerity has affected the poor.

Two panelists respond to the Henriot-Jameson presentation. Rose Spalding addresses the link between austerity and political instability, pointing out that behind the visual indicators of austerity-related discontent lies the more subtle erosion of confidence in basic institutions and of the legitimacy of the political order. Nicolas Barletta stresses the need for a new IMF-World Bank formula along with determined debtor country activities to enhance long-term economic growth and human development.

International Debt, Austerity, and the Poor

*PETER J. HENRIOT, S. J., AND KENNETH P. JAMESON**

The debt crisis. The debt trap. The debt dilemma. The debt bomb.

By whatever name, the current international situation of the massive external debt owed by the developing nations presents a monumental moral and political challenge to anyone committed to future global development. The World Bank reported that the total external liabilities for developing countries reached 1.017 trillion dollars in 1987. The consequences of such a situation are read in the daily news stories of economic instability, political unrest, social calamities, human sufferings.

The focus of this paper is on one aspect of the debt phenomenon and adjustment to it through austerity measures: *the impact on the poor.* Specifically, the paper surveys the recent history of external debt problems in two less developed countries (LDCs), Bolivia and Zambia, and the effects on the poor of the measures taken to stabilize their economies. The particular

---

*Peter J. Henriot, S. J., is the director of the Center of Concern, Washington, D.C. With a doctorate in political science from Chicago, Father Henriot focuses on research and education around questions of the political economy of international development and the church's response to justice and peace issues.

Kenneth P. Jameson is a professor of economics and faculty fellow of the Helen Kellogg Institute for International Studies at the University of Notre Dame. He has worked on governmental policy toward investment with the Ministry of Industry in Peru, the Ministry of Commerce in Panama, and on projects with the World Bank, the Inter-American Foundation, and the Agency for International Development.

focus is to analyze the social consequences of austerity programs, especially those following the pattern mandated or encouraged by the International Monetary Fund (IMF). The two
case studies are introduced by an overview of the roots of the
debt crisis to provide a common understanding of the state
of the problem at this moment. The review of the austerity
programs and their recent evolution will note their social consequences. The case studies are followed with concluding observations in an effort to provide a new focus on the
debt problem which could facilitate including concern with
the poor as an element in any program to deal with the debt
situation.

HISTORICAL BACKGROUND

The roots of the current debt situation are deep. Indeed, it
could be argued that the present crisis was being shaped decades, even centuries, ago in the policies of the countries of the
North which held colonies in the South. The inequity of the
current international economic order is a result of that historical process, and the debt overhang is but one instance of the
serious faults of that order.

In the late 1960s, the U.S. economy was seriously struggling with the burden of an unpopular war and a growing
social budget. "Guns *and* butter" was President Lyndon
Johnson's program, legacy, and downfall. The economy was
plagued with falling profits, lowered productivity and investment, and growing trade problems. Major U.S. corporations,
aiming to enhance their profits, moved some operations to
LDCs in order to take advantage of cheaper labor and benefits
and to be able to enter these markets. The large banks followed, lending to these firms and servicing their earnings. As a
result the so-called "Euromarket" (although not all the banks
were located in Europe) developed and operated without the
usual reserve requirements that central banks impose on commercial banks within their jurisdiction.

In the mid-1970s, considerable pressure built to encourage LDCs to borrow money in order to meet their develop-

mental needs. With the quadrupling of oil prices in 1974, commercial banks were flooded with "petro dollars" from the OPEC countries which were experiencing huge balance of payments/trade surpluses. The banks had the strong incentive to lend that money quickly, lest they would have to pay interest on it from their own assets. Hence they engaged in an aggressive, competitive effort to promote borrowing in the LDCs. As a report from the Overseas Development Council notes, "Individual loan officers were rewarded for the quantity more than the quality of their international portfolios."[1]

The LDCs readily responded to the offer of low interest rates and large volume loans, arranged quickly and generally with little or no interference in domestic economic affairs. They did so for a number of reasons. First, they desired to industrialize their economies, which required large imports of capital goods. Second, the rise of oil prices meant a greatly increased import bill for many countries. And third, the prices of manufactured imports also rose steeply, due to an oil-induced increase in the manufacturing costs in industrialized nations. These factors resulted in programs that could only be paid for with increased export earnings or with borrowed money.

During the mid- and late-1970s, many LDCs vigorously pursued a course of debt-led growth. This was particularly true of those oil-producing countries which lacked a capital surplus (e.g., Mexico) and the newly industrializing countries (NICs) which were involved in export promotion (e.g., Korea). This meant that today's trillion dollar developing country debt is concentrated in a few countries—almost half of it in Latin American countries.

In 1979, a second major oil shock hit the global economy when the OPEC nations doubled their prices. A second flood of petro dollars came to the banks. Yet this time, conditions were different from 1973, and both responses and consequences deviated sharply. Following the 1973 oil shock, the industrialized nations had tried to maintain economic growth; instead they now sought to restrain growth and to reduce inflationary pressures. The United States initiated severe anti-inflationary policies, with the Federal Reserve Board putting a tight squeeze on the growth of money and credit for the next several years. A general recession began in the industrialized nations.

For the LDCs that had been big borrowers, several severe consequences followed. First, interest rates on the debts to commercial banks generally floated with overall interest rates, and so the interest burden increased significantly. Loans were rescheduled and much higher interest rates were charged. "The 90-day variable rate loans that developing nations took on in the mid-1970s at, say, 6.5 percent, were costing as much as 19 percent when they renewed those short-term loans in 1980 and 1981."[2] One study estimated that higher interest rates increased the debt burden of the LDCs by some $34 billion in 1981–1982 alone.[3] Another study commented on the effect of the rescheduling:

> In 1980, interest rates on new loans in developing countries were rarely above the London Inter-Bank Offered Rate (LIBOR) plus 1 percent. By 1982–83, the rates were set at 2 percent or more above LIBOR, with refinancing commission of 1 percent or more. Given the scale of Third World debt, the burden of even small increases in interest rates was onerous. In 1985, an increase in the interest rate of 1 percent would raise the total developing world debt servicing burden by over $9 billion a year, or $25 million a day.[4]

Second, the export earnings of the non-oil LDCs began to decline sharply, as demand in the recession-prone industrialized countries declined and the price of commodities dropped precipitously. Prices of primary commodities relative to industrial goods fell some 40 percent between 1980 and 1982.

Third, faced with increased interest rates and decreased export earnings, the LDCs found it very difficult simply to keep up with interest payments on their debt. In August 1982, officials of the Mexican government announced that they would not be able to meet the service payments to commercial banks on their $58 billion external debt. In subsequent months, similar debt-servicing problems were announced by

Venezuela, Brazil, Argentina, and the Philippines. Banks in the industrialized nations were severely shaken. With the cooperation of the international private banks, the various ministries of treasury, and the IMF, new "packages" of loan reschedulings were worked out. The problem was compounded, however, by the fact that the commercial banks were at the same time curtailing the volume of new loans to the LDCs. New loans dropped from $50 billion in 1981 to $20 billion in 1982 to $10 billion in 1983.[5]

The LDCs now found themselves meeting their current debt crisis—paying the bills for servicing the loans—by means which would intensify a future debt crisis—borrowing more money at higher rates.

In many instances, inefficient domestic policies in the LDCs also contributed to the debt crisis. Much of the borrowed money had been invested in unprofitable projects such as huge energy plants and the latest armaments. Moreover, overvalued currencies encouraged capital flight out of the LDCs as local funds were exchanged for dollars, pounds, or francs, and for investments in the industrialized countries. "According to bank records in Europe and the United States, $51 billion moved out of the 15 largest debtor nations in 1981 and 1982—at the same time $81 billion of new loans were committed."[6] Former Prime Minister Michael Manley of Jamaica estimated that 70 percent of the loans received by eight major LDCs ended up in Swiss bank accounts, real estate in Miami, and other forms of capital flight.[7] Even Morgan Guaranty Trust has said that "on the admittedly oversimplified assumption that capital flight served only to inflate debt buildup and related interest charges, several . . . [LDCs] might have been practically debt-free today—were it not for capital flight."[8]

Overall, the LDC development that had been occurring came to a rapid halt. Burdened with the service of enormous debts, most countries now lack foreign exchange for development projects. IMF-imposed austerity programs have frequently caused stagflationary pressures which further stifle development and whose effects are felt acutely by the poor.

In understanding the debt crisis faced by the LDCs, Dornbusch notes that it is important to distinguish three different aspects:

—*Liquidity* problems involve the ability to service and amortize debts *now,* on schedule and for the amounts contracted.
—*Solvency* problems involve the ability to meet the financial liabilities of debt at *any* time.
—*Equity* problems involve the way in which large, unanticipated increases in the cost of debt service should be shared among lenders and borrowers.[9]

Liquidity problems can be addressed—and are in fact now being addressed—by the current approach of making additional loans to meet debt service payments, the "muddling through" approach. Solvency of nations is in theory no problem, for it could be addressed by depressing domestic economic activity and living standards low enough to free the foreign exchange revenues needed to service external debt, though with obvious and serious political consequences. And so it is equity problems which surface as central: *Which society and who in society should bear the burden of debt adjustment?* This is, of course, key to the topic of the impact on the poor.

THE DEBT SITUATION TODAY

Before moving on to examine debt and its relation to the equity problem, it will be helpful to have an overview of the debt situation today: What is the amount of debt owed, who owes it, to whom is it owed, how exposed are U.S. banks, and how has debt been renegotiated?

How Much Debt Is Owed?

The total 1985 debt owed by the developing countries has been estimated at $950 billion. Projected to 1986, the total debt is $1.01 trillion. As table 1 indicates, the debt in current dollars grew approximately 60 percent from 1980 to 1986.

Who Owes the Debt?

It is clear that the debt situation affects most critically Latin America. As column a of table 2 indicates, among the world's fifteen largest debtor nations that are the concern of the Baker Plan, ten are in Latin America.

TABLE 1

Growth of LDC External Debt, 1980–1986
(U.S. $ Billions)

	1980	1981	1982	1983	1984	1985	1986
Total Debt	632	729	809	871	908	950	1010
Percent Growth		15.3	11.0	7.7	4.2	4.6	6.3

Source: IBRD, The World Bank, *Development and Debt Service: Dilemma of the 1980s* (Washington, D.C.: World Bank, 1986), p. xi.

TABLE 2

The Fifteen Debtor Nations in the Baker Plan (1985)
(U.S. $ Billions)

	A	B	C	D
	Total Debt	Interest Payments	Interest % of GNP	Debt to U.S. Banks
Brazil	103.5	11.8	5.8	23.8
Mexico	97.7	10.0	6.3	25.8
Argentina	50.8	5.1	7.9	8.1
Venezuela	32.6	4.1	8.1	10.6
Philippines	27.4	2.1	6.2	5.5
Chile	21.9	2.1	12.9	6.6
Yugoslavia	20.0	1.7	3.6	2.4
Nigeria	18.0	1.8	1.9	1.5
Morocco	14.4	1.0	8.2	0.9
Peru	13.9	1.3	10.8	2.1
Colombia	13.9	1.3	3.3	2.6
Ecuador	7.9	0.7	6.0	2.2
Ivory Coast	6.3	0.6	8.7	0.5
Uruguay	4.9	0.5	9.8	1.0
Bolivia	4.2	0.4	10.0	0.2
TOTAL	437.4	44.5	7.3 average	93.8

Source: *Fortune* (Dec. 23, 1985), p. 101

To Whom Is the Debt Owed?

Of the current $1 trillion debt, approximately two-thirds is owed to commercial banks and the remainder to official sources such as government banks and multilateral lending institutions. Of the amount owed to commercial banks, two-thirds is owed to European and Japanese banks and one-third to U.S. banks. The total owed U.S. commercial banks is approximately $220–230 billion. Column D of table 2 indicates that the amount owed to U.S. banks by these fifteen debtor nations is close to $94 billion.

How Exposed Are U.S. Banks?

For several reasons, there is considerable worry in U.S. banking circles about the consequences of the growing debt problems in the LDCs. First, the interest revenue on the debt owed to U.S. banks by the fifteen largest debtor nations is approximately $10 billion annually. By comparison, total profits of the largest 100 bank holding companies were only $7.8 billion in 1984. Collapse of debt service would have tremendous impact on U.S. banks and could trigger a worldwide financial crisis.[10]

Second, the U.S. banks are more prone to difficulties because federal banking regulations require loan losses to be written off as incurred. By contrast, European and Japanese banks are allowed to write off bad loans over a period of several years.

Third, U.S. banks have a very high percent of their capital assets exposed in loans to developing countries.[11] The twenty-four largest banks are particularly vulnerable, as table 3 shows, although their vulnerability has decreased since 1982 because they are no longer making large loans to countries deep in debt.

As a specific instance of this exposure, the case of loans to Mexico is particularly illuminating. In June 1986, Mexico indicated it would be unable to meet its debt obligations without additional concessions and additional capital inflows. This initiated a process which by October had assembled a $12 billion package to confront this danger. The stakes for U.S. banks are large for most of the over $25 billion that Mexico owes U.S. banks is held by the ten largest banks in this country. A very large percent of the capital of these banks could be jeopardized by problems with these loans, as table 4 shows.

How Have Debt Payments Been Rescheduled?

As debts have mounted for the LDCs, their inability to meet payments have forced them to seek new arrangements

TABLE 3

Exposure of 24 Largest U.S. Banks to Non-Oil LDCs (1980–1985)
(U.S. $ Billions)

AS OF JUNE 30	TOTAL CLAIMS	CAPITAL	CLAIMS AS % OF CAPITAL
1980	54.4	33.8	160
1981	67.0	36.5	183
1982	79.3	39.8	200
1983	84.6	44.1	191
1984	89.0	49.7	179
1985	86.1	58.8	148

Source: IBRD, The World Bank, *Development and Debt Service*, p. xx.

TABLE 4

Mexican Loans of 10 Largest U.S. Banks
(U.S. $ Billions)

BANK	LOANS	PERCENT OF PRIMARY CAPITAL
First Chicago	1.0	63.7
Banker's Trust	1.3	55.5
Manufacturers Hanover	1.6	54.8
Chemical Bank	1.4	48.6
BankAmerica	2.5	48.0
Citibank	2.9	43.5
Morgan Guaranty	1.4	37.6
Chase Manhattan	1.4	34.8
Continental Illinois	0.6	25.9
Security Pacific	0.5	23.9

Source: Jack Anderson and Dale van Atta, "Mexican Debt Threatens U.S. Banks," *Washington Post,*
    June 19, 1986.

with lending governments and commercial banks. The government-to-government negotiations for rescheduling are handled through the Paris Club, with secretariat in the French capital.

The purpose of rescheduling is to allow both the lender and the borrower to structure a more acceptable relationship that promises continued effective interchange in the period ahead. "It aims (a) to smooth out humps in the repayment profile, so that countries are not faced with a huge bill because many debts are falling due in one year; and (b) to produce a new profile which, year-by-year, involves a debt-servicing cost that the debtor can manage."[12]

The number of reschedulings has increased rapidly in recent years. Averaging five per year in 1975–1980, the number has been around thirty in recent years. All in all, a total of 144 reschedulings have occurred in forty-two nations between 1975 and 1985. Table 5 indicates the amounts involved in the reschedulings from 1982–1985.

AUSTERITY PROGRAMS, OLD AND NEW

The bottom line from a developmental standpoint is that the indebted LDCs are presently required to export capital to the holders of their debt, and the international financial system has been relatively successful in enforcing this obligation. This has in general meant a reduction in domestic absorption, in domestic economic activity, in a fashion often dictated by the

TABLE 5

Multilateral Debt Reschedulings
(U.S. $ Billions)

	Paris Club	Commercial Banks
1982	0.6	1.7
1983	10.6	41.1
1984	3.9	8.8
1985	5.9	86.9

Source: IBRD, The World Bank, *Development and Debt Service*, pp. xiv–xv.

IMF which provides the resources necessary to maintain international payments until the policies take effect. Access to these resources is contingent upon specified policy changes, the "conditionalities." An outline of the common stipulations and the evolution of these packages over time will provide a base for understanding the effect of austerity programs on the poor in these LDCs.

As noted above, the period of debt-led growth for the LDCs was rapidly disappearing by 1980. The Mexican debt crisis of 1982 ended it with the finality of a brick wall. The goods and services that had been created during the period remained, though their life expectancy appeared to be far shorter than the life and drain of the debt load that had been created during the 1970s.

The cessation of dollar flows to the LDCs was like the loss of oil for an engine, or, in less benign terms, the loss of heroin to an addict. After imports had been reduced to their minimum levels, the only manner to maintain or improve functioning of the debtor countries' economies was to gain access to dollars once again. This required major adjustments on the part of the debtor countries to the changed international situation. The IMF has played an increasingly prominent role in this effort.

The IMF is the Bretton Woods multilateral institution charged with facilitating stability in times of a nation's difficulties with balance of payments. Its loans have traditionally assisted countries to meet short-term problems; however in recent years, the IMF's role has been expanded to that of a guarantor of the "creditworthiness" of the LDC seeking additional loans. Its stamp of approval—the granting of a standby agreement after detailed discussion with a debtor country about its economic policies and plans—has become a major factor in encouraging capital flows from other multilateral sources and from central banks and commercial banks.

As conditions for establishing those standby agreements and thus opening the door for future flows of capital, the IMF has required a set of domestic policy adjustments. These adjustments will, the IMF maintains, lead to a quick reversal of the balance of payments deficit, generating the necessary resources for the foreign loans to be repaid and the domestic economic situation to improve. The traditional IMF package has usually included the following conditions:

1. Devalue the currency: to discourage capital flight, to make imports more expensive, and the country's exports more price competitive in the international marketplace.
2. Curtail governmental purchases and subsidies: to reduce the national public budget which crowds out investment in productive areas.
3. Increase domestic interest rates: to encourage residents to keep funds in the country rather than invest in foreign countries and to attract foreign portfolio investment.
4. Slow money supply growth rate and restrict domestic credit: to counter inflationary pressures.
5. Remove price controls: to alleviate market distortions and encourage domestic production.
6. Increase taxes and tax enforcement: to curtail the domestic fiscal deficits.
7. Limit growth of wage bills: to curtail inflation by wage controls, limits on employment, and reduction of fringe benefits.

The IMF programs have been highly controversial on several grounds. First, they have been criticized for imposing "austerity" on a nation's economy—in a fashion that has special implications for the poor of the LDCs, as well as for a portion of the middle class. Currency devaluations increase the costs of imports, such as food, and of imports essential to developmental projects, such as oil. When combined with the reduction of subsidies and with wage controls, the resulting increase in the costs of food and transportation directly reduces the real income of the urban poor who spend a significant portion of their income on these goods. This may be offset in some measure by increased rural incomes through higher food prices, although structural factors often intervene to limit these gains, for example, credit restrictions force many rural shopkeepers and farmers out of the market. Imposition of wage controls and elimination of price controls cut workers' ability to meet basic human needs as prices rise and purchasing power is cut. Increased taxes, when levied on consumption or as value-added taxes, increase the cost of meeting basic human needs. Reduction of governmental spending lowers social services, food subsidies, and public employment—on all of which the poor and working class are disproportionately dependent.

In a December 1983 *Foreign Affairs* article, Johns Hopkins University professor Riordan Roett argued that the result of IMF programs for many developing nations has been widespread suffering, particularly among the lower classes. "The quality of life has deteriorated dramatically in most countries of South America, largely as a result of stabilization programs and austerity measures." A 1984 *Wall Street Journal* article depicted the human dimension of the suffering by citing the following statistics from Chile, a country that, by and large, has followed a program consistent with the IMF's austerity conditions: 1500 of the country's 4000 companies have gone bankrupt since 1982, the banking system failed as bad loans totaled 165 percent of capital and reserves, 25 percent of the work force was unemployed, with some middle class citizens taking jobs sweeping streets and driving cabs.[13]

In response to criticisms about the adverse human consequences of the austerity programs, Jacques de Larosiere, Managing Director of the IMF has presented an argument that the Fund does not in fact "impose austerity."[14] His five points are: (1) economic adjustment to external balances is inescapable; (2) the IMF does not see adjustment as synonymous with economic retrogression; (3) the programs do entail sacrifices but they must be compared to the alternatives; (4) the social costs of Fund programs are allocated according to the political decisions of the particular country; and (5) exchange rate adjustments may not adversely affect the least favored sectors of the population. It should be clear that even mild critics of the Fund would hardly be assuaged by such a bloodless defense of these programs.

A second criticism of the typical IMF program is that it contributes to political instability within countries that faithfully follow the program. The austerity measures have in fact created widespread unrest and caused "IMF riots" in several nations. A few years ago, an IMF austerity program in the Dominican Republic brought angry crowds into the streets; 55

people died, 2000 were wounded. Increases in food prices because of IMF programs have caused riots in Chile, Colombia, Peru, and Panama. While such political activity may have led to the replacement of a number of military governments, such programs create a particularly dangerous situation in Latin America today because of the fragility of the struggling newly democratic governments. Labor protests over wage cuts, urban unrest over increased food and transportation costs, and general strife fueled by a flagging economy all contribute to dangerous situations. One observer comments: "Workers now see themselves as paying for debt service on an external debt that reflects mismanagement and privilege from which they have had little benefit. For example, in Chile the real minimum wage is 30 percent below the 1981 level, and workers are clearly aware that they are paying a bill that is not their own."[15] Moreover, promotion of an export-oriented economy moves the countries away from self-reliance and makes them more vulnerable to future external economic shocks which could have significant political implications.

A third criticism of the traditional programs is that they simply do not work. The argument is that in the preponderance of cases where such programs have been adopted, the anticipated results of long-run growth and equilibrium in the international sphere have not in fact materialized. The clearest evidence of this is the incidence of "recidivism," the return to the international doghouse of many of the countries which have undertaken Fund programs. Prime examples of this have been Peru and Jamaica. At a more theoretical level, it is argued that Fund programs can be stagflationary and thus can give results directly opposite from those desired.[16]

The Fund has answered such criticisms by examining the numeric goals of a number of adjustment programs, and comparing them with the actual performance of the national economy. Its conclusion is that the general performance of the economies has corresponded to the Fund goals.[17] Again, the critics of the Fund-type programs remain unconvinced. They cite the evidence that Brazil has performed relatively well while resisting the demands that it undertake such a program as part of an agreement with the Fund, and that Mexico, despite its adoption of a Fund-inspired program, continues in repeated crises in recent years.

In the last several years there has been an evolution of Fund programs which makes it clear that the critics of the traditional adjustment programs are winning the day. There has been a quiet but significant change in the outlines of the IMF adjustment programs that can be interpreted as an admission that the traditional programs have not worked. The change has three elements: (1) a willingness to examine policies alternative to a devaluation of the domestic currency; (2) the demand that one element of conditionality for a standby loan be "structural adjustment" in the domestic economy; and (3) the requirement that specific steps be taken to deal with the external debt.

Evidence for these changes is available from a study of the elements of ninety-four Fund programs during the 1980–84 period.[18] Most of the traditional elements are contained in these programs: limits on credit expansion (98 percent); restraint on central government current expenditure (91 percent); measures affecting wages and prices (88 percent). However, only 55 percent of the programs incorporated liberalization and reform of exchange rate arrangements, an element which was previously inherent in any IMF program. In one sense this reflects the theoretical victory of the Fund critics who showed the many conditions under which devaluation would not measurably aid the performance of a country. In another sense it exemplifies a more pragmatic stance on the part of the IMF when faced with situations such as that of Guyana, whose only major exports, bauxite and alumina, would be little affected by marginal price adjustments. As a result the IMF has become more willing to accept alternative commercial policies such as import duties (57 percent of the programs).

The second change is to incorporate into a large portion of the programs (74 percent) requirements for "structural adjustment measures." This can mean anything from a complete tax reform to an overhaul of a social security program. The addition of this requirement clearly responds to the problem of recidivist countries. It sees the solution to this problem in the restructuring of those economies along lines that appear, to the

IMF at least, more efficient and effective. So the Fund has adopted the neo-conservative version of structuralism that grew during the 1970s in Latin America.[19]

In this step the IMF is following the lead of the World Bank which began to undertake structural adjustment loans in 1979–80 and has now put in place nearly forty such programs. The IMF recently created a special loan fund strictly for use in structural adjustment loans, in which it is supposed to cooperate on joint programs with the World Bank. Based on the Bank's experience, several things are clear about this new emphasis. First, this is yet another area in which the Fund and Bank will force their own views of policy on individual countries who have to call upon them to relieve the dollar starvation they are currently suffering. It will raise all the problems of conditionality to a new level. This has already been seen in a number of countries that have had World Bank structural adjustment loans where there have been street protests and claims of the abrogation of national sovereignty (e.g., Panama).

Moreover, there is an underlying "market model" in these programs which simply expands the logic of the earlier IMF programs to new realms. If a problematic economy's structures deviate from the norms of the market, these should be structurally adjusted to give the efficient results of the market. So the demand is for reform in the labor code or improvement in the pricing of agricultural goods. There are no demands for land reform, for attacks on domestic production monopoly, for international steps to limit the flight of capital or the financial machinations that accompany the international drug traffic. The effect of this reality on the poor sectors of countries which must adjust through Fund programs is far from clear. However, it is certain that the direct well-being of these groups is not paramount in the design and implementation of the program. Rather, creating the conditions believed to be necessary for a market system to function is a much higher priority.

The third element in the new approach is the requirement to take steps to deal with external debt, through renegotiation, restructuring, or some other alternative. A full 91 percent of the surveyed Fund programs incorporated this element, making it second in prevalence to limits on credit expansion. At one level, this is simply another element of conditionality in Fund programs. Yet, of even greater importance is the *symbolism* of this requirement. For it shows quite clearly the genesis of the balance-of-payments pressures on LDCs and the predicament they are in. It also points out that the IMF and the World Bank have continued as guarantors of the international financial system, and that agreement with them is in many cases a necessary prerequisite for additional funds to be freed for the offending/borrowing country.[20]

Thus it is clear that a new set of emphases is developing within the IMF as it approaches its "austerity" programs. It remains to be seen whether the poor will fare any better under the new forms of adjustment and conditionality, and whether the countries which adopt such new programs will be any less likely to become recidivists.

This background on austerity programs and their conditionalities leads to the major concern of this paper, the impact of such programs on the well-being of the poor in the countries which follow such programs. The two case studies, Bolivia and Zambia, pursue this concern.[21]

CASE OF BOLIVIA

Bolivia is a nation caught deeply in the web of poverty and international debt. It is the poorest of the South American countries with a per capita GNP of $510.[22] On a list of social indicators for Latin American countries, Bolivia generally is at the bottom (unless Haiti is included): the highest infant mortality rate, the lowest life expectancy, the lowest percent of required calories actually consumed, the lowest (except for Paraguay) share of the population with potable water, and the lowest school attendance rate.[23] It is also politically the most unstable of these countries; since independence it has suffered through an average of more than one government per year.

Its extreme condition might disqualify Bolivia as a case study of the relationship of debt and poverty. However, understanding Bolivia can provide a clear insight into the debt-poverty relationship simply because the economic pressures that the debt entails have clear repercussions on the level of poverty and on the lives of the poor.

The case study begins with an overview of Bolivian performance prior to its crisis which can be dated as starting in 1982. The emphasis will be on the evolution of debt and balance of payments and on performance on "basic human needs" indicators (BHN). The second section isolates the external pressures and the consequent deterioration in performance from 1982 through 1985. Of course the debt pressure was only one cause of the economic collapse, but it was a highly significant factor. The third section examines the effect which this debt-related collapse has had on the poor in Bolivia. The manner in which data are collected and the pattern of effects of the debt crisis suggest a threefold categorization of the effects: general effects, effects on the already marginal, and effects on the access to services.

Pre-1982 Bolivia

As was the case with most of Latin America, the decade of the 1970s was a period of relatively good performance for Bolivia, a pattern which wavered through 1981 and then collapsed. Although the stable progress of the 1960s was not matched, the general trends were positive. GNP growth was positive in every year until 1981, averaging a respectable 4.5 percent. Inflation was relatively stable at an average of 16.9 percent; the one incident of rapid inflation (45 percent in 1973–74) was quickly stabilized to 4.5 percent by 1976 with no loss in growth.[24] After a devaluation in 1972, the fixed exchange rate remained stable, with free convertibility, into 1979. There was a subsequent devaluation in 1982.[25]

This fairly healthy economic performance was facilitated by the favorable balance-of-payments situation. Terms of trade declined in 1971–73 and then rose significantly, especially in 1979–80. The current account was generally close to balanced except in 1978 and 1979 when there were substantial deficits and a significant drop in international reserves. Exports rose from $200 million in 1970 to $1.1 billion in 1980.

The balance of payments was also aided by capital in-flows, mainly in the form of loans. Total foreign capital inflows to Bolivia rose from an annual average of $37.8 million in the 1966–69 period to $41.5 million from 1970–74, and then more than doubled to $85.5 million annually from 1975–78. Transnational banks accounted for a mere 0.3 percent of new capital entering the country in 1970. By 1978, their share had risen to 61.8 percent. Likewise, their share in amortization and interest payments by Bolivia rose dramatically during this pe-riod, from 2 to 74 percent. Almost 70 percent of these funds were provided to state enterprises producing goods for ex-port.[26] Bolivia was a classic case of debt-led growth during the late 1970s.

Table 6 presents the evolution of Bolivia's international debt and its relation to exports. From that information the growing pressure of the debt can be clearly seen, with its impli-cations for the future evolution of the economy.

The 1970s also saw marked improvements in a number of social indicators and in the poverty situation in the country. Information is relatively dispersed on these issues, although the indicators are consistent.

Average real salaries rose over the period; unemployment remained relatively stable; life expectancy increased from 43.5 in 1960–65 to 46.7 in 1972–75. In the same period infant mor-tality fell from 225 per thousand to 157, while illiteracy of those over fifteen years of age fell from 61.2 to 37.3 percent. The index of per-capita food production rose from 100 in 1969–71 to 115 by 1976.

Between 1970 and 1973 the total number of students at all levels of education rose from 823,000 to 1,016,000; the total number of teachers rose from 28,641 to 40,648; and the total number of schools increased from 8,082 to 10,236. Between 1970 and 1975 the labor force covered by social security rose from 9 to 17.3 percent, representing an increase in the share of such costs in GNP from 2.9 percent in 1965 to 3.3 percent in 1974.

Thus the 1970s was a relatively positive period in Bolivia in terms of its economic and social performance. Yet the major difficulty which the economy would face—pressure from the

TABLE 6

Evolution of Bolivian External Public Debt
(U.S. $ Billions)

A Year	B Contracted Debt	C Disbursal	D Amortization	E Interests and Commissions	F Net (%)	G Debt Service/ Exports
1971	.782	.088	.021	.010	.591	17
1972	.966	.146	.042	.012	.681	25
1973	1,048	.056	.035	.018	.708	18
1974	1,210	.129	.055	.023	.786	13
1975	1,550	.171	.064	.027	.883	19
1976	1,979	.295	.072	.040	1,107	20
1977	2,442	.439	.101	.060	1,458	26
1978	3,102	.541	.271	.084	1,762	55
1979	3,499	.323	.124	.117	1,941	32
1980	3,642	.430	.122	.157	2,220	30
1981	4,535	.715	.174	.225	3,058	44
1982	4,553	.410	.172	.209	3,269	46
1983	4,820	.124	.116	.241	3,227	47
1984	4,947	206	154	202	3,317	50

Source: Rolando Morales, *La Crisis Economica en Bolivia y Su Impacto en las Condiciones de Vida de los Ninos* (La Paz: Papiro, 1985), tables A26 and A28.

external sector—was becoming clear. The international debt generated during this period would be a major component in Bolivia's crisis.

External Pressure and Crisis

The decline in international reserves and the devaluation of 1979 were the first signs of major economic difficulty for Bolivia. The international pressures emanated from a variety of sources.

Already by 1980 the disengagement of the transnational banks could be perceived. Their share of new capital fell by 50 percent and their transactions resulted in a net outflow of capital. This was offset in large degree by inflows of foreign official capital in the form of project disbursements during 1979. In 1980 this source of dollars also contracted by almost 50 percent to $201 million.

One effect was capital flight. Based on the Errors and Omissions element of the balance of payments, capital flight during 1980 was estimated at $370 million. International reserves declined further and net reserves became negative by 1980 and continued to decline.

The Bolivian government attempted to maintain currency convertibility by becoming involved with the private banks as well as by undertaking major loan agreements with international agencies. Notable in this regard in 1980 were the $240 million proceeds of a Structural Adjustment Loan with the World Bank and of a large loan from Argentina. The effort to maintain the flow of dollars in 1981 incorporated a second balance-of-payments support loan from Argentina for $125 million, the rescheduling of $167 million in commercial bank debt, and a further decline of $159 million in the reserve position of the Central Bank.[27]

By 1982, international factors made it clear that the progress of the 1970s was a thing of the past. The debt service load increased finally to 50 percent of exports in 1984 as loans came due and exports declined from $1.1 billion in 1980 to $782 million in 1984. The terms of trade had turned against Bolivia, the international recession had lowered demand for

Bolivian exports, and the scarcity of foreign exchange limited investment in all sectors, including exports.

The problems in the international sector set in motion a *process of declining output,* ever higher inflation, ever lower real wages, financial disruption, disarray in the fiscal sector, and unrestrained monetary growth. The formal economy came to be rivaled by the informal and illegal sectors.[28] Bolivia quit paying its debt to the private banks in 1984, although throughout it has maintained payment on its debt to public international lenders.

A new democratic government took office in August 1985. Its steps to stabilize the economy from a 10,000 percent inflation of 1985 resulted in further depression of wages, incomes, and overall economic activity. The government adopted a very stringent IMF-like stabilization program in September 1985. It then requested standby assistance from the IMF to carry out the program. Such aid, which would have been almost automatic in previous periods, was not forthcoming without further steps which went beyond the traditional variety of "conditionalities." Specifically, the government was required to adopt a thorough-going tax reform, which included a value-added tax, and to reach an agreement with its private international lenders, to whom Bolivia had been in arrears since 1984. Until these steps were taken, the standby loan was not considered by the IMF Executive Board. This new conditionality, this new adjustment program, was far more stringent than the previous version of IMF packages.

Of course, Bolivian economic policy and performance could have been better. However, the point to be emphasized is that the domestic disarray and the reversal of many of the gains of the 1970s had their source in the international sector. The remaining debts contributed mightily to that international pressure and continue to be a major drag on the economy. Indeed, much of the current economic policy in the country is a clear response to the debt situation.

The Effect of the Crisis on the People of Bolivia

The absolute decline in Bolivian GNP began in 1981, although in per capita terms it was underway by 1979 as external pressures came to dominate. The major declines came in 1982. This provides only a short period over which to assess the impact on poverty and on the lives of the people of Bolivia. Yet there are some clear indications available.

General economic trends

As might be expected, the general indicators of economic activity deteriorated quite rapidly. By 1982 real wages had fallen to 60 percent of their 1978 high points. At that time a wage indexation program was put into effect which resulted in very uneven behavior. But the general trend was still downward to an estimated 35 percent of the 1978 wages. The minimum wage showed a similar decline, although it may overstate the real loss in income because the informal sector expanded substantially as individuals searched for additional activities to offset the decline in formal sector income.

In a family survey in La Paz to reassess the consumer price index, based on a sample comprised of middle- to low-income families, over 4 percent had no income aside from gifts and donations, 53 percent had one person working, and 43 percent had between two and five wage earners.[29] Clearly one means of maintaining family income was to increase the number of family members active in economic activity, primarily in the informal sector. This offset in some degree the increase in the measured unemployment rate from 5.6 percent in 1979 to 9.2 percent in 1982. For those with no income, gifts of food or money were the difference between life and death.

Family income declined by over 8 percent from 1978–80 to 1981–83. As a result, families attempting to maintain their consumption lowered their saving in index terms from 100 in 1979, to 96 in 1980, to 9.0 in 1981–82, and finally to slightly negative saving in 1983. Despite these adjustments, consumption fell from 100 in 1980, to 98 in 1981, to 89 in 1982, and to 82 in 1983. On a per capita basis the decline was to 76. By 1985 it was estimated that the average minimum family consumption basket cost 8 percent more than the average income.[30]

There are no specific statistics on the poverty rate (i.e., numbers below a poverty line) in Bolivia in these years. Yet all of these changes in income and output could only have resulted in a substantial increase in the poverty rate measuring the general effect on the livelihood of large segments of the population. So at a global level the effects of the debt-induced crisis in Bolivia are clear: a deterioration in the standard of living for most segments of the Bolivian population.[31]

The effect on the already marginal

Different groups in a society in crisis will, of course, be affected in very different ways. When a society lacks a "safety net," those at the very margins of existence are quite likely to be forced below that margin with harsh effects on nutritional levels and on life expectancy. The only way to track this information is with continuous surveys over a long period of time, a type of information not available for Bolivia. So again the indicators will be partial at best.

Table 7 shows that by 1982–83 there are indications that the mortality rates in the first year or first two years had begun to increase, although the increase was small. Certainly the intensification of the crisis which began in 1982 and has continued until 1986 could only have moved performance even further in this direction. Additional indication of this effect is the substantial increase in infant mortality in the 1970–75 recessionary period, a period of much less disruption and deterioration.

The clearest of the available indicators are the patterns of malnutrition in children admitted to the Albina Patino Hospital in Cochabamba (see table 8). The percentage of children coming to the hospital with a normal nutritional level declined from 66 percent in 1977 to 44 percent in 1983. First-degree malnutrition varied with no strong trend; both second- and third-degree (acute) malnutrition increased substantially, although the increase in the third degree was only in 1983. That pattern is certainly consistent with the expectations of the effect of the crisis on the poor.

A similar pattern appears in urban surveys in 1983 and 1984. Children whose nutritional level was normal fell from 56.9 to 55.5 percent, while moderate malnourishment rose from 27.7 to 30.2 percent and acute malnourishment rose from 14.0 to 14.3 percent. This random sample did not overrepresent the children at the margin, so it understates the deterioration that would appear in a sample only of marginal children. As a comparison, a 1984 study which included rural children found only 39.2 percent with normal nutritional status, 38.5 percent with moderate malnutrition, and 21.4 percent with acute malnourishment.

The scarcity of good figures makes any conclusions very tentative. However, the evidence points to an important effect of the crisis on the sheer survival of the marginal group of the society. This is seen dramatically in a reversal of the infant mortality rates and in a clear deterioration in the nutritional levels of poor children, especially poor rural children.

TABLE 7

Early Mortality in Bolivia by Year, according to Indicators of Mortality and Contexts (Per 1000 live births)

Indicators and Contexts	1965–70	1970–75	1975–76	1982–83
Infant Mortality (up to 1 year)	160	165	167	168
Urban	125	133	131	127
Rural	180	178	199	178
Child Mortality (up to 2 years)	203	219	213	216
Urban	142	166	168	167
Rural	209	224	235	236

Source: Morales, *La Crisis Economica*, table E10.

TABLE 8

Nutritional State of Children Attended in Hospital Albina Patino (Percentages)

Nutritional State	1977	1978	1979	1980	1981	1982	1983
Normal	66	57	54	55	41	47	44
Malnutrition Grade I	8	12	13	12	15	12	7
Malnutrition Grade II	12	16	19	20	30	26	26
Malnutrition Grade III	13	15	14	13	14	15	23
TOTAL	100	100	100	100	100	100	100

Source: Morales, *La Crisis Economica*, p. 105.

Diminished access to human resource services

Another direct effect of the debt-induced economic disorder has been a restriction in access to basic human resource services which aid in maintaining and developing the capacities of persons, e.g., education and health. In Latin America such services for the lower and middle classes have traditionally been provided by the state; and, as noted earlier, there was a significant expansion of these activities in Bolivia in the 1960s and 1970s. This process was reversed with the 1980s as far as can be seen from the information available.

Had the 1970s pattern of increasing rates of school matriculation continued on into the 1980s, the annual increase in the number of children in school would have been between 4.3 and 4.7 percent in the 1980–83 period. In actuality, the rate was only 3.8 percent—indicating a significant number of students either not entering the school system or leaving it. It should be noted that enrollment did increase across all school years, although in all years the growth rate was lower than expected. The discrepancies in the matriculation rates were greatest in the lower pre-high school grades. This may reflect the inability of families to take on additional expenditures for starting a child in school and giving up the income if the child is working.

Another factor which influences this impaired performance on school matriculation is the decline in total education expenditures. In real terms education expenditures rose from B$448 million in 1970 to B$772 million in 1981. This growth in expenditures barely kept pace with the growth in students. However, the total expenditures began to decline rapidly in 1982 to B$643 in 1982 and then to B$612 in 1983. The most rapid decline was in capital formation in the sector as efforts were made to maintain current expenditures. Although there is no information on actual expenditures in 1984, it is clear from the 1986 budget that expenditures continued to fall, for the programmed expenditures were only 2.4 percent of GNP,[32] down from the 3.8 percent of 1983, which in turn is lower than the maximum share of 4.2 percent in 1974. In 1984 there were only 160 days of classes instead of the 200 generally required.

The same pattern occurs with overall social expenditure. These reached their height at 3.5 percent of GNP in 1981 and had declined to 2.9 percent by 1983, even as GNP declined dramatically.

The net result of these changes was a drastic disruption in the provision of public human resource services to the population of Bolivia, another effect of the debt-induced crisis on the welfare of the people of Bolivia.

Summary

Despite the serious blows to well-being which this economic disorder and decline have entailed, it is clear that many in Bolivia have discovered means of coping and surviving and of maintaining some basic minimal standard of living. One way of doing this has been through the growth of activity in the informal sector, that aggregate of activities which are illegal, semi-legal, or which take place outside the formal channels of the organized economy. These range from street-vending to cocaine traffic, from the gray market in foreign exchange to smuggling, from tax evasion to stealing. A second way is simply adjustments in the use of limited income to allow continued survival. For example, consumption behavior changed and food was grown, begged, given, or bartered in new patterns.

These coping mechanisms by poor Bolivians deserve further study outside of this present paper. They are mentioned here to indicate the impressive adjustments made by the popular sector in the face of the pervasive deterioration of life at least partially induced by the debt crisis.

Historically, Bolivia appears to be prone to instability. However, the recent debt experience has heightened this tendency. The 1982–1985 period has seen overall income decline and many economic activities have simply stopped. The President of the Business Federation recently stated that the national industry is working at only 40 percent of its capacity, due to competition from contraband, the lack of private investment, and the nation's dependence on imported primary materials. IMF conditionalities have required that expenses be cut back in the public sector, creating not only job losses but further curtailment of social services. In the first half of 1986, the public schools remained closed because of a teacher's strike.

Bolivia is in the news these days mainly because of the U.S.-supported war on cocaine production and the current wave of strikes and consequent state of siege. The larger picture of an economy in shambles because of debt overhang is not as well known. The impact on the poor is the most tragic part of that picture.

CASE OF ZAMBIA

With a per capita gross national product of almost $600, Zambia is not the poorest African nation. With a foreign debt at the end of 1985 of a little over $4 billion, neither is it the largest debtor in Africa. However, with a population of only 6.5 million, its debt is among the highest in the world on a per capita basis. As a percentage of GNP, 84 percent, the debt of Zambia ranks seventh in the world, and the impact of the debt and the debt adjustment programs on the Zambian poor has been tragic.

This case study looks first at the decline of the bright economic hope of Zambia, then explores the economic consequences of the austerity programs, and finally examines the social consequences.

Dimming of Early Hope

A landlocked nation in central southern Africa, Zambia was until 1964 the British colony of Northern Rhodesia. When it gained independence, it was one of the most promising of the new African nations. Because of its prospering copper mines, Zambia appeared to have a bright economic future. The mining industry exercised tremendous influence on the national economy as it had during the decades of colonial rule. Over 90 percent of the foreign exchange earnings came from the sale of copper and mining towns grew and set a pattern of urban growth which accounts for the fact that over half the country's population lives in cities of over 25,000 people—a remarkable exception on the continent of Africa.

The generation of large amounts of foreign exchange gave Zambia the ability to import a considerable number of products, including food. Its own agricultural development was seriously neglected as a result. Rural population is relatively low and agriculture contributes less than 15 percent to the GNP. This is contrasted, for example, with 40 percent in the Sudan and 50 percent in Ghana.

Zambia's bright hopes at the time of independence began coming apart when the world price of copper plummeted in 1975, dropping from an average price of 93.23 to 56.10 cents per pound. Export earnings declined by more than 40 percent and government revenues were reduced to less than one-fifth of their previous level.[33]

The collapse of copper prices was attributed to two sources: the recession in the industrialized countries and the introduction of substitutes, cheaper materials, and new technologies such as fiberglass cables. Moreover, Zambia and other major copper exporters—Chile, Zaire, Peru—were unable to form a cartel like OPEC to influence the market for copper. Despite the dire situation and grim predictions, both the Zambian government and the world banking community assumed that the trend of lowered copper prices was temporary. However, with the exception of a brief rally in 1979–80, the price of copper has—even in current terms—remained below its peak in 1974.

To meet the decline in earnings, Zambia began to borrow heavily in order to maintain its standard of living. With the assumption that copper prices would eventually turn around and with the eagerness of the international community to extend credit, Zambia did not find it difficult to secure loans. As a result, it moved heavily into debt. In 1974, its total external debt was less than $1 billion. As table 9 shows, this figure rose steadily.

Of the $3.89 billion debt in 1984, $2.78 billion was long-term public and publicly guaranteed debt, $23.4 million was long-term private debt, $388 million was short-term debt (i.e., debt that has an original maturity of one year or less), and

$698 million involved use of IMF credit. The 1984 debt was 84 percent of the GNP and almost 390 percent of export earnings.

Through a series of major loans, Zambia has fallen deeper and deeper into debt while experiencing increasing difficulty in meeting repayments. This has brought numerous reschedulings. There have been five major IMF loans over the past eight years (1978, 1981, 1982, 1984, and 1986). The servicing of the huge foreign debt eats up most of Zambia's foreign exchange, causing a severe shortage of foreign exchange throughout the country, with consequences for every aspect of the economy. This has led to debilitating shortages of imported items such as fuel, agricultural inputs, capital goods, and spare parts upon which the Zambian economy is heavily dependent.

The immediate future does not look any better for the Zambian economy. The debt service obligations for 1986 are expected to be close to 83 percent of the projected total export earnings of $933 million. This would equal over $110 per Zambian citizen being paid out in debt service alone. With export earnings expected to continue to decline further in 1987, debt service is projected to remain over 80 percent.

Economic Effects of Conditionalities

Under pressure from the IMF, the Zambian government has undertaken a number of economic reforms and a restructuring along the lines of the classic package of "conditionalities." These have generally been geared toward improving the country's balance-of-payments situation (i.e., decreasing the deficits) and toward liberalizing the economy (i.e., structuring

TABLE 9

Zambian External Debt (1978–84)
(U.S. $ Billions)

1978	1980	1981	1982	1983	1984	1985
2.58	3.25	3.59	3.64	3.74	3.89	4.05

Source: IBRD, The World Bank, *World Debt Tables,* 1985–1986 ed. (Washington, D.C.: World Bank, 1986), p. 190.

it more along free market lines). The reforms have included devaluation of currency (the kwacha), increased agricultural producer prices, removal of subsidies on basic goods, wage ceilings, and tightening of credit. Each of these has had significant impacts upon the lives of the poor.

Devaluation has had quite dramatic consequences. At its introduction in January 1968, the kwacha was pegged to the U.S. dollar. Since then it has been officially devalued three times (1976, 1978, and 1985). Moreover, after July 1983, the kwacha was tied to a basket of currencies which reflected Zambia's trading partners so that it could be allowed to depreciate slowly. This led to a 40 percent devaluation against the U.S. dollar from July 1983 to July 1985.

Since by IMF standards the kwacha was still considered to be overvalued, a new approach was undertaken in the fall of 1985 with the introduction of a weekly foreign exchange auction. Under this system, the government makes available a certain amount of foreign exchange each week and the rate of exchange (its worth in kwacha) is determined by the free competition of bidders. As had been widely expected, the first auction on October 11, 1985, resulted in a sharp *de facto* devaluation of the kwacha. It slipped from the previous week's 2.20 kwachas per U.S. dollar to 5.01 kwachas per U.S. dollar. Since then, the kwacha has continued to decline. The auction rate for July 5, 1986, was 7.71 kwachas per U.S. dollar.

As is usual with the IMF austerity programs, the devaluation of the Zambian currency is intended to decrease the relative price for Zambian exports, thereby making them more competitive on the international market, and to increase the price of imports, thereby inhibiting their consumption. It is also hoped that the increased kwacha earnings from exports will encourage Zambians to enter the export business and earn the desperately needed foreign exchange. Together these measures should, the IMF believes, significantly improve the country's balance-of-payments situation.[34]

However, the effect of the kwacha devaluation, especially recently, has by and large been extremely detrimental to the economy as a whole. While it is true that the devaluation of the kwacha had some positive effects on the country's kwacha export earnings during 1986, its inflationary consequences have already begun to be felt, with a significant inhibitive effect on the domestic economic recovery. The price of gasoline doubled and the cost of essential imported machinery and equipment rose beyond the reach of many companies. Especially hard hit was the very industry which was to be one of the main beneficiaries of devaluation, the copper industry. As the primary foreign exchange earner for Zambia, this industry nevertheless is itself a major importer of fuel, machinery, and tools, and must pay its expatriate workers in foreign exchange (workers who are valuable, indeed essential, to the running of the industry).

One commentator notes the impact of this policy of devaluation:

> Zambian industry, hamstrung by shortages of spare parts and imported raw materials, is currently running at less than 50 percent capacity. As of last November (1985), only 2000 of 6500 tractors in the country were operational; 320 of the national bus company's 555 buses were out of service; the airport at Livingstone, site of Victoria Falls and thus Zambia's major tourist center, was closed because the airport fire truck had broken down; two and a half million bags of harvested corn had not yet been hauled from the countryside to dry storage, despite imminent arrival of the rainy season, because of shortage of trucks, tires, fuel, and tarpaulins. At the nation's largest copper mine, only 57 of 190 ore-hauling vehicles were serviceable. Copper production, the country's main earner of foreign exchange, has declined for several years because of shortages of spare parts, fuel, and explosives. There is a vicious circle rolling here. The shortage of foreign exchange makes it impossible to buy the foreign goods necessary to increase production to reduce the shortage of foreign exchange.[35]

Another IMF-supported governmental policy that has added to the inflation is the increase in agricultural producer prices. The intent behind this move has been to realign policies in favor of the rural areas. The reasoning for such policies is that higher prices will encourage more persons to farm more land in pursuit of increased profits. Between the seasons of

1980–81 and 1985–86, the agricultural price increases ranged from 233 percent for rice to 80 percent for sunflower, with an average of about 132 percent. These increases, combined with additional non-price incentives, seem to have had some of the desired positive effects. The past few years have seen a 20 percent increase in cultivated area and considerable growth in output—8.6 percent in 1983 and 9.5 percent in 1984.

This is indeed good news for the increased agricultural production will benefit not only the nutritional health of the people but also the balance of payments as less food is imported. But the change is not without its negative side effect which also must be acknowledged: An increase in agricultural producer prices is passed along almost entirely to consumers. Those who feel the impact most acutely are the poor. Moreover, this measure stands the risk of increasing the gap between the minority commercialized sector in agricultural production and the traditional subsistence farming majority. According to USAID studies of Zambia, the increased income from improved producer prices have gone disproportionately to the few commercial farmers and not to small farmers.

> At present, only about 25 percent of all rural farmers regularly produce for the market. The others are too poor or lack adequate production resources to engage in commercial agriculture. The annual cash income of the majority of rural households is less than $300, much of that earned from non-farm employment. At such limited income levels, the great majority of small farmers will be unable to purchase costly inputs and thereby break into the agricultural economy. . . . The economic efficiency criteria of the IMF are efficiently excluding most rural households from participation in their own economy.[36]

While the increase in producer prices is designed to benefit the agricultural sector, other governmental "reforms" are hurting it. These reform measures tend to be rooted in the IMF loan conditions that are oriented toward "liberalizing" the economy (i.e., removing market distortions), and reducing the governmental deficits. Included among these measures are the decontrol of interest rates, establishment of tighter credit policies, and the reduction or removal of subsidies on agricultural inputs such as fertilizer. The consequences of decontrol of interest rates have been very unfavorable to the small farmer, as the rates have gone beyond the reach of all but the largest commercial and company farms. In November 1985, a special Zambian Parliamentary Committee on Agriculture reported that the escalation of interest rates and the tightening of credit available to farmers had the potential for serious disruption of investment in the agricultural sector.

A combination of factors, including the removal of subsidies and the devaluation of the kwacha, have brought about an alarming rise in the cost of agricultural production. Between April and November 1985, farm machinery prices doubled, diesel fuel went up 93 percent, chemicals and transport costs rose 75 percent, and labor charges increased 35 percent. Moreover, interest rates on seasonal loans rose from 15 to 17.5 percent.

Reduced subsidies on agricultural inputs are only part of the larger approach to subsidy reduction and price decontrol that have become the policy of the government. These subsidies were approximately 10 percent of total governmental expenditures in 1980 and 1981. In December 1982, the government removed the controls on all prices except those of maize meal, wheat, bread, and candles.

The program of IMF conditionalities has had a significant impact on the rate of inflation. Price decontrol, currency devaluation, a general shortage of goods due to recession and import cuts, and increased producer prices have all led to an accelerated inflation. Low-income earners are certainly hit the hardest by this development. Even before the introduction of the foreign exchange auction, official estimates of the inflation rate were at an all time high: 32 percent for low-income earners and 27.4 percent for high-income earners. These official figures are viewed as grossly underestimated, for informed estimates put the actual 1985 rate of inflation at between 200 and 300 percent even before the auction. The auction itself accelerated this trend, and the prices of most basic goods—detergent, soap, vegetable oil, milk, bread, sugar, and fuel—all rose by at least 100 percent in the weeks following the auction.

These price rises have not been accompanied by corresponding increases in the wages of workers. Only mineworkers—a well-organized political force—and civil servants received any minimal wage increase at all. And the majority of Zambians are not involved in wage-earning situations. Wage employment dropped from 27 percent of the total labor force in 1975 to 20 percent in 1984.

The impact of all of these factors on the cost of living in Zambia has obviously been severe, and the poor have been hit the hardest. The World Bank recently estimated that in 1986 individual incomes are less than 60 percent of their 1974 level.[37] An earlier estimate made by the Zambian government in 1984 put the real income per capita, measured in U.S. dollars and adjusted for the terms of trade, at less than one-third of its 1974 level.

It is clear that such a deteriorating economic situation has dangerous political effects. There is increasing conflict between the government and the unions, which are pressing for minimum wage guarantees. There is also growing unrest among the people at large. In both urban and rural areas, a people, already poor, are getting poorer every day. Toward the end of 1985, two serious disturbances required the service of riot police. The first involved bus and taxi drivers protesting the government's tardiness in approving fare increases in the face of the 100 percent rise in fuel prices. The second involved university students angered by increased fees. They specifically objected to the IMF pressures to reduce government expenditures.

Social Indicators of the Deteriorating Economy

When Zambia gained independence in 1964, President Kenneth Kaunda and his ruling United National Independence Party (UNIP) pledged great efforts to improve the social conditions of all Zambians. Buoyed by a healthy economy based on the copper boom, large investments were made in the social sector. It is precisely the social conditions of Zambia which are severely threatened today as the economy slumps under the impact of the IMF conditionalities.

Education

Providing mass education for Zambian children became a major priority of the new government. At independence, there were fewer than 100 university graduates in the country. Schooling was severely limited for the black Zambians. Today, 96 percent of primary-age children are enrolled in school, with another 15 to 20 percent continuing on into secondary education. This compares with 42 percent and 2 percent, respectively, just twenty years ago. Of the 20–24 age group, 2 percent advance to further education. There is, however, a high dropout rate throughout the entire school system. The national literacy rate is still only about 40 percent.

This decisive improvement in education facilities and levels was accomplished by a steady increase in real current and capital expenditures from the time of independence through to the mid-1970s, with education receiving an average of 15 percent of the overall budget allocations. The worsening economic situation in Zambia has forced substantial cuts both in real terms and as a percentage of budgetary allocations. This has occurred at a time of substantial population growth. "Education now accounts for only 6.5 percent of public spending, while in real terms expenditure was 26 percent lower in 1984 than in 1975. On a per capita basis the cut was even greater, at 42 percent."[38]

Shortages of books and equipment have begun to appear throughout the country. As part of general cost-cutting measures, the government is introducing some boarding school fees for accommodation and food, and considering the introduction of school fees for children from higher-income families. This has provoked the student unrest mentioned earlier.

Health-Nutrition

Throughout the mid-1970s, the overall health situation in Zambia improved considerably. Budget allocations for health services for this period were around 8 percent of public spending. This significant input of resources into health care had very beneficial consequences: The ratio of people per doctor decreased from 9500 to 1 at independence to 7600 to 1 in 1980. With the expansion of rural health facilities and para-medical staff, today there is one person with some medical training for every 1700 people, compared with one person for 9920 at independence. Life expectancy has increased from 40 years at independence to 51 years today.

With Zambia's economic deterioration, however, substantial cuts in health care allocations have resulted. Now only 6 percent of total budgetary allocations are spent on health, and there has been a per-capita decline in real expenditures of 19 percent over the last nine years. Cutbacks in capital development and shortages of drugs and equipment have become the norm. Rural health centers, experiencing severe shortages, have been forced to turn away seriously ill people. A recent visitor to Zambia noted: "Zambia's leading hospital . . . was chronically short of surgical gloves and scalpel blades; most surgery patients bring their own, and non-emergency operations are postponed until they do."[39] To add to the problem, falling standards have combined with a severe erosion of real incomes to produce a mass exodus of medical staff, particularly among expatriate doctors.

There are now indications that the health status of the population in general is in a state of decline. According to the Food and Agricultural Organization (FAO) statistics, the supply of calories as a percentage of daily requirements has markedly declined, as has the supply of proteins per capita (see table 10).

The lowered food supply, combined with the skyrocketing cost of food, has certainly led to an increase of malnutrition in Zambia. Unfortunately, the data on this topic are not

TABLE 10

Zambian Nutritional Data

	CALORIES % OF DAILY REQUIREMENTS	PROTEINS (GRAMS) PER CAPITA/PER DAY
1975	101.0	65.9
1980	96.2	59.9
1983	83.5	48.3

Source: Food and Agriculture Organization (FAO), *Country Tables*, 1986.

extensive. One study in 1980 showed that over 30 percent of the urban dwellers had incomes lower than minimum food need levels and could not afford spending at levels which would meet their basic dietary needs. Other studies indicated that there had been notable declines in the average weight and height of children in both urban and rural areas. "A 1981 study for the Zambian government suggests . . . that malnutrition and related ill-health problems have been increasing since the mid-1970s."[40]

Summary

It is clear that the Zambian economy is in need of restructuring. The full consequences of the decline of the copper industry had been delayed by the artificial action of an infusion of large amounts of capital through loans which can never be repaid. Unlike its neighbor Zimbabwe, until lately Zambia has not made the necessary moves to build up a strong agricultural base for the country's future. Its economic deterioration is serious, and the immediate future does not look bright. World copper prices will probably stay low and may even decline further.

The question remains: Has the severe medicine of IMF conditionalities been in the best interests of the nation? Certainly to date, the pressure to devalue, to cut subsidies, to raise prices, and other "restructuring" moves has had disastrous consequences on the lives of the poor.

Zambia's future also cannot be seen outside the geopolitics of the region. As a leading "front-line state" and host of the offices of the African National Congress (ANC), Zambia is inextricably caught up in the drama of tragedy of South Africa. Its own economy is tied into that of South Africa, both through trade and through transportation links. Nonetheless President Kaunda has recently repeated the call for economic sanctions against the racist regime in Pretoria, with the knowledge that this can only lead to retaliatory sanctions against his own country.

In May 1986, the United Nations held a Special Session of the General Assembly on the Critical Economic Situation of Africa. Central to the concerns expressed by African leaders was the need to deal more effectively and equitably with the debt crisis of the developing countries of the continent. The heavy burden of debt and debt-servicing has seriously constrained Africa's prospect for economic growth. As is clear from the case of Zambia, a particularly heavy burden is borne on the shoulders of the poor of the continent.

SOME CONCLUDING COMMENTS

In economic reports in the United States newspapers during the past two years, the global debt crisis has ranked second only to the debate over tax reform. Of particular interest in these stories, of course, have been the predicted consequences for U.S. banks and for the overall U.S. economy in the case of defaults of some of the major debtor countries. The relative merits of the "Baker Plan" or the "Bradley Plan"—or the potential of the "Castro Plan" (a cartel of defaulting nations)—are widely debated in the press.

Attention is also being given—increasingly so, it would seem—to the effect on the poor in the debtor countries. Major front-page stories in the *Wall Street Journal* and the *Washington Post* have focused on the increasing misery of millions of people in Asia, Africa, and Latin America. As governments struggle to reschedule debt payments and restructure economic policy, the population struggles with diminished food budgets and curtailed social services. Commenting on the situation of Latin American poor, an article in the *Wall Street Journal* noted:

> Statistics quantifying their misery are often nonexistent or unreliable, but to authorities and experts working in Latin America the empirical evidence leads to an inescapable conclusion: A whole region is being pushed backward, so that what was once the middle class now plunges toward poverty, and what was once the poorer class now lives hand to mouth.[41]

At the same time, the reality of the debt situation is constantly evolving. Lower international interest rates will gradually benefit the debtor countries, and those heavily reliant on imported oil will gain some resources from lower oil prices. Some proportion of the loans to the LDCs are being bought back at a heavy discount, and there is some small movement into equity positions to replace debt. With regard to equity swaps, however, few will make the mistake of the Bolivian representative who set off a firestorm of domestic discontent by suggesting that the Bolivian oil industry should be sold to retire the debt!

The reality remains, however, that the economic trajectory of many LDCs, particularly in Latin America, is highly conditioned by the reality of the international debt load which they bear. There is no question that the economic policy in these countries will be greatly influenced by the requirements of debt servicing.

The claim of this paper is that the traditional way of responding to these pressures through an austerity program that is either mandated by the IMF or resembles the IMF prescription has carried with it significant and detrimental effects on the poor of these countries. *How politically wise and/or morally acceptable is a process which stabilizes the international monetary system at the expense of the poor in the debtor nations?*

There seems to be a grudging agreement growing in the international financial community that something much more substantial must be done than simply to float more new loans on the basis of more old conditionalities. That this is true is indicated by the elements of the new IMF programs with Mexico and the prolonged negotiations with Argentina and Brazil—both of whose performances seem to have been better in recent years than that of countries which adopted the austerity package. The lessons of these efforts, along with those of the East Asian countries which have not confronted external pressures by undertaking domestic austerity measures, need to be applied to any major new set of proposals to deal with the debt problem. And the relatively good performance of the large Asian countries of India and China—both much less integrated into the international economy—should also be taken into account.

However, the key issue will remain the resolution of the debt overhang in many of the developing countries. As this study so clearly shows, any resolution must be based upon a new construct of conditionality, one defined much more broadly, shared much more equally, and implemented much more responsively to the needs of the poor of the less developed countries.

It has been suggested that the period of the 1970s can be usefully understood in terms of the "conditionalities" which implicitly or explicitly underlay the major public policies of the times.[42] Some of these conditionalities were:

—as long as the well-to-do benefit from it
—as long as future generations pay for it
—as long as foreigners pay for it
—as long as investment pays for it.

Any new approach to public policy dealing with the debt overhang should include a series of explicit conditionalities which incorporate directly the concerns of this paper. Examples of these proposed conditionalities are:

—the policy steps should deal with the causes of the problem
—the costs must be shared rather than passed to the poor and to the less-developed countries
—the poor must benefit
—structural change should be more comprehensive than simple economic liberalization.

The success to date in dealing with the debt crisis has been in keeping the international financial system operating. It is time to move substantially beyond that to solve the underlying problems and, in doing so, the needs of the poor of the Third World should remain a central focus.

Notes

We would like to thank Sophia Twarog for her research assistance. Kenneth Jameson also acknowledges support from the Jesse Jones Faculty Research Travel Fund of the University of Notre Dame.

1. Overseas Development Council, "Global Debt," *Policy Focus*, no. 5 (1985), p. 3.

2. Investment Responsibility Research Corporation, Inc. "International Debt Crisis," *Proxy Issues Report*, Analysis L (March 1986), p. L-4.

3. Overseas Development Council, "Global Debt," *Policy Focus*, no. 5 (1985), p. 2.

4. Debt Crisis Network, *From Debt to Development: Alternatives to the International Debt Crisis* (Washington, D.C.: Institute of Policy Studies, 1985), p. 33.

5. Andre Gunder Frank, "Coping with the Debt Crisis," *World Policy Journal* (Summer 1984).

6. Investment Responsibility Research Corporation, Inc. "International Debt Crisis," *Proxy Issues Report*, Analysis L (March 1986), p. L-5.

7. Frank, "Coping with the Debt Crisis," *World Policy Journal*, p. x.

8. Morgan Guaranty Trust, "LDC Capital Flight," *World Financial Markets* (March 1986), p. 15.

9. Rudiger Dornbusch, "Dealing with Debt in the 1980s," *Third World Quarterly* 7 (July 1985), p. 539.

10. Investment Responsibility Research Corporation, Inc. "International Debt Crisis," *Proxy Issues Report*, Analysis L (March 1986), p. L-4.

11. Jack Anderson and Dale van Atta, "Mexican Debt Threatens U.S. Banks," *Washington Post*, June 19, 1986.

12. "Rescheduling's Ways," *The Economist*, October 5, 1985, p. 26.

13. Investment Responsibility Research Corporation, Inc. "International Debt Crisis," *Proxy Issues Report*, Analysis L (March 1986), p. L-14.

14. Jacques de Larosiere, *Does the Fund Impose Austerity?* (Washington, D.C.: International Monetary Fund, 1984).

15. Dornbusch, "Dealing with Debt in the 1980s," p. 547.

16. Lance Taylor, "ISM/LM in the Tropics: Diagrammatics of the New Structuralist Macro Critique," in *Economic Stabilization in Developing Countries*, ed. William Cline and Sydney Weintraub (Washington, D.C.: Brookings Institute, 1984).

17. Thomas Reichman and Richard Stilson, "Experience with Programs of Payments Adjustment: Stand-by Arrangements in the Higher Trenches, 1963–72," *IMF Staff Papers*, June 1978.

18. Charles Sisson, "Fund Supported Programs and Income Distribution in LDCs," *Finance and Development*, March 1986.

19. Kenneth Jameson, "Latin American Structuralism: A Methodological Perspective," *World Development* (February 1986), pp. 223–232.

20. The August 1986 agreement between Mexico and the world financial community may represent a further evolution for the major debtors. It provided for resources designed to stimulate an already inflation-prone economy and built in optimistic growth targets for 1987. This contrasts with the June 1986 treatment of Bolivia, which had adopted a stringent austerity program but received no loan until a complete reform of the tax system was rammed through the legislature.

21. It should be made clear at the outset that neither Bolivia nor Zambia are offered as prototypes, as the "typical" LDC under adjustment pressure. Bolivia's poverty and political instability and its efforts to resist the effects of the debt overhang differentiate it from other Latin American coun-

tries. Nevertheless, the reality of the debt overhang and of its effect on the poor is certainly reflected in the experiences of other countries. Zambia's mineral reliance, its status as a front-line state, and its long neglect of agriculture also distinguish it from the "average" African nation. However, the reality of the IMF austerity program and of its effect on the poor of the country is again reflected in the experience of other African countries.

22. The World Bank, *World Development Report, 1985* (New York: Oxford University Press, 1985), table 1.

23. Much of the basic information presented here is based on Rolando Morales, *La Crisis Economica en Bolivia y Su Impacto en las Condiciones de Vida de los Ninos.* 2 vols. (La Paz: Papiro, 1985). To facilitate the flow of the paper, specific references to these volumes will be omitted.

24. Economic Commission for Latin America and the Caribbean, "The Economic Crisis: Policies for Adjustment, Stabilization, and Growth," typescript, April 1986, p. 68.

25. Banco Central de Bolivia, *Boletin Estadistico*, no. 255 (February 1986).

26. Michael Mortimore, "El Estado y los Bancos Transnacionales," *Revista de la CEPAL* (August 1982), pp. 124–150.

27. Unidad de Analisis de Politicas Economicas, "Analisis de la Gestion Economica en Bolivia," typescript, October 1985.

28. Unidad de Analisis de Politicas Economicas, "La Economia Informal; en Bolivia: Una Vision Macroeconomica," typescript, September 1985.

29. Unidad de Analisis de Politicas Economicas, "Analisis de la Gestion Economica en Bolivia," typescript, October 1985.

30. Julio Prudencio, "Crisis de Abastecimiento y Estrategias de Resistencia en Bolivia: El Caso de la Paz," manuscript, 1986.

31. Another offset to these trends was the rapid growth in drug (cocaine) related activity which occurred in certain more remote areas of the country. This provided major increases in incomes for some and acted as an escape valve for many farmers who moved into coca production.

32. Jorge Rivera, "Las Repercusiones de la Crisis Economica en el Proceso Educativo y las Politicas del Sector," *La Recesion Economica Mundial y Su Impacto en las Condiciones de Vida de la Infancia* (La Paz: Edobol, 1985).

33. The source for basic economic information for Zambia presented here is the *Quarterly Economic Review of Zambia*, published by the Economist Intelligence Unit, especially no. 4 (October 1985), Annual Supplement (October 1985), and no. 1 (January 1986).

34. Edward Zuckerman, "A Study in Red: Zambia Succumbs to Its Debts," *Harper's Magazine* (April 1986), p. 49.

35. Ibid., 52.

36. Bill Rau, "Conditions for Disaster: The IMF and Zambia," typescript, 1983.

37. The World Bank, *World Bank News*, July 10, 1986, p. 10.

38. The Economist Intelligence Unit, *Quarterly Economic Review of*

Zambia. Annual supplement, October 1985, p. 8.

39. Zuckerman, "Study in Red," p. 52.

40. Rau, "Conditions for Disaster," p. 9.

41. Mary Williams Walsh and S. Karlen Witcher, "As Debt Turmoil Ebbs and Flows in Mexico, Human Misery Persists," *Wall Street Journal*, June 12, 1986.

42. Marcos Mamalkis, "A North-South Dilemma: The Needs and Limits of Conditionalities in the Americas," *Journal of Interamerican Studies and World Affairs* 99 (February 1985): 103–121.

The Political Implications of Austerity

Few attempts have been made to specify the consequences of
austerity programs for the poor. The work presented by
Henriot and Jameson, therefore, makes a significant empirical
contribution to this discussion. Their detailed analysis of the
impact of stabilization programs in Bolivia and Zambia links
IMF-sponsored austerity policies to a contraction of basic
health and educational programs for the poor, growing problems with malnutrition and illiteracy, and a rising potential for
increased political instability. Although the underdeveloped
state of research on this topic makes it difficult to specify the
precise nature of those linkages or to control for other variables that may affect these developments, Henriot and Jameson's work calls our attention to these deepening social
problems and provides useful evidence in support of an alternative approach to economic stabilization.

Implicitly, their analysis sets out two important general
principles on which an alternative adjustment procedure might
be based. One is a commitment to shelter the poor from the
most harmful consequences of stabilization. This commitment
would encourage governments and the technical missions that
advise them to avoid policy adjustments that have a particularly detrimental impact on the most disadvantaged sectors of a
society. This approach would require governments to develop
mechanisms that buffer those social programs that address the

---

*Rose J. Spalding is a member of the political science faculty at DePaul
University. An authority on Central America, she has published extensively
on the politics of banking and agricultural systems in that region.

basic needs (food, housing, primary education, public health care) of low-income groups. Instead of approving across-the-board cuts in governmental spending or reductions that cut heavily into essential services, governments would be encouraged to carefully preserve these priority programs and locate other areas for budget reductions.

The second principle underlying Henriot and Jameson's paper is the understanding that solutions to economic problems should be closely tied to their causes. As the authors point out, the IMF's tendency to endorse a formulaic response, without much attention to the particular character of the country involved, makes it difficult to match causes and solutions. If one of the major causes of an economic crisis is that a military regime has engaged in profligate borrowing and spent unwisely for speculative or unproductive investments, then a reduction in, say, food subsidies or an increase in energy prices will not provide an appropriate solution to the country's problem. Or if the direct cause of financial instability is an abrupt decline in a country's terms of trade, the IMF injunction to cut the government's fiscal deficit may do very little to restore economic equilibrium. In such a case, a better course of action might be to urge further diversification of exports and to perhaps provide additional loans to finance the necessary economic restructuring. Or, as Henriot and Jameson suggest, the solution might require that the country avoid still deeper insertion into the international market and shift instead toward a more nationally centered, self-sufficient development strategy.

If we accept the two Henriot-Jameson principles—the importance of protecting the poor in the midst of an economic crisis and the need to tie policy solutions more closely to the causes of economic problems—then we are on our way to identifying a more equitable and developmentally sound approach to economic stabilization. If such an alternative is not pursued, the debt quagmire and recurring rounds of austerity crises will threaten much of the Third World with prolonged economic contraction, deepening impoverishment of the poor, and, as Henriot and Jameson note, rising political instability.

The link between austerity and political instability deserves further consideration. Henriot and Jameson note the angry riots in the Dominican Republic, Chile, Colombia, Peru, and Panama that were associated with the austerity-induced elimination of food and transportation subsidies. These open clashes are an important manifestation of the instability that austerity programs can trigger. They are, however, only the most visible and direct expressions of rising political discontent. The political systems of countries implementing austerity programs are being affected in other ways that are not so immediately apparent. Recurring economic problems and stabilization programs may lead to a decline of what political scientists have called "diffuse support." Healthy and vibrant political systems rely on widespread acceptance of the basic institutions of the government and a prevailing belief in the general legitimacy of the political order. When this kind of diffuse support wanes, sectors of the society begin raising serious questions about the legitimate authority of the regime. Under these circumstances, the willingness of the citizenry to accept the institutions of the state—ranging from elections to law enforcement to tax collection—declines and the potential for sweeping political instability rises.

With austerity "recidivism," these governments may lose not only mass acquiescence but also their capacity for innovative policy response. As governments attempt to abide by austerity measures, they forfeit national control over economic policy and turn short-term and even medium-term economic planning over to external agencies. In the process, they may curtail the research and planning activities of economic ministries and policy-oriented "think tanks" and lose the ability to investigate alternative proposals more in keeping with their own local needs. This process can ultimately erode the administrative capabilities of the state, as economic ministries wither and planning boards expire.

Prolonged adherence to austerity planning, therefore, can undermine "diffuse support" and contribute to a deepening legitimacy crisis, at the same time that it weakens the state administrative apparatus and undercuts policy innovation. This combination of rising opposition and a weakening state can be quite combustible. Persistent political instability is a likely result.

Henriot and Jameson tend to regard this instability as a troubling development. We should be cautious about making that assumption. Recent political changes in Latin America suggest that this political instability can be a constructive force. Since the end of the 1970s, the South American technocratic military regimes have been severely shaken, and several have been supplanted by civilian alternatives. This "redemocratization" process may be, at least in part, linked to the sharp economic contraction and the implementation of austerity programs that proved so socially, politically, and economically disruptive. We may look back on this period as one that had devastating social and political consequences in the short run, but that was ultimately politically constructive in that it undermined exclusionary regimes and supported the emergence of a new round of democratic rule.

Of course, technocratic military regimes are not the only ones that are being challenged by the pressures of austerity. Their more pluralistic successors face the same kinds of problems. Democratic regimes may be somewhat more resilient than their military predecessors, but their survival can also be threatened by prolonged economic stagnation and austerity programming. Several recent studies of the regional "transition to democracy" have concluded on a pessimistic note, suggesting that the process may be only temporary. Another round of authoritarianism may follow in its wake if the region's economic stagnation is not relieved.

Recognizing this, political leaders in reemerging democratic regimes like Peru and, to a lesser extent, Brazil have increasingly rejected the orthodox, IMF-sponsored austerity packages. They have begun to fashion different types of adjustment processes that cushion budget reallocations and allow continued growth. Studies like that by Henriot and Jameson may support this kind of innovation by clarifying the social and political costs associated with following the conventional austerity guidelines. Ultimately, this kind of work may encourage further exploration of alternative approaches to economic stabilization and promote different conceptions of national development.

A Time for Adjustment with Growth

NICOLAS ARDITO-BARLETTA *

I cannot disagree with the major thrust of the paper by Henriot and Jameson: We need a new formula to manage the debt problem; we need to define the problem more broadly; we need to share the debt burden more equally; we need to implement the new formula much more responsibly.

While the Henriot-Jameson paper contains excellent information, it needs more analysis. Certainly, there is a moral dimension to this question, and, equally important, in order to strengthen political action, there is a mutual advantage dimension in the solution to this problem. I have shared a similar position since 1983 when I was Vice President at the World Bank, but there are some caveats and important differences which should become evident in these comments.

The formula put in place in 1982 to try to resolve this crisis has not worked satisfactorily. A change is needed. However, the basic concept behind the formula is still a valid one. First and most important, it was recognized that the crisis was a worldwide responsibility, not just a problem of debt of developing countries or of the Latin American countries. The crisis affected all economic variables as well as all regions of the world. In 1983, for example, it was estimated that out of $320 billion of external debt in Latin American countries, $85 billion (that is, 25 percent of the total) was due to increases in oil

*Nicolas Ardito-Barletta is the general director of the International Center for Economic Growth. He is the former constitutional president of the Republic of Panama and has served as the vice president, Latin American and Caribbean region, of the World Bank.

prices, decreases in commodity export prices of Latin American products, and increases in interest rates. This illustrates the fact that it was a widely shared problem.

The actions adopted to resolve the problem would take into account the potential and the limitations of each one of the partners to this problem—developing countries, developed countries, and the international financial community. Concretely speaking, this meant taking into account the political opportunity and the political and economic limits of the capacity of each of these partners to apply solutions to the problem. This criterion of the basic concept remains critical today as we reevaluate the formula put in place four years ago.

That formula included three actions. The first was that the developing countries, especially the Latin American countries where the bulk of the debt is concentrated, would adjust their economies to the new world realities. This has happened: Imports dropped by 40 percent in Latin America over the last four years—a total of $40 billion. The trade account (exports over imports) improved by $35 billion in two years. The net transfer of resources to Latin America went from plus $5 billion to minus $30 billion in three years.

We are transmitting resources from Latin America to the developed countries, and this has created a severe level of social sacrifice. In Mexico, real wages went down by 35 percent in three years. Imagine what would happen in the United States if real wages should drop by 35 percent in three years? What would happen to the political system? Mexico and its institutions are still there. The gross domestic product of Latin America as a whole declined by 12 percent over the last four years. Currencies have been devalued by between 25 to 40 percent in real terms in at least eight countries. But, fiscal deficits have been reduced, and adjustment has been taking place, in some countries more than others.

The second action of the formula was that the banks and the financial community would reschedule and restructure the debts and would provide additional funding in order to ease the adjustment. The latter has not happened. Instead, there has been a net negative transfer of resources out of the region. The banks have cooperated and have worked very hard—this has to be recognized. But at the same time they have received $142 billion worth of interest over the last four years. Interest rates remain high in real terms, and they are a big burden in the servicing of the debt. So in this second action, the effort to help the countries ease their adjustment has not been sufficient. It is estimated that $20 billion per year additional funding is needed over the next three years to complement the countries' efforts to grow again.

The third action was that the developed countries, which were also adjusting and reducing inflation four years ago, would grow again and would help improve the terms of trade for the commodities that are the major exports of the debtor countries. The United States did grow again; it now has a large trade deficit. Other developed countries have not had dynamic economic growth and have not contributed as much. At the same time they are putting in place more protectionist measures than the United States. We have to credit the United States that, so far, it has not increased in a significant way the level of protectionist barriers to trade. However, the developed countries can contribute much more to world recovery and to an easier process of adjustment through their own growth.

In evaluating that tripod of actions to correct the world economic imbalance evident in 1982, the 1984 results were good, and the 1985 results were unsatisfactory. The 1986 performance does not look much better. Obviously, with the lower interest rates, the lower oil prices, and some commodity price increases (e.g., coffee), the situation will show some improvement. Some countries are beginning to grow again, especially Brazil, but also Colombia, Chile, and Peru. It is an open question whether that growth can be sustained. But a new formula under the same criterion is needed—a formula which requires a greater contribution from the financial community and the developed countries. This would permit adjustment with growth in the developing countries, which would ameliorate the unemployment and the plight of the poor.

I disagree with the implication of the Henriot-Jameson paper that there is no need for adjustment by the developing countries. Countries were not obliged nor forced to borrow. The opportunity was there. They took advantage of it. They overborrowed at negative real interest rates thinking that such a situation was going to continue and they got themselves in trouble when the overall economic situation changed due to the policies of oil exporting countries and of the developed countries. Colombia is an example of a country that managed much better, not overindebting itself, and Colombia's present situation is better than that of other countries.

Bolivia is not really the best example to highlight the point that adjustment with recession is increasing poverty levels. The information presented on Bolivia may illustrate a point but the country has had other long-standing difficulties not caused by the international settings which have deeply affected its situation.

At this point, these countries can and should do more for themselves. The key here is that they should get into a position of adjustment with growth, because with growth, some of the poverty problems will be reduced or even eliminated. We need to regain the track to growth. More funding is needed from the international community, either in positive net quantities or perhaps through a formula to avoid paying interest on old debt for three years. At the same time, these countries can do more to adjust their economies and prepare them for growth, while simultaneously diminishing the burden on the poor. They could decrease expenditures in armaments; they could reduce corruption; they could reduce waste and mismanagement; and they could target better expenditures to help the poor. A global perspective is needed to identify a realistic solution.

In addition, help is needed to make self-adjustment politically viable for these countries. We cannot ask so much of them, without giving additional support, that they would fail because of the political situation or the weakness of institutions. We need to allow them to return to growth as they continue adjusting. The actions have to be phased differently, on a country-by-country basis, with more flexibility, to provide more financial support and greater export opportunities.

While the debtor countries need to continue to work for themselves, the international community, because of moral concern and the mutual advantage opportunities that derive from enlightened self-interest, has a commitment to provide more help than it is doing at the present time. Better trade and financial flows are necessary. The interest rates must continue to go down in real terms. Better policy coordination is needed among countries. Through meetings for economic policy coordination, the seven key countries are making a more concerted effort to solve the economic problems. There is also the need for better coordination between those seven countries and the key debtor countries, in Latin America and the rest of the developing world.

Four years of stagnation is too much. One or two years would have been acceptable, but with four years social indicators are showing that it is too costly, too socially and politically painful for these countries to continue to adjust in a way that does not demonstrate *to the people* that effective and positive results are achieved. The political implementation of the optimum policies requires that some positive results are achieved beyond abstract financial indicators, results that can be appreciated by the people at large. The new wave of democratic governments in Latin America needs the external support to succeed. The stability of these democratic governments will depend on their ability to show that difficult and often unpopular policies do succeed and that the situation of the majority of the people can again be improved.

The crux of the matter depends on the ability of developing countries to turn the increasing savings generated as a result of the adjustment policies into larger investment flows so that growth can be regained. With growth regained, policies that increase savings faster than consumption are needed in order to permit both investment and debt service to be maintained. This way both greater solvency and social improvement will again be feasible. But to achieve that, more external financing and open markets for developing country exports are needed.

Adjustment is needed, but it can be achieved more effectively over a longer period of time through growth and human development. It would be self-beneficial as well as morally right for developed countries and the international financial community to now give the financial and the trade support required as a complement to the efforts of the indebted countries. The developed countries would gain in trade, financial stability, reduced immigration, and world stability. These are not insignificant gains. Developing countries should not be forced to choose between serving external debt or providing for the welfare of their people.

PART II

Debtor Country
Developmental Strategies

As Third World governments respond to the debt crisis and the various policies imposed as conditions for rescheduling old debt and obtaining new funds, they initiate domestic changes that will have enduring effects. In the second part of the volume, we explore alternative national coping strategies, their potential effectiveness in the long term as well as in the short term, and how policies are helped or hindered by externally imposed conditionalities.

There are important differences in the nature of the debt crisis as well as in alternative responses available to governmental policymakers in Africa, Asia, and Latin America. Both Latin American and sub-Saharan African countries find themselves in difficult circumstances. However, even though Latin American countries have accumulated a heavier debt burden, they have greater promise for renewed economic development than countries in sub-Saharan Africa. Asian countries seem to be coping very well.

In a careful analysis of Latin American experience and prospects, Alejandro Foxley argues that through new social contracts those countries can rekindle development with revised internal policies and adjustments, combined with only a modicum of support from the international financial system. He expresses severe doubts about the viability of the strategies implemented so far and stresses the importance of creating an environment that stimulates productivity at the plant level.

Kwan Kim traces the deterioration of sub-Saharan Africa over the past ten years indicating that, short of massive external support, even the barest, minimally acceptable levels of development simply will not occur. In contrast to the African and Latin American experience, the newly industrializing countries of East Asia have fared well through the debt crisis. Kim outlines the coping strategy of Korea and how Korea was able to minimize the effect of the external shocks that led to the severe debt crisis in so many other countries.

Four panelists comment on governmental strategies and how they are influenced by conditionalities imposed by multilateral institutions such as the World Bank, the International Monetary Fund, and the Inter-American Bank. Paul Streeten points out the double paradox of conditionality and calls for greater freedom in debtor country policy selection with measures of performance tied to results, including human rights, rather than to the policies. Guillermo Chapman distinguishes between short-term and medium-term adjustment with the policies for near-term stabilization and medium-term structural changes coordinated within an overall long-term national developmental strategy. Richard Webb shares the Peruvian experience, asking how Peru can adjust at minimum cost to what he sees as a permanent deterioration in the balance of payments. He outlines the Peruvian decision to tie debt service to exports and observes that the resulting restrictions on new funds is probably fatuous. Chandra Hardy argues for a complete change of mindset in which we recognize that a new conditionality will not solve the problem; that development is losing the race against population; and that balanced development which reaches the poor depends upon a redistribution of assets and redirection of investment.

The participants' reaction to these papers and responses is overviewed in a discussion summary at the end of the section. The focus is on growth—its importance, possibility, and long-term implications.

Latin American Development after the Debt Crisis

ALEJANDRO FOXLEY *

Latin America has reached an impasse. After five years of harsh adjustment programs, the prospects for economic growth in the major debtor countries are far from promising. Current projections, based on an oil price of $18 per barrel and interest rates around 8 percent, show a likely rate of GDP growth for the rest of the decade of not higher than 3.7 percent per year.[1] At this growth rate, Latin America would be barely recuperating its precrisis levels of GDP by 1990. A full decade of growth would be lost.[2] Moreover, given this growth rate and a labor force that grows at more than 2 percent a year, the employment prospectives for the rest of the decade do not look favorable. Total external debt would reach $480 billion by 1990. The debt-export ratio would still be, on average for the region, higher than 300 percent and, by some estimates, Latin America would still be needing something on the order of $30 billion a year in net capital inflow.[3]

These figures are important because they confirm widespread doubts about the viability of the strategy implemented so far. This strategy was formed at a time when Latin America's economic prospects appeared more promising. By the end of

*Alejandro Foxley is the Helen Kellogg Professor of International Development at the University of Notre Dame, and the president of the Corporation for Latin American Economic Research (CIEPLAN) in Santiago, Chile. He is a member of "The InterAmerican Dialogue" and the executive committee of the International Economic Association.

69

the 1982–1983 debt crisis, expectations for a more permanent solution to the problem had been bolstered by the rapid growth in world trade, which would have enabled significant expansion in the economies of the debtor countries and increased their ability to pay back their debts. This optimistic perspective was influenced by the views of the creditor banks on the best method of resolving the crisis, and it prevailed until early 1985.

The strategy of the banks consisted of trying to achieve two simultaneous objectives. First, they wanted their financial position to improve rapidly. They planned to achieve this by reducing their credit volume in Latin America and capitalizing a high proportion of their profits so as to cover themselves against the risk of nonpayment by some of the debtors. Their success in fulfilling this objective meant that by mid-1985, their financial position was already equal (in terms of the ratio between the banks' capital and their claims in debtor countries) to the level in the years preceding the debt crisis.[4]

Second, the banks wanted to improve the ability of three major debtors—Mexico, Brazil, and Argentina—to make their payments. The banks closely followed the performance of these economies and in-depth studies were undertaken to evaluate their prospects at the end of the decade.

Banks measure a country's creditworthiness on a variety of aggregate ratios. The one that is probably used most often is the debt-export ratio. A country is considered to be solvent and creditworthy when this is under 200 percent. It should not be surprising, then, that the banks felt confident when some financial institutions made projections for Brazil and Mexico and found, under plausible assumptions, that these countries seemed capable of reaching the year 1990 with a debt-export ratio under 200 percent. There was still concern about Argentina whose situation was particularly difficult to forecast, both because of the government's unclear position on the debt payment and the uncertainty surrounding the application of an internal economic adjustment policy which Argentina did not appear ready to accept. However, in June 1985, when Argentina implemented a shock policy that was even harsher than the IMF's and showed a willingness to catch up on foreign debt interest payments, it seemed that the main obstacles to solving the debt problem in Latin America had dissipated.

Of course, the banks were aware that the situation of the other countries in Latin America was not necessarily the same as that of the major debtors. In fact, projections for the small and medium-sized countries, such as Chile, Peru, Bolivia, Nicaragua, Jamaica, and others, showed that their debt-export ratios did not reach the minimum necessary to be regarded as creditworthy. The position the banks took on these other countries was that governments and multinational agencies should aid their economies with easy credit terms.

The current situation of the principal debtors has modified the banks' optimistic outlook. The September 1985 issue of *World Financial Markets* reviews its previous projections for the economies of Argentina, Brazil, and Mexico so that none of the three countries even approaches, by the end of the decade, the threshold of a 200 percent debt-export ratio. The levels projected for 1990 are about 300 percent for Brazil and Mexico; 350 percent for Argentina.[5] These estimates do not take into account the impact of oil price reduction on the Mexican economy, which is already having a devastating effect on that country's capacity to meet its debt obligations.

The deterioration of the economies in these countries is not an isolated occurrence. It is clearly a problem affecting the entire region. According to bank sources, around October 1985, ten Latin American nations were behind in their interest payments; six others had not been successful in meeting the goals of the adjustment programs established by the IMF; and two others refused even to negotiate with the IMF. In 1985, Bolivia and Nicaragua fell behind in their payments, and Peru unilaterally announced a ceiling on the interest that it would pay and refused to negotiate with the IMF. The Dominican Republic and Jamaica struggled to maintain a precarious level of domestic stability in the face of extremely severe austerity policies. Chile entered into a new period of economic stagnation. Mexico held back payment of nearly one billion dollars and requested more than six million dollars to keep up with its payments in 1986. The IMF declared Mexico to be out of compliance with the established goals. Brazil kept up its interest payments, but was not able to settle differences with the IMF regarding an adjustment program.

Against this economic backdrop, Latin America's main debtor countries were applying political pressure for a new approach to solving the debt problem; one that would be compatible both with the banks' goal of avoiding a solvency crisis and with the resumption of the economic growth in Latin American economies which was seen as indispensable to payment of the foreign debt. Some analysts interpreted these political reactions of the governments as a symptom of "adjustment fatigue."

BEYOND "ADJUSTMENT FATIGUE"

As has been indicated in the previous section, growth expectations for Latin America do not offer much hope for improvement in living conditions in the reasonable future. In light of this, some countries tend to regard efforts to comply with the current adjustment policy as simply pointless. It is important to note, in spite of this perception, that most countries have not considered the option of a moratorium, such as the one that occurred in the 1930s. This is because they have believed until now that the costs would be too high. On the one hand, considerable emphasis has been placed on the possibility of a liquidity crisis, which could arise if the flow of credit to a country were suddenly interrupted. On the other hand, there has been hope that "good behavior" in the form of timely payment of the debt would create conditions to quickly reestablish voluntary credit channels through the international banking system.

Another important consideration in the past was the internal political situation. Authoritarian governments, who saw their internal base of support weakening, attempted to strengthen links with their principal sources of outside political and economic support—the U.S. government, multinational institutions, and creditor banks. This was the case in Chile, which became the most faithful observer of conditions favored by the IMF, the banks, and the U.S. government, and main-

tained this observance despite the catastrophic social consequences of the imposed adjustment.

Paradoxically, Latin America's new democracies arrived at
similar political conclusions, but for different reasons: The
fragile nature of these new democratic systems and the absolute importance of avoiding any economic disaster set off by a
sudden break in the flow of credits from banks led governments, such as those in Argentina, Uruguay, and Brazil, to be
overly cautious in their approach to the debt questions and,
despite their reluctance, to follow the policies suggested by the
IMF and the banks. The perception of the costs of not having
credit available, however, has been changing because the flow
of credit toward these countries has actually been decreasing
dramatically since the end of 1984. Despite their "good performance," several of these economies are currently going through
various liquidity problems. Recent events in Mexico are a sali-
ent example. One has only to look at the figures to see where
the problem lies: The net credit from private international
banks to the seven major debtor countries in Latin America
grew by only 2.5 percent in 1983 and by 1.6 percent in 1984;
during the first quarter of 1985, the net flow was negative.[6]

The threat of loss of access to voluntary bank loans in the
future is also diminishing in effectiveness in view of the general impression in financial and political circles that the banks
will not voluntarily renew a normal flow of credit before the
end of this decade, except perhaps to larger countries, such as
Brazil, which have been able to sustain solid recovery with significant levels of economic growth.

The cost of reducing concerted actions with banks in favor of more concerted actions among countries is considered
lower now, not only for the reasons mentioned above, but also
because in several cases these governments have been able to
considerably strengthen their internal basis of political support. The examples set by Alfonsín, Sanguinetti, García, and
Sarney illustrate this point very well. It could be argued that
precisely this perception of the economic crisis, combined
with the impossibility of improving the economic situation by
depending, as in the past, on high levels of external credit,
might make it possible for Latin America's new leaders to

launch an appeal for large-scale nationwide mobilization in order to solve the debt crisis through domestic savings and internal efforts.

The recent experience of Argentina could serve as a lesson. So long as the country's economic situation did not deteriorate drastically, it was impossible to attain the political support necessary for economic adjustment. Alfonsín's political talent enabled him to recognize the critical point of crisis and convert it into an opportunity. When the gravity of the crisis became well known and there was no other alternative open to Alfonsín's government, it took harsh economic measures—the so-called "Plan Austral"—which the population as a whole supported despite the immediate costs to each particular group. Alfonsín came out of the crisis stronger and was able to gain time before tackling the structural problems underlying the current economic crisis in Argentina. The same happened in Brazil in early 1986, when the "Plan Cruzado" was put into practice with widespread popular support.

The point is that it *is* possible for a country subject to severe external constraints to achieve dynamic levels of growth. But it needs leadership capable of mobilizing the population through a national developmental plan which spurs the country's imagination and encourages it to make a special effort to save and work in order to free itself from crisis. What countries need are their own national strategies for overcoming constraints. Much historical experience points in this direction. What blocks this path for Latin American countries in the 1980s is their governments' limited autonomy in defining national developmental plans in response to their own institutional structures, experience, and knowledge, on the basis of past successes and failures.

A New Conditionality?

Current efforts by the U.S. government point to a shift in the focus of its approach to the debt problem by acknowledging the need for economic growth in order to pay off debt. Greater emphasis is now being placed on the importance of structural change for renewed growth. Structural readjustment could be a necessary condition for the proper use of capital that agencies such as the World Bank might make available to debtor countries at higher levels. This increase in resources would be subject to compliance with long-term developmental policies consistent with the "correct policies" view held by these agencies and/or the governments that have the greatest influence on them. This would represent a new form of conditionality which would be superimposed over that defined so far by the IMF.

However, the extension of the principle of conditionality to the sectoral or structural change programs undertaken by developing countries may imply limiting the ability of each country to find the developmental scheme most effective in mobilizing its creative energies. Public statements by Secretary Baker seem to be saying to the multinational developmental organizations that their new mandate is to loan preferably to those indebted countries that are willing to try in a serious way to move toward "reaganomics": privatization of public enterprises, free-market policies, free trade practice, liberalization of financial markets, supply side incentives through lower taxes. It would seem that this new form of conditionality takes little account of the past experiences of some countries who have used such policies, particularly in the Southern Cone in Latin America.

Jamaica is another instance. This country has been subjected to simultaneous and superimposed conditionality by the IMF and the World Bank over its economic policy and developmental program. Its structural adjustment program included more than twenty simultaneous conditions that cover domestic concerns (such as privatization of state-run bus companies and publically held land, reorganization of the stock exchange, a program for reforming public administration, altering government-run hotel rates and public radio commercials rates, and introducing staff-reduction quotas in specific state-run companies) in addition to the more standard conditions on foreign trade, taxation, and finance.

If this form of conditionality becomes more widespread, countries will be severely constrained in defining their own developmental programs and will have no leeway in their application; in some cases, they will be led into the same errors committed by those Latin American countries who hurriedly liberalized their economies in the 1970s. The alternative for these countries would be to seek a deliberate delinking from the international economy. This may become an appealing alternative for some countries in the area. But the historical lesson is well known: Isolated, autarchic countries with "wartime economies" inevitably end up restricting civil liberties and developing very authoritarian-looking "wartime policies."

We will return to these topics shortly. First, however, it is useful to critically examine the basic assumptions of the current strategy for solving the debt problem.

EXTERNAL AND INTERNAL ADJUSTMENTS

There are two aspects that contribute to the fragility of the current strategy for solving the debt problem: The first is related to the notion that industrial countries' growth will be the basic mechanism by which debtor countries will be able to solve the debt problem in the long run. The second has to do with the difficulty of sustaining the massive transfers of funds from debtor countries to developed countries that have been occurring since the inception of the debt crisis.

The Locomotive Theory

According to this theory, the debt problem could be solved, without the need for governmental intervention, if stable, strong growth rates were achieved in the industrial economies.

Strong growth rates—above 3 percent for the OECD economies—would make it possible to expand the exports of developing countries to annual rates of at least 6 percent.[7] With real interest rates in the international markets projected between 4 and 5 percent, the higher growth of exports would make it possible for these countries to allocate even fewer exports to debt service maintenance than before. Thus, the solution for the problem would not be short term, but a favorable result would be guaranteed in the medium term, with no other intervention than that necessary for maintaining sound macroeconomic policies.

The developed economies in 1984 grew at a respectable 5 percent, a high rate which stemmed from the 6.8 percent economic growth in the U.S. economy that year. This rapid growth, aided by unusually high U.S. demand for imports as a consequence of the high dollar, made it possible for Latin American exports to the United States to grow at an astounding rate. This higher growth of exports actually began in 1983, providing for that two-year period an annual expansion rate of 32 percent in exports from Latin America to the United States, although the impact was partially offset by a drop in Latin American exports to the rest of the world. These results seemed to fully validate the strategy currently being used.

In 1985, however, the situation took a sudden turn for the worse. Industrialized nations as a whole grew only at a rate of 2.8 percent. This modest growth was accompanied by continued deterioration in the purchasing power of Latin American exports. In 1985 alone, it decreased by 4.6 percent;[8] and most analysts agree that the deteriorated terms of trade for Latin America are not likely to recuperate in the short to medium term.[9] These figures show the fragility of the mechanism on which the debt-payment capacity of debtor countries is based.

The "locomotive" mechanism, which presumes that rapid, stable growth in the industrialized economies would create a sweeping demand for Latin American exports as well as an automatic improvement in the region's terms of trade, does not seem to be reliable enough to bring about an "automatic" market solution to the debt problem in Latin America. There is a need for intervention from governments and international lending institutions in order to "guide" the process, neutralizing the negative impact of external "shocks," until the economies are able to recover their ability to grow in a sustained manner and pay off the debt.

Can Internal Efforts for Paying the Debt in Latin America be Sustained?

Since 1983 Latin America annually transferred about US$30 billion to the industrialized countries. This represents approximately 5 percent of the region's GNP. To effect this transfer, Latin American economies had to free resources that would otherwise have been added to internal savings for investment. Transfers were paid with the foreign exchange produced from surplus trade balances. If the economy is at full employment, these surpluses are achieved by reducing internal spending in order to generate the savings that need to be transferred abroad.

In order to ensure their ability to transfer resources for paying the debt, countries apply adjustment programs negotiated with the IMF. Although the nature of these programs is well known, two aspects should be emphasized: the dual conditionality to which the countries are subject, and the fact that the IMF programs tend to ignore particular circumstances and new economic constraints arising from the debt crisis itself.

Dual conditionality occurs because different entities—the banks on the one hand and the IMF on the other—each impose their own conditions. After the debt crisis, the international banks decided to limit the total amount of loans a given country may receive. They use three criteria to determine these totals: their need to reduce banks' exposure in a given country, their aim to increase reserves in order to cover the risk of non-performing loans, and their decision to give out new loans only to the extent required by a given country in order to allow it to continue interest payments without affecting its creditworthiness. As a consequence, the internal effort that the country has to make is determined by the size of its debt and the level of the interest rate, as well as by the banks' upper limit in their desired lending to the country in question as derived from the above-stated criteria.[10]

The resource constraint for the country is thus determined by the amount of new external credit the banks and official agencies are willing to provide. The magnitude of the internal adjustment effort that the country must make is in turn conditioned by the ceiling imposed by the banks on the new lending that is available. This is the first conditionality constraint.

A second type of conditionality is present when the country asks the IMF to help finance a balance-of-payments deficit. The IMF usually sets two types of conditions. First, the country should reduce imports by tightening spending, and second, the country has to take measures that would allow it to divert resources to the production of either exportable goods or goods that can be used to replace imports.

The adjustment that began in 1982 in Latin America showed just these features, and the results were as expected. Imports dropped very rapidly. Significant reductions in production followed. The drops in production resulted from Latin America's traditional dependence on imported raw materials and imported capital goods for full capacity use and internal production expansion. When imports fall 40 percent in two years, as was the case in 1982–1983, the resulting shortages in raw materials and intermediate goods inevitably brings down output levels in the economy.

Internal adjustment policies have also created huge complications in the fiscal sector. The IMF has always placed emphasis on reducing the fiscal deficit. The recommendation is often very simple. The rule of thumb seems to be: Cut the deficit in half each year, regardless of its relative level.

Following the period of financial liberalization in Latin America, two events occurred. The governments, state-run companies, and the private sector borrowed excessively abroad. When external funds evaporated, the renegotiation of loans became inevitable. At this point the international banks pressured governments to take over external liabilities contracted by the private sector. This was achieved by either government guarantees on the private debt or by having the public sector assume the obligation to make payments in dollars.

In order to make the interest payments on the foreign debt, governments had to purchase dollars with surplus internal resources obtained either by reducing spending, or by printing more money, or by issuing bonds that were placed on local financial markets. If the choice was to reduce spending, this only accentuated the contractionary trend set in motion by the IMF adjustment policies regarding the non-financial deficit. Contractions in government expenditures usually had the largest impact in the area of investment and in spending for social services.

The other options for the government consisted of either borrowing in the domestic capital market or, alternatively, printing more money. When the first alternative was chosen, the consequence was a rise in the interest rate which accentuated recession; on the other hand, when the second alternative was chosen, inflationary pressures immediately increased, as could be observed in the cases of Argentina and Brazil where inflation catapulted to the three-digit level.

Furthermore, the requirement to convert government savings into foreign exchange in order to pay the debt in dollars meant that the government had to purchase this foreign exchange, thereby creating upward pressure on the exchange market. The fear of devaluation caused by this pressure could only be assuaged by providing a strong inducement to hold domestic currency which, in turn, implied increasing domestic interest rates. This was the mechanism chosen by Alfonsín's economic team; variants of this mechanism have also been used in Mexico and Brazil, which explains the extremely high real interest rates that prevailed in these countries during the adjustment period.

All of these aspects have obvious repercussions on the economic climate of the countries during the post-crisis adjustment phase. The undesirable consequences of austerity policies against a background of excessive borrowing can be summarized as follows: slow growth or outright stagnation in production levels, aggravation of the financial position of firms, high rates of real interest, pressure on the dollar, and a permanent climate of economic uncertainty.

Uncertainty is perhaps the most significant unintended consequence of the drastic adjustment effort. IMF targets for the main macroeconomic variables have to be continually revised, due to the inability of most countries to meet them. While this occurs, the IMF interrupts the flow of external funds until negotiations with each country's policy makers are reinitiated. These negotiations take months, during which time the economic agents can do nothing but wait.

In this environment it is impossible to maintain a stable economic policy, and frequent changes make the public lose confidence in the policy makers. What suffers most are investment levels. Economic agents do not feel they can make rational decisions in such an uncertain environment, and they often choose to hedge against uncertainty by buying dollars. Capital flight turns out to be the last escape valve in the face of a climate of economic deterioration and uncertainty. In fact, the figures for capital flight from Latin America are impressive: During the 1983–1985 period alone, it reached $31 billion for the ten largest Latin American debtors.[11]

Lessons to Be Learned from Dual Conditionality

The picture drawn in the previous section would not be balanced if one did not also recognize the valuable role the IMF played during the crisis in preventing a collapse in the international monetary system. The IMF's key function was to put pressure on countries and banks to maintain payments flows and minimum levels of new credit that were essential to prevent the "debt bomb" from exploding.

On the other hand, it cannot be denied that the debt-burdened countries had to adjust their economies to the new conditions of scarce credit. To achieve this, greater fiscal discipline was necessary, along with internal savings efforts and a redirection of national production toward external markets. It is also clear that the achievement of greater international competitiveness continues to be the best basis for a solid solution to the debt problem.[12]

But what is often not recognized by international lending agencies is that economic policy approaches in Latin America in the 1980s are more sophisticated and pragmatic than old stereotypes would admit. Most governments and policy makers in Latin America today would stress the importance of the market and its proper functioning as a necessary, although insufficient, condition for the efficient allocation of resources in these economies. This approach recognizes the reality of mixed economies in Latin America as a valid historical formation that has existed and will continue to exist in the future, whatever the ideological intents of the extreme left or right.

Latin America today has a greater understanding than ever of the need to promote more incentives for the development of entrepreneurial capacity. What is needed is a dynamic private enterprise sector that is productive and competitive at the international level.

Furthermore, critical evaluations of past free market experiments are currently underway in Latin America. It is generally accepted now that a naive and radical hands-off attitude on the part of the governments leads to serious distortion in resource allocation: low investment, high capital flight, etc. This was often due to poor performance in specific markets, such as domestic capital markets that in some countries produced real interest rates in the range of 20–50 percent for several years; to persistent goods and labor market disequilibrium, to unchecked speculative behavior by economic agents that led to capital flight, to imperfect world markets for key export products, etc. Thus it seems that an active regulatory role for the government is needed, as well as governmental intervention for the protection of the poorer sectors through vigorous development of social programs.

The difference between this sort of active governmental presence and old-fashioned statism lies in the fact that what is stressed now is a decentralized, smaller government that opens channels for the private sector and organized labor to participate in the decision-making process. Discussions in Latin America today focus more on decentralized development, social pacts, and concerted action; and less on an omnipresent state role or the advocacy of unrestricted free markets.

With this in mind, we can now discuss some of the lessons that can be drawn in Latin America from the experience with "dual conditionality."

The IMF's mandate is to promote international financial order by conditioning its financial support of countries in difficult situations on their compliance with measures to normalize the balance of payments. In addition to the necessary emergency measures, the success of external adjustment depends most importantly on strengthening the ability of the economy to export and to substitute imports efficiently. An aspect that is usually ignored in the redirection of production toward export goods is that success hinges on the impact that the macroeconomic adjustment policies will have at the microeconomic level, i.e., on the firms themselves.

Adjustment policies during and after the debt crisis were characterized by reductions in investments of up to 30 percent and by the persistence of a recessive trend in the economy. For firms, this meant low sales levels and chronically idle capacity. Stagnation in sales weakens the ability of the companies to pay off debt. Recessive adjustment with restricted credit pushes interest rates up and sales down. This, in turn, sets off an *internal* debt crisis: Firms cannot pay back their credit and the proportion of banks' nonperforming loans goes up sharply, resulting in bankruptcy among some banks and financial institutions, and governmental intervention to stave off bankruptcy in others. Efforts to save productive firms from bankruptcy lead either to liquifying the debt through inflation, as in the case of Brazil and Argentina, or to repeated renegotiation of the debt with the banks, as in Chile. In the latter case, the governments, through their central banks, subsidize the renegotiated interest rates and assume the exchange risk if, for any reason, the private debt is "dedollarized."

Private enterprise, saddled with debt, is unable to contribute to the economy's recovery because of prevailing recessive conditions affecting sales. Investment in projects to modernize production and expand capacity cannot be undertaken because the cumulative effect of the prevailing recession and its accompanying uncertainty forces business to turn to purely defensive, survival-oriented strategies. The government is pressed to accept a write-off of private firms' debts and reduce the size of the work force, as well as reduce wages and benefits for employees. When the situation becomes critical, the private sector lays off even its most highly skilled workers. It then enters a period of stagnation and sluggishness; the morale of both managers and employees drops. Uncertainty over work and wage conditions decreases interest in work, and this affects productivity levels. Under such conditions, no incentives remain for the internal creativity which is essential for achieving international competitiveness.

Can the successful export experience of East Asia be repeated in a microeconomic climate that stifles innovation, creativity, and modernization of the production process? The real cause of the recent decline of private enterprise in Latin America is not so much crowding-out by the government or an excess of government control: On the contrary, the economic climate was on the whole quite permissive for private enterprise during the 1970s. Latin America's current problems can better be explained by errors committed during the period of liberalization, such as excessive borrowing and the prevalence of interest rates far above the rate of return on assets. Without a doubt, the greatest source of problems was the adjustment policy, conceived as a purely macroeconomic process without sufficient consideration of its potential effect on industry at a micro level.

The lesson is that if the IMF's conditionality is to strengthen export capabilities, attention must be focused on the microeconomic conditions necessary for production firms to recover from their current debilitated state.

The first requisite is internal financial house-cleaning of the firms. The IMF, however, normally limits itself to imposing conditions at the macroeconomic level for the central bank to tighten credit, a large part of which is used precisely for salvaging companies, private or state-run, which would otherwise go bankrupt. Reducing this credit has a negative effect on the position of these firms. Naturally, their ability to pay back their debts depends on their profits, which, in the short run, depend on anticipated sales levels. An adjustment policy without prospects for a reactivation of demand makes it impossible for the firms to move from a purely survival-oriented strategy to another, more active, strategy that would normalize their financial position, while preparing the ground—through relatively high exchange rates and low tariffs—for directing firms toward the external market.

How can private enterprise be strengthened when it simultaneously faces debt problems and a decline in markets? Who will take on investment projects to put the paralyzed economy back on its feet? Government and public sector enterprises have important roles in this situation, as was shown by the successful strategy used by industrial and Latin American economies to recover from the Great Depression in the 1930s. At that time, private enterprise suffered from problems which, like those faced in Latin America today, kept it from becoming an active factor in ending the recession and reinitiating growth.

Even with private enterprise on the way to recovery, there would still be the problem of strengthening export capabilities. This depends on more than just financial rehabilitation and favorable exchange rates. It requires research into new products, improvements in product quality, and access to new markets. Future conditions in external markets, according to most estimates, will be difficult: World trade is expanding at a slower rate than in the 1970s; there is more protectionism; and more countries are attempting to increase exports simultaneously to the same markets. It is unlikely that this type of export strategy will be successful unless it is based on a close relationship between current or potential exporters and the government. This was the method used in post-war Europe and, more recently, in East Asia.

Finally, world economic conditions in the 1980s are characterized by instability, volatile interest rates, and potential external shocks from adjustments in industrialized economies. The presence of these factors indicates the advisability of clear rules of the game set by the government to reduce uncertainty and stabilize expectations of domestic economic agents so as to allow them to consider new investment decisions and modernization plans aimed at increasing productivity and international competitiveness. Mechanisms for coordination and exchange of information with private enterprise, and involvement of labor organizations could aid in reducing uncertainty and stabilizing expectations about the future.

Other lessons related to the IMF's conditionality have to do with the acknowledgment of various structural complications that may interfere with the economy's recovery. One is the high prominence of the financial component—payment of the foreign debt—in current governmental budgets in Latin America. If this is not adequately recognized and the condition is imposed mechanically that, regardless of the level of spending, the deficit of the public sector must be cut in half, the government will find itself facing a dead-end. For it would be forced then to suspend the very same investment projects necessary for reactivation and to reduce spending for social services, which are aimed precisely at compensating the worst effects of the recession on lower-income groups. Moreover, the policy will ultimately produce a rise in the interest rates that the government has to pay in order to attract resources to finance the payment of interest on the public debt. Overkill in the reduction of public spending has gone so far in some cases as to prevent countries from using World Bank credits because the required counterpart of domestic public resources is just not available.

Another valid lesson to be learned from recent adjustment policies is that the combination of tight domestic credit policies and the liberalization of the foreign exchange market are likely to induce capital flight which is very difficult to reverse once it has started. The point of the lesson is that the government should control the foreign exchange market and actively regulate the flow of external funds in order to avoid the worst consequences of procyclical behavior on the part of external creditors and domestic borrowers alike. This, in turn, is what will allow the country to recover some degree of autonomy in monetary and financial policy.

A final lesson can be drawn from the dual conditionality imposed by the IMF and the banks: The banks' strategy of rapidly reducing exposure forces governments to adjust too drastically. Since adjustment occurs through import reduction in the short run, this has a negative impact on the exports of industrial countries, leading to loss of jobs.[13] The magnitude and speed of the productive employment loss generated by this process in industrialized economies is ultimately determined by the velocity at which the major private international banks decide to withdraw from the credit market in debtor countries, because this is what regulates the intensity of the adjustment effort needed by their domestic economies and, thus, their required import reduction. In this way, the policies of private international banks toward developing countries have an indirect, but significant, effect on unemployment rates in industrialized countries.

Of particular concern is the drop in net capital flows to debtor countries. These fell from a peak of $37 billion in 1981 to $4.7 billion in 1985.[14] This tight lending policy on the part of the banks will probably accent, rather than moderate, the contractionary characteristics of the adjustment programs that, as argued before, tend to weaken production units the most and, therefore, to jeopardize the ability of Latin American economies to pay off debt, recover, and grow in the medium and long term.

How to Ease the Foreign Exchange Constraint

The concern of the banks and the U.S. government over the apparently unsuccessful debt strategy has resulted in a policy shift. A proposal has been made to increase the role of the multinational organizations by expanding the credits granted by the World Bank and the Inter-American Development Bank. This would entail a $9 billion increase in net new loans over a period of three years, plus the creation of mechanisms which would allow cofinancing by the World Bank and private banks, as well as World Bank guarantees on some of the loans made by private banks, as has already occurred in the Chilean case. It is hoped that this will help the debtor countries attract $6 to $7 billion per year in private credit.[15]

Some of the proponents of these measures want the World Bank, possibly in cooperation with the IMF, to condition new loans on obligatory structural reforms and economic policy reforms on the part of debtor countries. The proposed changes include the privatization of state-run companies, the liberalization of trade and financial flows, and, in general, the active promotion of a free market and pro-private enterprise policy. This new form of conditionality would be a third dimension added to the conditions already imposed by the banks (ceiling for the total of new external credits available) and IMF conditions pertaining to the specific type of economic policy the country should adopt in order to adjust the economy in the short run. This new conditionality would be based on the process now being applied by the World Bank in its structural adjustment loan (SAL) programs which, in turn, reflects current U.S. governmental policies of promoting liberalization and privatization.

The proposed increase in the availability of government and private funds constitutes a move in the right direction. However, the new forms of conditionality are not necessarily helpful. The basic challenge, which is now all but unanimously recognized, is to create conditions that will enable Latin American economies to resume their normal economic growth. Otherwise, their ability to pay the debt will become increasingly weaker with time.

Growth in Latin America has come to a standstill as a result of the insufficiency of the level of imports that the region is currently able to finance. Around 1981, imports to Latin America were approximately $100 billion. In 1985 they totaled $57 billion. A "normal" level, based on that which existed in the second half of the 1970s, would be around $80 billion in 1985. In order to recover this level, an additional $20–25 billion will be required each year. This would make it possible to increase imports by one third. Using the import elasticities estimated by Lessard and Williamson, this could lead to an 8–15 percent increase in the region's GNP, with a probable 5 percent reduction in the unemployment rate.[16]

Latin America's new inflow of capital in 1984 and 1985 was approximately $8 billion annual average. Adding between $20–25 billion in new resources would produce a net capital inflow similar to the one that existed immediately prior to the boom period of 1978–1981. So long as reserves remain constant, this would represent a deficit in the current account of the balance of payments similar to 1976 and 1977 levels, a period when growth rates could be characterized as "normal" with annual GNP growth at about 5 percent. The availability of $30 billion in net new external funds would be equivalent to 8 percent of Latin America's combined debt. Assuming annual rates of growth in the 5 percent range and 3 percent inflation, net credit expansion would be consistent with maintaining the ratio between the region's debt and its GNP constant in the future.

How can this capital expansion be financed? Fishlow and others have suggested a formula based on two principal components.[17] The first puts a ceiling on the interest rate paid on credits. Any excess over this limit would be capitalized; as a result, the real value of the debt would remain constant. The second aspect of the formula would require an expansion in official credits—from governments and from multinational lending agencies.

If a reduction of four points in nominal interest rates could constitute an acceptable target for the maximum rate to be paid in any one year by indebted Latin American economies and if the difference with respect to market rates were capitalized, Latin America would reduce by this means its current net transfer of capital outside the region from $30 billion to $18 billion. How can the difference be financed in order to attain $20 billion per year?

In a climate of resumption of economic growth and rational, more stable economic policies, one could expect current low levels of direct foreign investment of around $2 billion per year to return to their previous levels. Foreign investment in Latin America as a whole exceeded $4 billion annually in the 1981–1982 period. Hence, it would be possible to obtain an additional $2 billion per year.

The remaining $6 billion would still have to be financed with new official credits to the region. Two points of significance should be noted. First, this amount is equivalent, in 1985 dollars, to the annual average level of external government financing available to Latin America in the 1961–1970 period (the Alliance for Progress years). Second, under the Marshall Plan, U.S. government transfers were equal to 14 billion in 1985 dollars per year between 1948 and 1951. Over 85 percent of these funds were grants. That financing effort represented 1.2 percent of the U.S. GNP each year. A similar percentage of the U.S. GNP today would represent an average annual level of aid of $46 billion.[18]

A Latin American Development Fund could be established to grant long-term credit at interest rates not in excess of 2 percent in real terms. These credits would be used to aid countries' development programs and investment plans by cofinancing with the countries themselves. The decisions of the Fund would be made jointly by representatives of the government agencies providing resources to the Fund and by representatives from Latin America chosen on the basis of their technical capabilities and their political significance in the region.

The conditionality criteria to be applied to these credits should avoid the exaggerated forms of "policy conditionality" often required by multinational agencies. The criteria should be tailored to specific circumstances. It would be advisable for the IMF to continue to supervise the adjustment of imbalances in the external sector of the economies. The forms for internal adjustment should vary, however, depending on the nature of the imbalance and the structural characteristics of the particular economy. As Bacha points out, the IMF should not, as it frequently does, apply a rigid conditionality for the internal adjustment of the economy. Rather it should leave the country free to design its own domestic adjustment program as long as the goals set for the balance of trade and the balance of payments are met.[19]

It has been noted that Brazil improved its balance of payments at the end of the 1970s through highly unorthodox domestic economic policies.[20] It increased, rather than decreased government investment, directing it toward sectors of tradable goods and thereby creating conditions for the subsequent expansion of exports and substitution of imports. Thus, Brazil in recent years has been able to generate strong trade surpluses (about $12 billion a year) which have enabled it to continue paying the interest on its gigantic foreign debt.

Countries should be able to proceed more selectively in their internal adjustment. IMF-mandated adjustment policies have the strongest impact on wage earners (because they increase unemployment), and on the poorer strata of society (because these groups are most affected by the general drop in income and by cuts in public spending that reduce social services). A strong argument, based on equity considerations, can be made that a selective fiscal and spending policy should be applied.

Conditionality in a development fund should concentrate on increasing investments, particularly in the areas of exports and substitution of imports, and on the absorption of unemployment. The instruments for achieving these goals should be tailored to the specific characteristics of each country. These criteria contrast with the current concept of policy conditionality, which assumes that a particular instrument of economic policy, if used in a certain way, will necessarily produce the same results in any context. Albert Hirschman has called this view "mono-economics," arguing that it tends to ignore the entire achievement of developmental economics.

The discipline of developmental economics arose in the post-war era with the growing awareness of the specific nature of economic problems in developing countries, and the need to identify those factors that distinguish between developing and industrialized countries as well as those that distinguish among developing countries themselves. Within the discipline, attempts were made to design specific strategies and select appropriate policy instruments to remove obstacles to development in a particular historical and structural situation.

The same policy instrument used in the same manner in structurally different developing economies can produce very different results. Dornbusch shows this by comparing the effects of devaluations of the exchange rate in Korea and in Brazil.[21] In Korea, exports account for 37 percent of the GNP, whereas in Brazil, they only reach 10 percent. While income distribution in Korea is rather even, in Brazil it is not. Under these conditions, devaluation in Korea will have a much greater impact on the balance of payments than in Brazil. Indeed this is the factor that explains why Korea was able to adjust quickly to the debt crisis by devaluating its exchange rate and producing an immediate response in terms of greater production of internationally tradeable goods.

In Brazil's case, however, the impact of devaluation is smaller for two reasons. First, tradeable goods play a smaller role in the country's overall production. Second, the uneven distribution of income imposes a ceiling on the tolerable level of real devaluation for the local currency. Real devaluation normally implies a loss of purchasing power for the population—that is, a drop in real wages. Drops in income will be poorly distributed if the differences in income between groups are very large. Wage earners at the lower end of the scale often push for cost-of-living adjustment clauses in their contracts. This wage indexing, while protecting them from loss in purchasing power, greatly hampers the effectiveness of devaluation as an instrument for adjusting the balance of payments in the case of Brazil. The limits of "mono-economics" and the dangers of a uniform conditionality that ignores countries' structural characteristics and developmental levels should be evident in this example.

The key issue in the theory and practice of developmental economics is the mobilization of existing resources to revitalize the national economy. It is equally important to find a combination of local production factors which encourages innovations in technology and production methods in order to achieve sustained growth in production and productivity levels. When a country finds its own formula for development—a scheme capable of mobilizing and promoting creativity and innovation—it reaches a level of development that has the potential to sustain itself in the future because the conditions for achieving permanent increases in productivity are met.

If this view of the developmental process is accepted, then it follows that conditionality should not stifle the search for the developmental formula best suited to a particular country's needs, and it should not impose economic conditions that will leave the government with nothing to offer in the future to motivate economic agents. The combination which should most be avoided, as the result of excessively restrictive conditionality, is that of tough, uniform policies applied by weak governments. From greater rigidity in conditionality will come greater weakness in government.

Conditionality should be consistent with the idea of energizing a society, i.e., putting it in creative tension for development. It should increase, not restrict, the society's degrees of freedom and enhance, not reduce, its indigenous problem-solving capacity. What follows is that conditionality should be flexible enough to allow nonuniformity in the policies applied in different institutional, structural, and even historical contexts. Why recommend further financial and trade liberalization in the countries of Latin America's Southern Cone when their current economic crisis was at least in part due to an unrestricted application of the very same policies being recommended now by some lending agencies? What would be the purpose of pushing for the privatization of banks and state-run firms in those countries where public firms have often endured external shock better than private firms?

Chile provides an example. During the boom, the State Bank was careful to lend only to firms whose projects—after careful evaluation—proved profitable. In addition, it did not engage in the extended practice of private banks of lending (in fact, over-lending) without guarantees. It might also be useful to note that many public enterprises were able to perform better than their private sector equivalents during the recession (as a consequence of their quasi-monopoly situation that allowed them to stay in the black by upward adjustments in utility rates).

The recognition of different situations and of flexibility in conditionality criteria are part of the necessary ingredients in a suitable economic policy which should be more pragmatic and draw from the evidence of past successes and failures, rather than from ideological preferences. In economic policy, simplistic, ideological criteria are no substitutes for good sense. The conditionality that is applied to adjustment in the short term must be consistent with long-term development. If the outcome of adjustment policies is a drop in investment of 25 percent to 30 percent for four or five years in a row, as has recently been observed in Latin America, then something is inconsistent between the short- and long-run elements of the desired policy package.

The problem is no mere technical matter. If what is required is a government with broad support and ability to lead the country in mobilizing human and physical resources in order to overcome the external constraint, then an excessively rigid and premature conditionality may nullify the process through which the government is gaining the credibility and legitimacy necessary to actually implement the required economic program. As the case of President Alfonsín illustrates, it is the expansion in political legitimacy—which can only occur under a full democracy—that will enable a government to achieve the levels of freedom that are needed to later apply economic measures that may involve harsh sacrifices for the population.

This sequence of actions is essential for any adjustment-with-growth program to be successful.

THE DOMESTIC TASK FOR LATIN AMERICAN COUNTRIES

By the end of 1986, no significant advances had been made that would allow Latin American economies to resume growth as a condition for enhancing their capacity to meet payments on foreign debt.

A hastily arranged package for Mexico consisting of financing over $12 billion over a period of fifteen months to allow that country to continue paying interest on its external debt has been estimated as a positive emergency measure but one that does not deal with the underlying factors causing the problem. At the same time, the solution implies effectively locking in all resources that the Baker Plan envisaged as desirable for the fifteen largest debtors. Where are the other countries going to obtain the external financing they so desperately need?

Meanwhile, the international economic scenario does not seem to evolve in the direction envisaged by the architects of the muddling-through strategy on the debt question. Japan and West Germany do not seem prepared to go into more expansionary policies in order to compensate for slow U.S. growth. U.S. trade and budget deficits continue to increase. A trade deficit of $170 billion, after a 30 percent devaluation of the dollar, has prodded the Administration in Washington to push for trade concessions from U.S. trading partners.

In the recent General Agreement on Tariffs and Trade (GATT) meeting in Punta del Este, Uruguay (September 1986), the U.S. delegation pushed for trade liberalization in services and in some high-tech industries such as computers. That this is part of a self-serving strategy is demonstrated by the fact that these are precisely the sectors where the U.S. might have the competitive edge in its favor, whereas in other areas in which it does not have clear comparative advantage, like textiles, shoes, steel, sugar, and beef products, the U.S. is still imposing non-tariff restrictions to producers in the rest of the world. It is relevant to mention, in this context, that trade figures for 1980 show that 46 percent of the U.S. trade was subjected to non-tariff restrictions by this country.[22] The figure for the European Economic Community (EEC) countries is 45 percent and for Japan it is 60 percent. Thus, the push toward free trade seems to be extremely selective and generally following a pattern of industrial countries maximizing short-term gains vis-à-vis other countries.

This is a serious problem that Latin America will have to face in the new developmental strategies that are being designed now for the post-adjustment period, where growth has to resume and equity considerations must be brought into the picture again, after years if not decades of forced neglect. Brazil and Argentina seem to be leading the way. A recently unveiled ambitious and well-formulated integration scheme for the Argentinian and Brazilian economies that takes into account existing barriers for significant expansion of their trade to the countries of the EEC will surely establish a pattern to be followed by other Latin American countries.

This is a first significant consequence of the shift in developmental strategy in Latin America. The transition from debt-led growth to export-*cum*-savings growth, will have to support itself in significant South-South trade, making use of any advantage that integration between the various national markets will provide for additional export expansion, or for intra-region import substitution schemes.

But this is not the only consequence. A second one is related to the fact that debt-led growth ended in economic stagnation and debilitated productive structures in Latin America. At the heart of this phenomenon is the fact that investment rates severely declined during the post-boom adjustment period, to the extent that net investment decreased by 50 percent.

The difficulty that this poses cannot be overlooked. The main problem does not lie in the lack of investment projects. The main bottleneck is domestic savings. Since external resources will not be available in an amount consistent with the need to expand investment rates by more than 25 percent these economies will have to rely on domestic savings generation.

The problem is not that Latin American countries are not providing the effort. In fact, belt tightening during the adjustment period has allowed them to generate acceptable levels of domestic savings. But the problem has been that a significant proportion of those are being transferred abroad as "net payments to factors," to use a national accounts expression. These are largely interest payments on the debt.

The point can be illustrated by looking at table 1, where it can be seen that national savings, that is those resources that stay in the country—available for investment purposes—show a significant fall, which can be explained by the increase in payments abroad shown in the third and fourth columns in table 1.

The way out of this low-investment trap has many dimensions. The first and obvious one is that the part of savings being transferred abroad has to decrease, so that it can be made available for investment purposes. Proposals like Senator Bradley's seem quite relevant in this respect. Many proposals today agree that interest rate caps and partial write-downs of the debt seem necessary for highly indebted countries to be able to resume growth. This was detailed earlier in this paper.

Policies designed to increase domestic savings are a natural complement to actions that attempt to ease the transfer problem. But the limits of these policies to enhance savings are

TABLE 1

Domestic Savings for Selected Latin American Countries, as % of GDP

	NATIONAL SAVINGS		PAYMENTS TO FACTORS ABROAD		DOMESTIC SAVINGS	
	1980	1983	1980	1983	1980	1983
Argentina	19.8	13.6	1.0	8.8	20.8	22.4
Brazil	18.0	17.8	3.1	5.1	21.1	22.9
Chile	14.3	4.8	3.1	8.9	17.4	13.7
México	25.3	27.2	2.7	5.6	28.0	32.8
Perú	18.1	15.0	4.7	6.0	22.8	21.0

also clear. If the standard of living is still significantly below normal levels, it does not seem possible to expect much in terms of additional savings efforts on the part of households.

Business savings are constrained by the severe financial difficulties imposed on firms by the recurrent recessionary policies that have prevailed after the debt crisis. Government savings, on the other hand, might be raised by upward adjustments in tax rates or in utility rates. The latter have a clear inflationary impact.

This leads us into a related but different aspect. If what one wants is to attack the roots of the problem of low savings capacity of firms, households, and the public sector, or—to look at the other side of the coin—the roots of low investment in the economy, one is forced to say something about the adjustment process itself.

Economic orthodoxy declares that recessionary adjustments are inevitable if inflation and balance-of-payment difficulties are to be overcome. What is not recognized is that there are alternative adjustment mechanisms that are better for avoiding domestic falls in output and employment levels, while at the same time being quite effective in reducing "inertial inflation" and the external sector deficit. The "Austral," "Cruzado," and "Inti" stabilization programs in Argentina, Brazil, and Perú—while not exempt of problems—do suggest that alternative stabilization strategies are possible and that much more effort should be devoted—and surely will be devoted—in the future for better policy design in this area in Latin America.

What these adjustment programs have not been able to provide is a clear-cut answer to the question of how a transition can be achieved from stabilization-*cum*-price freeze toward sustained growth without high inflation resuming again.

The answer to the latter part of the statement—avoiding the resumption of high inflation—is being sought by recurring to the old (and always new) idea of social pacts. What policy makers in Brazil, Argentina, Uruguay, and Perú are saying is that, if inflation is the result of claims on shares of national income by competing groups that exceed 100 percent then surely something has to be done to make those claims compatible with the fact that there is not enough income generated to satisfy all competing claims. The problem is basically a political one, and thus requires a political solution. That is why the predominant themes in these countries today are coalition- and consensus-building, concerted action, income policies, and the like.

The question is how to change—through persuasion, social pressure, and government incentives—the revealed preference of labor unions for higher wages and of business for a hands-off attitude on the part of government, which is the opposite of what is required to make competing claims mutually consistent. How to develop preferences for disinflation, for a shift of attention toward employment—generating activities toward production and productivity—as a way out of the low growth–high inflation syndrome, are the basic issues that are very much present in public discussion in Latin America today.

If what is needed is responsible, growth-oriented action on the part of government, business, and labor, what is it that should be done in order to mobilize scarce domestic resources in a most efficient way?

The debt situation is forcing Latin American economies toward export-oriented and import substitution-oriented growth. How can this be achieved given current protectionist trends in EEC countries and the U.S., and given the relatively "backward" structure of Latin American trade in the early 1980s? It is interesting to note that manufacturing exports for Latin America as a whole did not represent more than 20 percent of total exports as recently as 1982. The rest is mainly primary sector exports, whose terms of trade have been systematically falling in the last few years. Industrial development has regressed by at least fifteen years if current output indexes are compared to historical peaks. The region is lagging in the production of capital goods, chemical products, and high-tech items. Given these conditions, how can Latin America reverse this trend and find "niches" in world markets that represent overcoming the limits involved by too much specialization in primary products exports? How can the region create new comparative advantages in production and trade?

This is a key issue to tackle if the new developmental strategies are going to be successful. Surely Japan, Korea, and indeed post-war Europe have shown the way. As early as 1945

Jean Monnet was writing about "l'economie concertée"; about the need for countries to produce—in a concerted fashion—a "vision" of what it is possible to achieve in the various branches of production through a joint effort of government and private sector with the cooperation of labor. "Strategic planning" is the fashionable term to describe such a process of identifying high-priority sectors to be developed, with international competitiveness in mind.

The organization of the effort at mobilizing scarce resources as a function of those goals should be a responsibility of the state, as indeed has been the case in countries like Japan, Korea, Taiwan, Brazil, or Mexico. The experience of newly industrializing countries (NIC) is one that deserves more attention and will certainly receive it from other countries in Latin America, struggling to find a way to mobilize human and physical resources seeking a more dynamic development of those sectors with highest potential for export expansion or efficient import substitution. This approach, rather than naive versions of "reagonomics," is likely to dominate the scene in Latin America in the next decade.

On the other hand, international competitiveness in manufacturing will not be achieved if Latin America is not able to bridge the technological gap vis-à-vis industrial countries. There are no simple "recipes" to achieve this, but there is no doubt that Latin American policy makers do visualize a key role that multinational companies could play in the process of transferring new technologies to the relatively less developed countries in the region.

Direct foreign investment will not perform a significant role in solving the external financial bottleneck facing Latin America in the foreseeable future. At best, foreign investment could contribute about 15 percent of total external financial needs of the region. But there is a very important role, of a more qualitative nature, which is possible—to contribute by providing either new technologies or access to new markets. This is the role that foreign investment was induced to play in Korea.[23] The trend is already visible in Latin America too.

Much needs to be done in Latin America in order to be able to meet the challenge of a new developmental strategy centered in the creation of new comparative advantages and in sustained domestic savings effort. The final target should be to develop conditions such that endogenous increases in productivity are possible through creative and innovative production processes. What has been said about technology is also true about the need for new industrial organization schemes at the plant level.

There is a revolution going on in the world today concerning how to achieve higher productivity growth in the shop floor. The revolution includes spheres such as labor-management relations, organization of the labor market, job stability, wage flexibility, and incentive systems. All these are being reappraised and subject to serious scrutiny.

Productivity has been mostly absent in Latin American discussion. Again, this is an area where foreign firms could play a role in introducing new schemes and concepts that could have the virtue of effectively challenging approaches and methods still prevalent in most of Latin America and inherited from the import-substitution industrialization that dominated developmental patterns throughout most of the post-war period.

NOTES

This paper is an extension of Kellogg Institute Working Paper #72, Notre Dame, July 1986.

1. Projections by Project LINK at the University of Pennsylvania, March 1986, and by BID, March 1986.

2. CEPAL, "The Economic Crisis: Policies for Adjustment, Stabilization and Growth," April 1986.

3. Estimates by BID, March 1986.

4. Morgan Guaranty, *World Financial Markets,* February 1986.

5. Morgan Guaranty, *World Financial Markets,* September 1985.

6. Ibid.

7. There has been much discussion on the relation between the economic growth of OECD countries and the expansion in exports of developing countries. The most complete discussion of the topic is found in R. Dornbusch and S. Fisher, "The World Debt Problem," a report to the Group of Twenty-Four, September 1984. See also A. Fishlow, "Coping with the Creeping Crisis of Debt," Working Paper No. 181, Dept. of Economics, University of California, Berkeley, February 1984.

8. CEPAL, "The Economic Crisis."

9. See Project LINK projections.

10. The ratio is: $v^* = (i-y) D/E$

where:

v^* = net transfer of resources outside the region
i = international interest rate
y = rate of increase (reduction) of exposure
D = amount of the debt
E = volume of exports

See R. Dornbusch, "World Economic Issues of Interest to Latin America," mimeograph, Inter-American Dialogue, September 1985.

11. Morgan Guaranty, *World Financial Markets*, February 1986.

12. Krueger develops this point. She argues that most countries have already adjusted their economies. The main problem now is how to reduce the debt overhang that constrains the export capacity of many countries. See A. Krueger, "Developing Countries, Debt Problems and Growth Prospects," World Bank, August 1985.

13. The Chemical Bank has estimated that 800,000 jobs were lost in the U.S. economy due to this effect alone. See *The Washington Post*, September 29, 1985.

14. CEPAL, "The Economic Crisis."

15. The official figure is $20 billion in three years.

16. D. Lessard and J. Williamson, "Financial Intermediation Beyond the Debt Crisis," Institute for International Economics, *Policy Analysis*, No. 12, September 1985.

17. A. Fishlow, "Coping with the Crisis."

18. This information was supplied by Konrad Stenzel.

19. E. Bacha, "The Future Role of the International Monetary Fund in Latin America," mimeograph, Dept. Economics, P.U.C., June 1985.

20. R. Cortázar, "Employment, Real Wage, and External Constraint: The Cases of Brazil and Chile," PREALC, September 1985.

21. R. Dornbusch, "World Economic Issues."

22. D. Ibarra, "Crisis y Sector Externo en America Latina," forthcoming in R. Feinberg and R. Ffrench-Davis (ed.), *Más Allá de la Crisis de la Deuda* Santiago: (Ediciones DIEPLAN, 1986).

23. K. Kim, *Política Industrial y Desarrollo en Corea del Sur* Mexico: (Nacional Financiera, 1985).

Continuing Crisis
in Sub-Saharan Africa

KWAN S. KIM *

The oil crisis of 1979, subsequent worldwide recession, declining terms of trade, and soaring world interest rates had altogether a dramatic impact on Third World countries as these nations were suddenly faced with declining outputs and the ensuing problems of servicing increased external debts. An intriguing aspect of the crisis is the marked differences observed in economic performance and debt situation in the early 1980s between different regions of the developing world. Latin American countries which were able to maintain sustained growth in the 1970s[1] have turned into highly indebted nations, with most now considered as "problem borrowers.". As shown by table 1, they contrast with developing countries in Asia and Africa in the size of debt burden, as measured by the ratios of debt to exports, debt services to exports, and debt to GDP.

On the other hand, the developing Asian economies that pursued an outward-oriented developmental strategy seem to have fared far better in facing the debt crisis.[2] For instance, debt services as a percentage of exports have been steadily held below 10 percent in Asian countries. The debt service ratio, on the average, for Latin American countries was as high as 54 percent in 1982, more than five times that of Asia's, while that for African countries rose to about 20 percent, twice

---

*Kwan S. Kim is a professor of economics and a faculty fellow of the Helen Kellogg Institute for International Studies at the University of Notre Dame. Formerly a senior economist for the Agency for International Development, he has taught in Holland, Mexico, Tanzania, Kenya, and Minnesota.

that of Asia's (table 1). Again, comparing the groups of major borrowers, in 1983 the seven largest Asian borrowers had, on the average, a debt-service ratio of 36 percent compared with 117 percent for the eight largest in Latin America (table 2).

The level of indebtedness in the low-income, sub-Saharan African region is still low in comparison with other parts of the developing world. The size of external debt in sub-Saharan Africa, which comprises 44 countries, pales considerably in relation to that of Latin America: The region's total debt roughly equals Brazil's, accounting for less than 10 percent of the total developing country debt. As a result, Africa's debt has not yet been perceived as posing serious problems to the international financial community. Nevertheless, because of the fragility of African economies, the external shocks have been inflicting a most damaging impact. The rapid buildup of the debt over the past decade has been accompanied by a continuous, inexorable economic decline, thereby clouding prospects for sustained growth of the continent.

The main purpose of this paper is to explore the full implications of external debt and adjustment policies pursued or to be pursued by African governments for the continent's long-term development. A brief review of the debt situation and

TABLE 1

Debt Situation in Non-Oil Developing Countries
(Percentages)

	AFRICA	ASIA	LATIN AMERICA
Debt/exports			
1973	71.5	92.9	176.2
1978	111.4	77.7	211.5
1982	147.4	80.9	245.6
Debt-service/exports			
1973	8.8	9.6	29.3
1978	12.0	9.6	41.7
1982	20.1	9.8	54.0
Debt/GDP			
1973	19.4	19.7	23.0
1978	29.4	22.3	30.3
1982	35.2	26.7	38.2

Source: IMF, *World Economic Outlook.*

economic performance in Africa will be followed by the discussions of adjustment strategies, in particular, the new strategies that stress policy reform toward increasing liberalization and "marketization" of the African economies.

ECONOMIC PERFORMANCE AND DEBT SITUATION

Until well into the mid-1970s, sub-Saharan African countries had on the whole experienced a moderate rate of growth

TABLE 2

External Debt and Debt Services of Major LDC Borrowers

	GROSS DEBT AT END-1982 ($ BILLIONS)	DEBT SERVICES IN 1983 AS % OF EXPORTS*
Latin America		
Argentina	38.0	154
Brazil	85.5	117
Chile	17.2	104
Colombia	10.3	95
Ecuador	6.6	102
Mexico	80.1	126
Peru	11.5	79
Venezuela	29.5	101
(Subtotal)	278.7	117
Asia		
Indonesia	25.4	28
S. Korea	36.0	49
Malaysia	10.4	15
Philippines	16.6	79
Taiwan	9.3	19
Thailand	11.0	50
(Subtotal)	108.8	36
Middle East and Africa		
Algeria	16.3	35
Egypt	19.2	46
Israel	26.7	126
Ivory Coast	9.2	76
Morocco	10.3	65
Nigeria	9.3	28
Turkey	22.8	65
(Subtotal)	112.8	58
Total of 21 LDCs	501.2	71

*Interest on gross debt plus all maturing debt, including amortization of medium- and long-term debt and all short-term debt as percent of exports of goods and services, including net private transfer payments. Source: Morgan Guaranty Trust Company.

that was less than satisfactory but not poor as it exceeded the rate of population growth. For instance, per capita real income even for the 29 least developed African countries grew at an average rate of 1.2 percent during the period from 1959 to 1975. The long phase of lackluster but positive growth was followed by an economic crisis in the wake of the first global oil crisis and the ensuing worldwide recession in the early 1970s. The crisis has been characterized by a broadly experienced deterioration of the economy exemplified by declining levels of output and income, widening trade deficits, food production lagging behind population growth, rising inflation, and unemployment.

From 1974 to 1984, per capita income for the region as a whole declined by nearly 10 percent and its trade deficit rose from $4 billion to $14 billion by 1984. In terms of current-account balance, the deficit reached $6.9 billion in 1985, about the same as the total net transfer of external resources to the region.[3] The total net resource flow to sub-Saharan Africa was $11.8 billion in 1980, which declined by 40 percent over the next five years. It is estimated that sub-Saharan Africa needs $26 billion a year for the next five years—$9 billion of it from external resources—just to restore their 1970–73 levels of per capita real growth in food production.[4] The region's 29 poorest countries will face yearly a $2.5 billion gap in the investments required to maintain 2 to 3 percent of real growth in their economy.

Africa's decline can be attributed to factors both external and internal to the region. Externally, throughout the decade of the 1970s and the early 1980s, the African economies experienced substantial shocks from the slowdown of industrialized country growth, the sharp fall in the terms of trade, and the soaring rise in world interest rates accompanied by declining aid flows in the wake of two oil-precipitated recessions. Of course, the adverse impact of the shocks was not limited to Africa; other developing countries were also seriously affected by unfavorable external developments. The difference, however, is that low-income African countries have been subject to external shocks much greater than any other group of developing countries: Their terms of trade declined by nearly 15 percent during each of the two three-year periods of 1973–76 and

1979–82, and in 1982 the index of terms of trade for sub-Saharan Africa was the lowest since the Great Depression.[5] As a result, given the fragile nature of African economies, the impact of the negative exogenous factors has been more damaging than in any other part of the developing world.

In terms of the internal factors, the major explanation for the dismal economic performance rests on the inherited frailty of the economic structures in low-income Africa. Despite the obvious country-specific variations, there are several features of structural deficiency common in the African economies that render them highly vulnerable to external shocks. The African economy is typically an agrarian society with a small pocket of urban-based industry; infrastructural developments, both in human and physical capital, are inadequate with a resulting low efficiency in industrial production; agricultural output is highly vulnerable to the vagaries of weather conditions; and the economy is heavily import-dependent with exports concentrated in a few primary commodities.

The structural characteristic of the African economies can best be summarized as being at a fundamental disequilibrium in the sense that even at a "competitive" exchange rate, external payments equilibrium can be obtained only at an extremely low-income level. The perpetual gap between investment needs, on the one hand, and domestic savings and exports, on the other, requires continuous inflows of foreign capital. Since the mid-1970s, this gap has widened as concessional capital inflows diminished and as the terms of trade for primary commodities declined. In Africa, external indebtedness has become a function of this widening gap.

Many discussions of Africa's crisis have focused on state *dirigisme*. In sub-Saharan African countries, state activism is generally seen as the major means of solving a country's economic problems. The usual criticism of African states does not rest so much on the extent of state activism as on the effectiveness of its activities. A stereotypic African state would fit into the category of what Gunnar Myrdal described as "the soft state," which is in essence seen as ineffective and often unable to formulate and implement cohesive developmental strategies. African governments are also perceived as maintaining an authoritative, clientele-oriented, administrative structure. The development of African societies is undermined by corruption, patronage, personal rule, and bureaucratic inefficiency. Especially, corruption in government is seen as genuinely stifling Africa's developmental potential.[6]

As for the patron-client relationship, many African governments seek political coalitions favoring urban interests. This is because a relatively small proportion of masses—consisting mainly of city dwellers—is politically conscious. It is this urban group's political support that immediately matters to the ruling class. Thus, for instance, the chronic food shortage in African countries may be seen in part as resulting from the government's deliberate policy to keep food prices low in an attempt to appease the urban populace. As will be discussed later, the issue of state activism is an important one as it forms the basis of the recent argument for structural reforms in African countries.

As a result of growing current-account deficits accompanied by steadily declining aid flows, the buildup of external debts in the region has been at an exceptionally rapid pace. The long-term total debt of the sub-Saharan region jumped from $10 billion in 1971 to about $125 billion by 1984.[7] If a series of debts not covered by government guarantees are included, the total can be estimated as high as $175 billion for 1984.[8] Moreover, the debt-servicing obligations have become increasingly burdensome. The total official debt relative to annual export earnings doubled to more than 200 percent in the period from 1977 to 1983. The debt-service as a percentage of export earnings, including short-term debt obligations and arrears in debt payment, similarly increased from 11 percent in 1971 to more than 35 percent by the mid-1980s.[9] The situation is far worse for the 29 poorest African countries—their average debt-export ratio reached close to 350 percent at the end of 1984, compared with 203 percent for the 17 major indebted countries in the developing world that have been targeted for assistance under the Baker Plan.

Africa's debt situation has worsened by steadily aggravating borrowing conditions. With the decline in foreign aid, many African countries had no alternative but to turn to floating rate loans or loans provided under unfavorable conditions by commercial banks. Over the period from 1977 to 1981, the average maturity of foreign loans declined from 20.4 years to 15.8 years; the average grace period fell from 5.9 years to 4.3 years while the concessional elements in the loans dropped from 37.2 percent to 6.7 percent.[10] There was also a shift in Africa's debt structure in favor of private sources. Loan disbursements from private sources amounted to about 90 percent of those from official creditors in 1971, and steadily rose to 110 percent by 1981. Increased private sources in external financing were largely responsible for high average interest rates; the interest rate charged by private creditors rose from 6.7 percent in 1977 to 14.2 percent by 1981.

Africa's difficulties with external debts have been reflected by the rise in frequency of debt reschedulings. Since 1979, 15 African countries have rescheduled debt and in the period between 1979 and 1982, 20 out of 38 cases of the multilateral debt renegotiations were for African countries.[11] Debt reschedulings are only a short-term response to debt-servicing problems and are clearly not meant to deal with the country's external payments imbalances that would require longer periods of adjustment. The net effect of repeated reschedulings in Africa has thus been only to increase the debt burden. An increasingly common problem has been that payments arrears on the remainder of the loan balance start to inhibit its rescheduling.

THE STRATEGIES FOR ADJUSTMENT

The domestic strategy for debt management in Africa has generally followed IMF programs for correcting external payments imbalances. The IMF's influence became a decisive factor in African countries' economic policy in the aftermath of the second oil crisis in the late 1970s when the IMF emerged as an exclusive source of non–project financing. The lending from the IMF has since become highly conditional on the borrower's adopting an IMF adjustment program. IMF lending imposes on recipients certain performance requirements that include exchange–rate adjustments, money supply controls, import reductions, fiscal austerity, and tax revenue increases.

IMF prescriptions soon proved to be largely ineffective in Africa. After a decade of active involvement by the IMF, African economies are deeper in economic stagnation and debt crisis. The austerity measures aimed at correcting Africa's external disequilibrium—with the consequent depression, rising unemployment, disinvestment, inflation, and fall in living standards—have caused extreme hardships in sub-Saharan Africa. On a number of occasions, the conditionality of the IMF was in part responsible for social unrest and political destabilization as the food riots in Tanzania, Ghana, Sudan, and Egypt clearly attest.

There are a number of reasons for the IMF's poor record of effectiveness in Africa. First, the period of adjustment specified in an IMF agreement was typically three to five years, which must be considered too short a period for the effects of adjustment measures to be felt in the economy. Given the need for restructuring of the export sector, Africa's balance of payments adjustment should require much longer-term financing. Second, IMF-disbursed credits to Africa have been too limited in size to be of much help for adjustment efforts. Compliance with an IMF program is usually required as a condition for the credit recipient to obtain additional funds from other sources. Since 1979, however, not only has the Fund's net lending slowed to a trickle but both concessional and private capital flows to Africa also diminished drastically. Finally, the fundamental reason for the IMF's failure in Africa is that the Fund's program is designed to provide short-term support to the demand management of troubled debtors, whereas the problem of African economies must be seen as basically a structural one on the supply side. For example, the African economies, particularly their industrial sectors, crucially hinge on essential imports. Policies to cut back on imports by belt-tightening measures are, at least in the short run, inconsistent with any efforts for Africa's resumed growth—a requisite for the payment of external debt on a sustained basis.

Faced with the inadequacy of the IMF intervention,[12] and in conjunction with the initial move made under the Baker

Plan,[13] the World Bank and other multilateral development agencies began in the very recent past to take more initiatives in favor of structural adjustment in the debt-ridden Third World countries. The new policy thrust currently advocated by the international financial community stresses the benefits of reliance on markets, "privatization" of the economy, and liberalization of trade and capital movements. The policy reforms suggested are different from the IMF stabilization programs in the sense that the former are more far-reaching, including schemes for the establishment of "realistic" prices and rehabilitation programs for such key sectors as export and transportation.[14]

The liberal version of proposed policy reforms, pointing to the harms done by African government, argues that a retreat from government activism is the major means of improving economic performance in Africa. In this regard, conditionality of the future lending from the World Bank and other donor agencies is likely to center increasingly on the improvement of the climate for private capital in the recipient country. Thus, African markets will have to be gradually opened to foreign trade and investment.[15] Also, in line with increased efforts for "privatization" and integration to world markets of the domestic economy, the country's domestic prices, wages, and exchange rates need to be allowed to find their own levels as determined by market forces. Tariffs and protection of import-substitution industries should similarly be reduced with the economy gradually transforming itself into an outward-oriented one.

As external financial resources are in increasingly short supply and bound by the continuous need of debt-rescheduling, Africa's access to external resources will continue to hinge upon the government's willingness to comply with the policies that would be acceptable to the lenders. Thus, with a policy restructuring imposed as a condition of access to international capital, many African governments now face an awkward choice of either accepting the new policy prescriptions or suffering a drastic reduction in future resource inflows.

NEO-LIBERALISM: THE LONGER-TERM IMPLICATIONS

While existing government structures and governmental policies may have been partly responsible for Africa's decline, now the question is whether or not the alternative process of market-oriented development can indeed revitalize the faltering economies in contemporary Africa. Although under exceptionally propitious external circumstances, the new strategy could conceivably help relieve Africa from its pressing debt burden, there will be a number of real difficulties and problems in enforcing the policy shift. What follows is a discussion of the major problems and implications—both economic and political—of implementing policy changes for Africa. The fundamental issue concerns the feasibility and efficacy of implementing a market-oriented developmental strategy.

The peasants and urban poor are much less integrated into the cash economy in Africa than they are in Latin America or East Asia. Africa's peasant economy is rooted in communal ties based on familial relations or common residence. African peasant farmsteads are typically self-reliant, dependent neither on the market economy nor on governmental services for subsistence and reproduction. Thus, as noted by G. Hyden,[16] neither modern capitalism nor modern socialism, will prevail in Africa until they find ways to subvert the familial mode of production in African peasantry. In addition, even the formal, commercialized sector in Africa is often characterized by monopolistic or oligopolistic market structures because of essentially limited domestic market size. "Perfect competition" as found in the textbook model is a remote reality in Africa. There is thus no guarantee that a greater reliance on market forces will be a route toward improvement in the quality of life for Africans. The Western version of laissez-faireism does not appear a promising orientation in the African context.

Price incentive systems, however desirable they may be from the perspective of efficiency in resource allocation, are likely to work in Africa only if implemented in the context of a comprehensive, supportive policy package that must include the enormously costly programs of improving transport and the marketing system.[17] Furthermore, free-pricing orientations are bound to result in higher prices of domestic foodstuffs as removal of subsidies in food production and a devaluation of the domestic currency—important components in the "getting prices right" policy—will encourage substitution in production from food crops to cash or exportable crops. Finally, the food-deficient continent is currently faced with the urgent task of building the infrastructure to support agriculture, stemming the tide of desertification, and developing human resources. Infrastructural development in Africa will be very costly and require substantial investments. Obviously it can not be left to private-sector initiatives. Thus, the implications of the policy shift for longer-term food supplies in Africa are not very encouraging.

Entrusting resource-allocation decisions to the dictates of market forces enhances the possibility of further marginalizing the rural and urban poor in Africa. While the policy shift in favor of economic growth in the debt-ridden African countries may sound sensible, there remains a large issue of how much benefit from the new strategies can really trickle down to the poorest.[18] For instance, devaluations will likely help only the large-scale cultivators in export crops, not necessarily the small food-crop farmers. Also, as imported basic goods' prices tend to rise with devaluations, urban workers who tend to spend relatively greater proportions of their income on consumer goods will be affected more severely. It is by now widely accepted that the burden of devaluation and inflation in developing countries falls more heavily on the more vulnerable groups of society. Furthermore, reductions in the role of government will inevitably lead to a curtailment of governmental services. Clearly, expenditure cuts in such areas as education, health, or nutrition services will most directly affect the poor.

Unless carefully orchestrated with other macroeconomic policies, exchange rate adjustment in the context of a structurally rigid, import-dependent African economy is likely to exacerbate the external payments as well as the debt situation. A crucial factor that has contributed to the balance-of-payments problems in Africa has been the lack of diversification of the economy, especially in the export sector. In the absence of

structural reforms for a more diversified, efficient export economy, devaluations alone will do little, if anything at all, to restore growth on a sustained basis. Past evidence in many
African countries supports this view: Permissive devaluation
policies resulted in high inflation rates, frequently more than
offsetting the initial effect of the devaluation. The classical case
is that of Ghana. In conformity with IMF-imposed conditionality, Ghana has devalued its currency fourteen times since the
mid-1970s with the resulting, cumulative deterioration in its
external payments position.[19]

Success in the African countries' move toward export-
orientations will crucially depend on the recovery of OECD
countries' growth, as indebted countries cannot be expected to
solve their debt problems in the absence of a complementary
growth of demand in the world market for their exports.[20]
Since 1979, however, African exports have been severely curtailed by sluggish OECD growth, and the possibility of OECD's
resuming growth rates comparable to those which prevailed
during the 1960s is considered extremely unlikely throughout
the remainder of this decade. Nor are the worsened terms of
trade for Africa likely to be reversed in a major way during the
1980s. Thus, African exports will have to compete for shares of
very low-growth world markets against the opposition of more
experienced exporters from other developing countries. Furthermore, African countries have not had much success in
building domestic enterprises to carry out export activities nor
in mixing import substitution with export promotion in a complementary manner. In this regard, it is well to remember that
East Asia's export success was achieved by strong states that
provided organizational as well as fiscal-financial support to
export drives.[21] It is difficult to foresee that any initial success
in nonprimary exports can be achieved for Africa without
some public-sector support.

An important part of the adjustment strategy continues to
be the demand management. Expenditure cuts include reductions in imports, thereby leading to decreased industrial output
and employment since a typical African industry depends
heavily on imported inputs. The alternative policy of import
liberalization would be worse: The dismantling of import-

substitution industries by encouraging import competition is likely to accelerate the pace of deindustrialization in Africa.

The current climate of policy reform is toward increased "privatization" of African economy and industry. While the reformist argument is quite correct in that unproductive state-run industries have been an important cause of Africa's decline,[22] immediate "privatization" of industry will not be a panacea for African problems. For example, the main difficulty with African industry has always been the critical shortage of entrepreneurs. Manpower constraints have severely curtailed industrial development in the past. Also, the restructuring of the economy toward increased competition will have to seek an expanded role for small and medium-sized private firms. It is not obvious, however, that financial mobilization to support the restructuring will take place on an adequate scale in the current context of debt difficulties. The problems of shortages in both investable and human resources must be resolved before any full measures of replacing public-sector activities by private sources can be implemented.

In Africa, political stability often hinges on economic conditions.[23] In this regard, the new strategies could cause considerable political instability. In low-income Africa, devaluations and reductions in food subsidies have been opposed by the urban poor, quite frequently by open violence. In many African countries, the support of the urban sector provides the political legitimacy of the regime. A vehement urban-based political opposition would be almost impossible to withstand by any regime. An additional implication worth noting is the possible formation of a new class structure in African society. Policies for increased integration of the domestic economy into world markets are likely to result in a diminution of the accountability of national leaders and an expansion of foreign-based influences. This can create a foreign-allied domestic elite structure, and possibly a new form of political division in society. At the same time, such policies can easily initiate a reverse process of the "indigenization" policies that have so far been successfully implemented in many black African countries (Kenya, Tanzania, Nigeria, etc.).

CONCLUDING REMARKS

The key to the neo-liberal version of African development is to "privatize" and capitalize African industry and society: African society is expected to be transformed into an entrepreneurial one, competitive with the rest of the world. The fundamental issue, then, is: Can contemporary Africa really be sold a capitalism freed of the inherited chains of state control? The preliminary observations made in this paper are intended to highlight the difficulties and problems inherent in African society for implementing Western-style laissez-faireism. There is thus little reason to expect that a market-oriented development strategy will suddenly unleash a self-sustaining process of economic development in Africa. Such success is all the more unlikely since the fortuitous external developments needed to mitigate reductions in external resource flows and increases in debt-servicing requirements are very unlikely within the immediately foreseeable future.

The crucial point to remember is that because of the fragility and vulnerability to external shocks of the African economy, the average African is poorer today than he or she was twenty years ago. Furthermore, the increased debt burdens are now turning into a critical factor that constrains the implementation of any policies for economic revitalization. The indebtedness of these countries, which up to the mid-1970s had shown considerable stability in relation to the size of their economy, has since jumped far out of proportion with domestic economic activities. For low-income Africa, possibilities of satisfying the IMF conditionality—a precondition for securing new resources from outside sources—seem far more remote today than several years ago. It is now projected that even under the unlikely events of high, sustained industrialized–country growth[24] and of resumed annual flows of concessional capital at the pre–first oil crisis level, the majority of sub-Saharan African countries will not see any gains in living standards over the coming decade.[25]

What is required in Africa's restructuring efforts must not be based on a clear-cut choice between the "invisible hand" or the "grip of the fist"; there are a wide range of possible measures the state can provide to support private sector initiatives. The *sine qua non* for Africa's future is the establishment of a stable, businesslike, non-bureaucratic relationship between government and private sector.

NOTES

1. In the 1970s some Latin American countries grew at a rate no less rapid than the average East Asian newly industrializing country.

2. These countries include all non-Communist economies throughout East and Southeast Asia with the exception of the Philippines (see table 2).

3. The net amount is obtained after deducting payments of capital, interest, and dividends.

4. IMF, *International Financial Statistics 1985*; and *Economist* 7 (June 13, 1986): p. 81.

5. World Bank, *World Development Report 1983* (Washington, D.C., 1984).

6. For an extensive account of governmental corruption, see Gideon S. Were, *Leadership and Underdevelopment in Africa* (Nairobi: Gideon Were Publishing Co., 1983); and K. Kotecha and R. W. Adams, *African Politics: The Corruption of Powers* (Washington, D.C.: University Press of America, 1981).

7. For the sources of data, see IMF, *World Economic Outlook*; and World Bank, *World Debt Tables*, 1984–85.

8. The total figure is an estimate by the Economic Commission for Africa, according to which non-government guaranteed debts are assumed to constitute about a third of the total.

9. A maximum of 25 percent and 100 percent, respectively, for the ratio of debt-service to exports and for that of total debt to exports is normally considered by the bankers as affordable by a developing country.

10. For a fuller exposition of the structure of external debt, see E. C. Onwudiwe, "Africa's External Indebtedness: Structure and Inner Politics," paper presented at the Global Development Conference, University of Maryland, September 1986. Also see World Bank, *World Debt Tables,* 1982–1985.

11. For details of debt-reschedulings in Africa, see C. S. Hardy, "Africa's Debt: Structural Adjustment with Stability," in R. J. Berg & J. S. Whitaker, ed., *Strategies for African Development* (Berkeley, Calif.: University of California Press, 1985), pp. 453–475.

12. For a case study of the futility of IMF programs, see Ajit Singh, "Tanzania and the IMF: The Analytics of Alternative Adjustment Programs," forthcoming in *Development and Change*.

13. There is not much that is really new in the substance of the Plan itself, except that the Bank-sponsored conditionality is certain to include provisions of wide-ranging structural reform.

14. The Economic Recovery Program launched by the Ghanaian government in 1983 represents a case of an extensive reform along the lines of neo-liberal policy measures. U.S. Department of Commerce, *Foreign Economic Trend: Ghana,* December 31, 1984, pp. 1–4. It is also an official U.S. Agency for International Development policy to promote the channeling of aid resources directly to private sectors in Africa. Also for an extensive nature of the World Bank's structural adjustment program, see P. M. Landell-Mills, "Structural adjustment lending: early experience," *Finance and Development,* December 1981, pp. 17–21.

15. The World Bank advocates the foreign direct investment solution to the debt crisis. Recently, the Bank sponsored the Multilateral Investment Guarantee Agency, whose main function is to provide insurance against the risks of direct investment in developing countries.

16. For a fuller exposition of peasant motivation in Africa, see Goran Hyden, *Beyond Ujamaa in Tanzania: Underdevelopment and an Uncaptured Peasant* (Berkeley: University of California Press, 1980).

17. There are conflicting views concerning how price incentives really work in Africa. While a number of studies have shown various degrees of sensitivity of food supply to price changes (see, for example, K. A. Malima, "Determinants of Cotton Supply in Tanzania," in K. S. Kim, R. Mabele, and M. Schultheis, ed., *Papers on the Political Economy of Tanzania* (London: Heinemann Education Books Ltd., 1979), pp. 223–227), other studies, including that of Hyden (1980, p. 24), have concluded fundamental limitations of price incentive systems in stimulating African peasants' marketing products. See also Marian E. Bond, "Agricultural Responses to Prices in Sub-Saharan African Countries," *IMF Staff Papers* 30 (1983), pp. 716–725. Nevertheless, the general consensus that emerges is that price incentives by themselves are unlikely to be effective in Africa unless accompanied by a more comprehensive policy package.

18. On the other hand, the alternative policy of directly helping the poor can have a trickle-up effect on the rest of the economy, possibly generating a higher, sustained economic growth in the long run. For instance, many World Bank studies tend to indicate that the Bank's projects directed at poverty alleviation in Africa have achieved an economic rate of return greater than the conventional, commercially oriented projects.

19. John Kraus, "The Political Economy of Conflict in Ghana," *Africa Report* (March-April 1980), pp. 8–10.

20. For simulation studies of the global economy, see W. R. Cline, *International Debt and the Stability of the World Economy* (Washington, D.C.: Institute for International Economics [Distributed by MIT Press], 1983), pp. 44–73, and Morgan Guaranty Trust, *World Financial Markets,* June 1983.

21. For details, see Kwan S. Kim, "Industrial Policy and Industrialization in South Korea: 1961–1982—Lessons for Other Developing Countries," Kellogg Institute Working Paper 39, 1985, University of Notre Dame.

22. For an empirical study of state enterprises, see Kwan S. Kim, "Enterprise Performances in the Public and Private Sectors: Tanzanian Experience, 1970–75," *Journal of Developing Areas* (April 1981): pp. 471–484; and for a more recent argument, see George B. N. Ayittey, "The Real Foreign Debt Problems," *The Wall Street Journal,* April 8, 1986, p. 30.

23. See P. M. Johnson and W. R. Thompson, *Rhythms in Politics and Economics* (New York: Praeger Press, 1985).

24. In this scenario, the growth rate of world trade is assumed at around 7 percent to 8 percent, comparable to the level before the first global oil shock. Given the lackluster performance of the U.S. and other OECD economies in the recent past, however, a considerable slowdown in the growth of world trade from around 6 percent to 8 percent to less than 3 percent has been projected for the remaining decade. See H. Rowen, *The Washington Post,* September 14, 1986, p. 9.

25. See World Bank, *World Development Report 1985.*

East Asian Coping Strategies: The South Korean Case

KWAN S. KIM *

A striking feature that has emerged from the recent, global debt crisis is the contrasting developments in the debt situation between the two most heavily indebted Third World regions of East Asia and Latin America. East Asian countries generally suffered more from the unfavorable world-market conditions that developed in the early 1980s.[1] Yet despite the larger impact of external shocks, they have been more successful in coping with debt difficulties. For all major Asian borrowers excluding the Philippines, interest and amortization payments as a share in exports have continued to remain at a level considerably below that of any single large borrower in Latin America.[2] Asian countries have also been able to maintain relatively high growth rates and low inflation throughout the 1980s.

Among the East Asian countries, South Korea stands out as a striking example of successful debt management.[3] As a rapidly industrializing country, it is, in absolute terms, Asia's most heavily indebted nation with gross external debt of $36 billion in 1982 that accounted for no less than a third of the region's total. Korea was also one of those indebted countries in which the adverse balance-of-payments impact of external shocks was most severely felt, in 1974–82 the adverse impact accounted

*Kwan S. Kim is a professor of economics and a faculty fellow of the Helen Kellogg Institute for International Studies at the University of Notre Dame. Formerly a senior economist for the Agency for International Development, he has taught in Holland, Mexico, Tanzania, Kenya, and Minnesota.

119

for about 30 percent of the outstanding debt, which was above the Latin American average of 25 percent.[4] The country, nevertheless, proved to be quite successful in averting a deteriorating debt situation.

This paper focuses on the recent experience of South Korea (referred to hereafter as "Korea") in an attempt to explain how an East Asian country's situation is different from that of Latin American or African debtors, and how it has avoided the latest debt crisis. As the model of debt management, the Korean case deserves closer examination. There is by now a growing literature comparing economic performances of the early 1980s in East Asia and Latin America.[5] Some have argued that the external shocks of the late 1970s affected East Asia with much less force than Latin America. As already mentioned, there is evidence to suggest that the contrary was the case.[6] Korea's success in debt management has also been attributed to its outward-oriented policy or exchange rate management. However, attention to a particular policy alone would be uninformative. Korea's adjustment strategy involved more than exchange rate and trade policies. Thus, the causes of the interregional differences must be sought within the context of a broader, integrated analysis that includes the role of other complementary policies and factors as well.[7] This paper has chosen to take a closer, integrated look at Korea's overall adjustment strategies in recent years.

The plan of the paper is as follows: The first section traces the origins and evolution of the recent crisis in Korea, followed by an examination of structural causes of the crisis in section 2. Section 3 focuses on Korea's adjustment policies in response to the crisis. Section 4 discusses the consequences and long-term implications of these strategies. Finally, tentative conclusions concerning Korean policies are summarized in the concluding section.

THE RECENT CRISIS

The origin of the rapid buildup in international indebtedness in Korea can be traced to the early 1970s when the government launched ambitious programs to develop large-scale heavy and chemical industries. After spectacular economic growth during the decade of the 1960s, there was a need for the Korean economy to move away from the emphasis on labor-intensive exports as rising domestic wages began to erode the international competitiveness of Korean exports.[8] Thus, Korea's target-oriented policymakers were eager to borrow from abroad whenever domestic saving fell short of required investment. Korea started to borrow heavily as the financial resources required to develop capital-intensive industries continued to exceed the domestic saving potential.

The domestic saving ratio rose slowly, reaching the level of 27 percent by 1979. This was largely the reflection of increased corporate savings. In the late 1970s the households' savings propensity actually declined as a result of negative domestic real interest rates and an anticipated real exchange rate depreciation. On the other hand, with the rapid increase in government-financed investment projects, investment as a proportion to GDP, which reached as much as 35.4 percent by 1979, began to exceed the domestic saving ratio. As a result, the inflow of resources from abroad had to be kept high throughout the 1970s.

The crunch came in the wake of the oil crisis of 1979 and the ensuing industrialized country recession. In addition, the Korean economy was severely jolted by declining terms of trade and rising foreign interest rates on its accumulated debt. For instance, by 1980 the relative price of Korean exports in importables fell to about 85 percent of the 1978 value (table 1), and would amount to only two-thirds of the relative price of Korean exports in 1972. The volume of Korean exports in the period of 1979–1981 also increased at a rate much slower than that obtained during the preceding decade. To make matters worse, the assassination of President Park in 1979 left the country to face the economic crisis without firm political leadership. There was then a poor harvest in 1980, which necessitated substantial food imports.

As a result, the growth rate of GDP plunged from a 10 percent average registered during the period from 1970 to 1978 to a low 6.5 percent in 1979, and to a negative 5.2 percent in 1980 (table 2). Industrial and mining outputs showed a similar pattern of decline. The government's investment-oriented, expansionary policies continued to fuel inflation. As fixed investment as a proportion of GDP reached as much as 33 percent by 1979, the rate of inflation rose to 40 percent in 1980 from an average of 17.7 percent during the 1970s. Exchange rate adjustment, on the other hand, was generally insufficient in relation to international inflation differentials, which eroded the international competitiveness of Korean exports. In 1980 Korea's current-account position deteriorated by $1.7 billion.

The declining outputs and widening current-account deficits began to cause concern in the international banking community as to Korea's ability to pay its huge debt.[9] It was the group of non-oil, newly industrializing borrowers that was the source of growing concern to bank creditors. In 1979 Korea was already cited as a "potentially problem country" by Morgan Guaranty Trust Company,[10] and was indeed in the fourth position in the IMF's country-ranking in terms of unfavorable

TABLE 1

Major Economic Indicators in Korea

	1978	1979	1980	1981	1982	1983	1984	1985
GNP[a]	52.0	62.4	61.2	67.2	70.9	75.3	81.1	83.1
Exports[a]	12.7	15.1	17.5	21.2	21.9	24.4	29.2	30.3
Imports[a]	15.0	20.3	22.3	26.1	24.3	26.2	30.6	31.1
Per capita GNP[b]	1,487	1,662	1,589	1,719	1,773	1,912	2,041	2,032
Gross debt outstanding[a]	17.3	20.6	29.3	34.2	38.3	40.4	43.1	46.8
Terms of trade	100.0	97.9	84.9	83.1	86.3	87.5	89.4	89.9
Debt service as percent of exports	10.6	13.3	11.9	12.4	13.1	13.0	13.5	
Debt service as percent of GNP	3.6	4.0	4.4	5.1	5.2	5.2	5.6	

[a]In current U.S. $ billion.
[b]In 1980 U.S. dollar.
Sources: Korea Development Institute, *Quarterly Economic Outlook;* The World Bank, *World Debt Tables.*

TABLE 2

Changes in Macroeconomic Indicators
unit: rate of growth (%)

	1979	1980	1981	1982	1983	1984	1985
Real GDP	6.5	−5.2	6.2	5.6	9.5	7.5	5.1
Real investment	−20.0	−23.0	6.0	0.1	18.0	19.0	2.0
Inflation	18.3	28.7	21.3	7.3	3.4	2.3	2.5
Budget balance[a]	−11.4	−67.2	77.0	30.4	64.0	32.0	
Exchange rate[b]	0.0	36.0	6.2	6.8	6.2	4.0	7.6
Money supply (M2)	24.6	26.9	25.0	27.0	15.2	7.7	15.6

[a]Difference between government revenues and expenditures.
[b]Nominal domestic currency per U.S. dollar.
Sources: Economic Planning Board, *Major Statistics of Korean Economy,* 1986; Bank of Korea, *Statistical Year Book;* IMF, *International Financial Statistics.*

debt position. For Korea, the need for policy adjustment was inevitable.[11]

IMBALANCES AND DISTORTIONS

Although Korea's recent crisis may be seen as precipitated directly by external shocks, the declining growth performance in the late 1970s must not entirely be attributed to external factors. Increased business concentration, growing numbers of ailing firms, weakened corporate financial structure, and insufficient interindustrial linkages reflect only a few syndromes of structural distortions facing Korean industry in the late 1970s. Such syndromes were caused by the industrial policy of the two previous decades, which had concentrated on a few large-scale, key sectors as the points of growth.

The Korean government pursued an outward-oriented industrialization strategy based on a system of "administrative guidance." The efficiently functioning Korean bureaucracy was typically assigned some quantitative target goals to achieve. For this, all the support and incentives would be unspared to those firms in the targeted sectors. In the course of implementing such a strategy, the governmental officials' obsession with achieving quantitative results produced considerable success,[12] although from a qualitative point of view, the results can be judged as disappointing in many areas. There are three issues worth considering in this regard.

First, in order to satisfy the growth targets quickly, it was considered important to capitalize on scale economies in industrial production. This naturally meant concentrating policy support on large, indigenous enterprises, which were favored for bank credit under the banking system controlled by government interests.[13] As a result, large business concentration developed in Korean industry as smaller firms were discriminated against in bank lending.

Second, the government's policy of targeting products specified only what sectors of the economy should be promoted for expansion. Loans tended to be approved on the basis of superficial compliance with the administrative guidelines and not on merits of individual projects. Many worthwhile projects failed to be undertaken. These weaknesses were manifest in the late 1970s when a number of government-supported projects had to be discarded. Too many production units were crowded into a few sectors, resulting in overcapacities of these industries. In addition, the bias in favor of large-scale efficiency encouraged excessive borrowing by large firms, which often resulted in a very unstable debt-equity position. By the late 1970s it was not uncommon to find large firms having liabilities five to ten times as much as their net worth. As these firms were burdened with interest payments excessive in relation to their equity, their operation was made particularly precarious in bad times, as was the case in the early 1980s.

Third, the government, in an attempt to expedite attainment of the target goals, tended to reward the more successful exporters by basing its support on the quantitative results of their exports. Not only has this led to an economy-wide inefficient use of resources, but has also created a serious structural imbalance biased against the development of domestic goods industries. In addition, such a support system tended to favor production of assembly-type exports that generally relied heavily on foreign raw materials. This usually led to the need for more imports through exports with the consequence of chronic pressures on the trade balance as the economy became increasingly dependent on foreign capital.[14]

THE GOVERNMENT'S RESPONSE

The causes of declining economic performance in the late 1970s can be traced as much to external shocks as to the long-accumulated distortions in Korea's industrial structure. In this context, the government adopted a two-pronged approach to the resolution of the crisis: Short-term macroeconomic policies were designed to respond to a continuously changing external environment, and the long-term measures were aimed specifically at correcting the structural distortions in a move to enhance the efficiency of the economy, to maintain high sustained growth, and to improve equity in the distribution of income. High sustained growth has been the most important policy objective. The labor force in Korea has been growing at an annual rate of 3 percent, and it will be necessary for the economy to grow at least 5 to 6 percent in order to create new jobs sufficient to absorb about a half million new entrants to the labor market every year.

The Short-term Response

The initial concern in 1980 of the caretaker government in the aftermath of the assassination of President Park was to improve the current account. Given the hostile environment of rising world interest rates, diminishing availability of external finance, and deepening world recession, it was then considered sensible to enforce a stabilization program that included increases in imported energy prices and domestic interest rates, and a devaluation of the Korean won. The economy was quickly pushed into a recession. Concerned with this development, the Chun government, after coming into power, decided to reverse the earlier course. To the extent that additional borrowings could be made possible, the government decided not to sacrifice target growth for the balance of payments or other objectives.

Two distinct periods of 1980–1982 and 1983–1985 can be identified in the shift of adjustment policy under Chun's regime. During the initial phase the government adopted a moderately reflationary measure clearly intended to overcome the recession-led debt crisis. This was against the background of a still depressed world market but with some hopeful signs for the recovery of Korean exports, as there was a surge in export orders in the latter part of 1980.

In efforts to stimulate domestic investment, particularly in housing, construction, and exports, from the negative growth experienced the previous year, the government implemented a number of measures including a reduction in bank interest rates and increases in essential imports (table 1). The decision not to curtail essential imports was an important one as the reductions in imports could quickly decelerate industrial growth. The money supply increased by more than 50 percent during the period of expansionary policy (1981 and 1982). The rapid liquidity expansion, however, fueled a modest rate of inflation in 1981, followed by a sharp drop in inflation to a low 7.3 percent growth the next year (table 2). This fall in inflation was largely due to a decline in commodity prices abroad, but there was also a high degree of coordination between the monetary and fiscal authorities through Korea's efficient planning process. The government took actions to finance budget deficits with a minimum effect on the money supply. The government exercised fiscal discipline by reducing expenditures on the farm price support program, phasing out the system of policy lending to targeted enterprises, and increasing tax revenues. As shown in table 2, the budget balance which was drastically reduced in the years of high inflation (1979–1980) registered a very modest reduction by 1982. On the whole, government budget as a percentage to domestic absorption fell by 2.5 percent over the years between 1980–82.[15]

Domestic investment was maintained at a relatively high level throughout the early 1980s, as shown by the fact that GDP grew more rapidly than real consumption expenditures. The increase in the saving ratio in Korea seems to be correlated with the rise in labor-force participation rates: In the past the growth rate of labor force absorption in Korea has been in the range of 2.5 to 3.0 percent, while population has grown at 1.0 to 1.5 percent. Thus, the average worker has fewer dependents to support and is able to save more. Although domestic saving to a certain extent responded to investment opportunities,[16] the investment and saving gap had to be made up by additional borrowing.

In this regard, Korea, despite the hardened borrowing terms, was still able to borrow altogether some $5 billion new funds during the critical years of 1980 and 1981.[17] This was an important factor that contributed to an early recovery of the economy. Despite a growing concern by banks about political and economic conditions in Korea, Korea was still considered as a more dynamically viable economy in comparison to other developing countries. Also, conditions of high market liquidity and resulting competition among bankers continued for new borrowers. Thus, in addition to $1.7 billion fresh loans from official sources, of which Japan accounted for the lion's share,[18] Western banks in late 1980 had already begun to compete to arrange Korea's next big syndicated loan. As a result, close to two-thirds of the new loans contracted during the critical period came from private sources which were obtained mostly on short-term, commercial terms.[19]

The second phase of adjustment started in late 1982 against the background of an expected recovery in the world market. Following the fall in oil prices and foreign interest rates in 1983, planners switched from the emphasis on domestic growth to export expansion. The immediate task was seen as restoring price stability to strengthen Korea's international competitiveness. Hence, the maintenance of competitive exchange rates through a control over inflation was accorded utmost priority.

In an attempt to reduce inflationary pressures and further increase domestic saving, the government resorted to measures to finance budget deficits with minimum impact on money supply and an interest rate policy that guaranteed a positive real rate to savers. The earlier policy to phase out agricultural price support programs continued at an accelerated pace. Preferential and subsidized loans provided to large conglomerates were mostly abolished, which generated substantial savings to the government. The nominal exchange rate was devalued to parallel domestic inflation. The real exchange rate, on the whole, remained at a competitive level throughout the post-1982 period.

Structural Reforms

In view of the structural problems mentioned earlier, the government's long-term policy has been concerned with structural adjustment and institutional reforms to achieve the twin goals of increased efficiency of the economy and improvement of equity in income distribution. Specifically, the Fifth Five-Year Plan (1982–1986) called for reforms in the following areas.

The priority goal of the reform has been the "rationalization" of industries to increase industrial efficiency by streamlining troubled firms and industries. The past practice of policy lending resulted in inefficient corporate management and a weak corporate financial structure in several sectors of the economy. The credit exposure in the form of loans and guarantees by a bank to individual borrowers has often been many times the borrower's net worth.[20]

With the enactment of the Anti-Monopoly Act in 1981, the new ground rules of business proscribed cartel arrangements, barriers to market entry, and other monopoly practices. The domestic market was to be open to increased foreign competition.[21] Tax preferences and preferential interest rates for a large number of "strategic" industries were abolished. Ceilings on bank borrowing by companies were imposed. The new strategy was to eliminate the ailing sectors and companies through freer competition. The role of government in economic management is now seen as a provider of the "functional incentives" that should not discriminate between sectors and should be used to stimulate the development of new technologies, products, and markets.

The structure of conglomerates was considered too diversified and inefficient. Taking advantage of governmental protection in the past, the *chaebols* (giant conglomerates) in Korea have managed to filter into side businesses in various forms of horizontal integration. An integral part of the "rationalization" measures is to enhance industrial efficiency by forcing conglomerates to stay in mainstream specialization. The ultimate policy goal is the development of a vertically integrated, internationally competitive industrial structure instead of the grouping of diversified subsidiary firms.

The government has already taken actions to create a better business climate for small and medium-sized firms in terms of access to credits and export markets.[22] By law, at least 35 percent of bank loans must now be allocated to small and medium-sized firms. The increased participation of small businesses in exports would be in line with the country's effort to diversify export products and markets, which would keep exports less vulnerable to changes in international market conditions.[23] In addition, the role of small firms in developing technology-intensive and parts industries must be considered important, as Korea's new strategy calls for increased governmental support of high-tech industry. For this, a new integration scheme, called "the systematization scheme," is being pushed ahead by both the government and business community. It is a device aimed at increasing efficiency through a division of labor between the process of assembling at the parent firm and parts-making by small, subsidiary firms.[24] Intraindustry specialization is thus expected to strengthen the international competitiveness of Korean products.

Approaches to a more equitable income distribution are sought by enhanced employment opportunities through high, sustained economic growth and by increased access to education and training by all groups of society. For these purposes the government has been increasing expenditures on education and technical training. Within industry the increased support given to small firms is expected to reduce business concentration. The government has also been promoting rural industrialization, thereby making non-farm employment opportunities available to farmers. The loss of the agricultural price support program is, however, likely to widen the rural-urban gap.

Finally, in pursuing the new strategies, there will be an increasing reliance on market mechanisms and less governmental intervention. The painful experience of picking "wrong winners" in the early 1970s led the policy reformists in the early 1980s to reevaluate the government's ability in industry-specific assistance in an already diversified and sophisticated economy.[25] The reform has called for liberalization, specifically, in such sectors as import, finance, and foreign investment.[26]

CONSEQUENCES AND IMPLICATIONS

The changes in economic indicators during the period of adjustment are summarized in table 2. In interpreting the results, one must not attribute the observed changes entirely to the effect of adjustment policy. The table clearly shows that the speed of the recovery in all aspects of macroeconomic performance was impressive: Real output bounced back into a positive growth of over 6.2 percent in 1981 and 5.6 percent in 1982 from the decline of 5.2 percent in the previous year. The economic downturn in the U.S. and other industrialized countries during the last quarter of 1981 halted the recovery of the Korean economy. The resumed growth in 1982 was made possible by increased domestic construction activities. The current account improved in 1981, and within three years the current account deficit as a fraction of GNP declined to the 1978 level. Exports were on the rise again, recovering from the level of $18.9 billion in 1980 to an annual average of more than $25 billion in the subsequent three years. By 1982 expansionary monetary policy through influencing interest rates resulted in a full recovery of domestic investment to the pre-crisis level.

The annual growth of 26 percent in money supply during the initial phase (1980–1982) was lower than the average growth (33 percent) experienced in the previous period between 1968 and 1977. Furthermore, the rapid industrialization in Korea had been accompanied by a growing need for liquidity, requiring a slow increase in the ratio of money to GDP.[27] Thus, the observed rate of growth in money supply should not be considered excessive. The moderately expansionary policy, however, proved to be somewhat inflationary. The inflationary consequences resulted from the decline in the rate of output growth experienced in the earlier 1980s. Nevertheless, any contractionary policy in those critical years would not have been acceptable to Korean decision-makers, since it would have meant a retrenched economy leading to debt difficulties.

It must be pointed out, however, that there were fortuitous circumstances for Korea that enabled the government to pursue an expansionary policy. Largely because of Korea's long-standing credibility in the international financial community, Korea, although limited in amount and in much hardened borrowing terms, was still able to borrow from abroad. This ability to borrow prevented Korea from the need to cut back on essential imports. Had imports been curtailed due to the unavailability of foreign credit, the recovery of the Korean economy may not have been that easy. On the other hand, the expansionary policy based on continued borrowing during the first phase has caused a casualty in the economy. During this period borrowing was mostly short-term with extraordinarily high interest rates. The debt service as a share in exports in 1983, if the rollover of short-term debts is excluded, comes to only 17 percent, as compared to the ratio of a whopping 49 percent if all short-term debts are included.[28] Korea still has an extremely unfavorable debt composition. The reduction of the unfavorable debt accumulated in the early 1980s has indeed been a priority in recent government policy.

During the second phase of adjustment, perhaps the government's most remarkable achievement was its success in restoring price stability. The government simply concentrated on measures to control inflation to assure stability and international competitiveness of Korean exports. Due in a large measure to the efforts to reduce budget deficits and to raise domestic saving, and in part to the decline in commodity prices abroad,[29] the rate of inflation dropped from 21.3 percent in 1981 to 7.3 percent in 1982 (table 2). Reflecting the rise in real exchange rates as well as the improvement in the external environment, Korea's balance of payments quickly improved: The current account deficit which had been projected at $4.4 billion early in 1982, fell to $2.5 billion.[30]

Beginning in late 1985, the Korean economy started to show signs of added vitality, having fully recovered from the 1980 crisis.[31] Benefiting from the decline in oil prices, the easing of foreign interest rates, and the weakened value of the U.S.

dollar to which the Korean won is tied, Korean exports picked up rapidly with the resulting rise in GNP that attained a real growth rate of more than 11 percent in the first half of 1986. The nation consequently generated, for the first time on record, a current-account surplus of $1.75 billion in the first eight months of 1986. All this happened despite the general decline in world trade in 1985. Sustained export growth was in part the reflection of increased diversification in the range of Korean products, which made exports less sensitive to cyclical fluctuations.

Although the recent surge in the economy can, to a certain extent, be attributed to favorable external developments, due credit should also be given to domestic policies that promoted industrial efficiency and export diversification to stimulate high growth. This growth-oriented strategy proved to provide the most satisfactory resolution of debt problems for Korea. As exports and GNP continued to expand and were reinforced by an interest rate policy that guaranteed a positive real return to savers, Korea was able to satisfy increased portions of its financial requirements from domestic resources.

With the continuation of the current world market trend, and barring the possibility of dramatic political or social unrest,[32] prospects for Korea appear promising in comparison to other developing countries. The country's export base has been substantially broadened with the diversification of the range of products, making exports less vulnerable to the uncertainties of the world market. It has already established a competitive position in heavy, capital goods, automobile, and high-tech industries in international markets, and the government considers these industries—particularly in the product areas of automobiles, electronics, and machinery—as key to Korea's success in the decades ahead. On the anticipated strength of Korean exports, the nation's current-account surplus is projected to further rise to $3.0 billion by 1991.[33]

As a result, Korea will be able to reduce dependence on foreign loans. As shown in table 3, the nation's net debt (outstanding foreign debt minus net foreign assets) is projected to decline from a 1987 peak of $35.7 billion to $29.3 billion in 1991, the target year of the Sixth Five-Year Plan (1987–91). More important, outstanding debt as a share in GDP will gradually be trimmed from 56.3 percent in 1985 to 31.1 percent by 1991. Along with the decline in debt burden, per capita income is scheduled to rise from $2094 in 1985 to $3714 in 1991. Of course, Korea's debt management performance will depend on continued economic growth and export expansion. The rising danger of industrialized country protectionism poses a major threat to the plan's goals. However, Koreans have consistently overcome adversity.

CONCLUDING REMARKS

Despite the rapid rise in the size of external indebtedness, Korea has successfully avoided the debt difficulties other developing countries currently face. The Korean experience shows what can be done in a short time to avert a possible debt crisis. It is true that in contrast to countries pursuing an inward-oriented economic policy that usually leads them toward debt problems, those moving toward greater integration into world markets on a more diversified basis can gain increasing access to both equity and debt finance. Indeed, Korea's outward orientations seem to have fostered a high degree of resiliency for the economy to cope with external shocks: The Korean economy with an internationally competitive industrial structure made itself adaptable to changing world market conditions, and has been better positioned to deal with debt problems.

Nevertheless, outward orientations by themselves are not

TABLE 3

Projections for Foreign Debt and Economic Performance

	1985	1987	1988	1989	1990	1991
Population (in millions)	41.3	42.1	42.6	43.1	43.6	44.7
GNP[a]	86.3	103.9	117.7	131.9	147.8	166.0
Per capita GNP (in U.S. $)	2,094	2,468	2,763	3,061	3,389	3,714
Current account[a]	−0.9	1.0	1.4	1.7	2.4	3.0
Outstanding debt[a]	46.8	49.3	50.6	51.6	52.0	51.7
—Share in GNP—	56.3%	46.7	43.0	39.1	35.2	31.1
Net debt[a]	35.5	35.7	34.8	33.6	31.6	29.3

[a]In billion U.S. dollars.
Source: Economic Planning Board.

a sure safeguard against debt problems, particularly during a world recession. Korea's success can be attributed to its effective economic policy and efficient debt management. There is evidence to indicate that not only have Korea's borrowed funds been used mostly for investment purposes but also they have been used efficiently.[34] The highly efficient use of capital has enhanced Korea's credibility to lenders. The availability of foreign capital even in adverse times has largely been the result of Korea's exceptional economic performance.

The positive effects of economic policy were of course reinforced by other complementary factors including Korea's efficient labor force, political stability, effective government-business collaboration, and among others, strong government management. Strong management is a distinct feature of Korean bureaucracy, shared by other East Asian newly industrializing countries.[35] The ability of Korean decision-makers, undeterred by external influences, to swiftly formulate and implement corrective measures considered to work best in response to changing circumstances is what has generally been lacking in other developing countries. Another factor should also be considered. Unlike other developing countries, Korea has had no serious problems with capital flight. Apart from the reason of attractive yield to capital in a growing economy, Korea is an example of a country in which controls on capital movements have been very effective.

Thus, in the case of Korea, domestic policies had a clear impact on the external debt situation.[36] One fundamental conclusion that can be drawn from the Korean experience is the importance of structural adjustment if the debt problem is to be resolved without undue damage to long-term performance of the economy. For Korea, the timely shifts in export composition, streamlining troubled industries, and industrial reorganization for greater efficiency formed an integral part of the overall adjustment strategy, which proved to be as important as financial stabilization measures.

NOTES

1. According to a recent study, during the period of 1974–1981 external shocks were responsible for 38 percent of the outstanding debt for the

group of major East Asian borrowers, as compared with 25 percent for the group of major Latin American borrowers. The group of major borrowers in Asia in the study included South Korea, Thailand, the Philippines, Malaysia, and Indonesia; major Latin American borrowers were Brazil, Mexico, Argentina, Chile, and Venezuela. P. Nunnenkamp, *The International Debt Crisis of the Third World: Causes and Consequences for the World Economy,* (New York: St. Martin's Press, 1986), p. 67.

2. Refer to table 2 on p. 123.

3. Within the East Asian region, there are, of course, country specific variations in recent economic performance. More agriculturally oriented nations, such as Indonesia and the Philippines, have struggled with falling international prices for their export commodities. Despite considerable improvements of their economies in the early 1980s, both countries recently have had problems of high inflation and reduced productivity. Singapore has been suffering from over-investment in the domestic construction industry and its high-wage labor force is beginning to feel the pinch as the overall economy has not responded adequately to governmental measures aimed at stimulating growth to create new jobs. Oil-exporting countries such as Malaysia and Indonesia are trying to cope with the fall in oil prices. Taiwan and South Korea, currently taking advantage of cheaper oil and low foreign interest rates, are maintaining strong growth rates.

4. P. Nunnenkamp, *International Debt Crisis of the Third World,* table 24, p. 66.

5. For instance, J. D. Sachs, "External Debt and Macroeconomic Performance in Latin America and East Asia," *Brookings Papers on Economic Activity,* 2, 1985, pp. 523–573; B. Balassa, "Adjustment Policies in Developing Countries: A Reassessment," *World Development* 12 (September 1984): pp. 955–972; R. Solomon, "Brazil vs. Korea: Differing Experiences as Debtors," *International Economic Letter* (Washington, D.C.: R. S. Associates, Inc., November 12, 1984).

6. See note 1.

7. Such factors as Korea's efficient labor force, political stability, strong government management, and relative ease of access to international credits should be taken into consideration.

8. In the second half of the 1970s real wages rose faster than productivity. This exerted cost-push inflationary pressure.

9. In the late 1970s close to 60 percent of Korea's borrowing came from private sources. Korea was Asia's largest borrower with an outstanding private debt of over $20 billion in 1979.

10. David Kern, "Neither alarm nor complacency," *Euromoney* (April 1979): p. 128.

11. IMF, *International Financial Statistics,* Tables 10–15, pp. 41 and 198.

12. These measures quickly led to the targeted sectors' increased share in exports.

13. The policy-lending system to provide special support to selected firms worked very well for Korea in the early days of industrialization. With-

out this governmental financing, it would have been impossible for Korea to develop for exports in a short space of time such sectors as light manufacturing, construction, steel, automobile, and shipbuilding industries.

14. For details, see K. S. Kim, "Industrial Policy and Industrialization in South Korea: 1961–1982—Lessons for Other Developing Countries," Kellogg Institute Working Paper, 39, University of Notre Dame, 1985, p. 80.

15. During the period of 1979–82, Korea's average budget share was about 17.2 percent, about the same level as in Mexico. The difference was that Korea's defense budget accounted for a much larger share of 6 percent in GDP. IMF, *International Financial Statistics*.

16. See for example, M. J. Kim & Y. C. Park, "A Study on Savings Behavior, 1953–1972," in C. K. Kim, ed., *Planning Models and Macroeconomic Policy Issues* (Seoul: Korea Development Institute, 1977).

17. This estimate is based on the "net flows" figures reported in World Bank, *World Debt Tables* (1985), p. 214.

18. These funds were in addition to the Japanese reparation settlement of 1965, by which $300 million in grants and $200 million in loans were provided to Korea over the ten-year period from 1965 to 1975. Nevertheless, as A. Krueger points out (A. O. Krueger, *The Developmental Role of the Foreign Sector and Aid* [Cambridge, Mass.: Harvard University Press, 1979], p. 158) Japan has not been a "significant factor" in total exchange availability in Korea.

19. The unfavorable terms under which these loans were contracted in the early 1980s were responsible for Korea's somewhat worsened—but still manageable—debt situation in subsequent years.

20. The recent incident was the dissolution of the Kukje Group, one of the ten largest conglomerates in Korea, when the lenders refused to roll over Kukje's debt because of its precariously high debt-equity ratio.

21. The government has recently adopted more liberal policies to induce foreign investors for joint ventures. Foreign capital and technology are to complement Korea's efficient labor force and well-developed, productive infrastructure. In a typical joint venture setting, the locally produced components will be shipped to the United States for assembling. These are the kinds of combinations that are considered a better match for the Japanese advantage in technology.

22. The centrally controlled credit management practiced in the past discriminated against small and medium-sized firms which, taking advantage of cheap labor, tended to specialize in labor-intensive products including textiles, toys, stationery, and food. Heavy industries, on the other hand, have relied on imported parts and material. Despite the strong rise in the export of heavy industry products in recent years, the trade balance failed to improve for this reason. Korean industry's limited value added can be attributed to the underdevelopment of small and medium-sized businesses.

23. The Taiwan experience attests to this fact.

24. For instance, it is argued that Japan's market dominance in electronics, automobiles, and machines comes from a closely woven integration

of myriad small parts suppliers into the primary manufacturers.

25. The earlier excessive investments in heavy and chemical industries, in which the government thought Korea would have a comparative advantage, only produced a sharp decline in capacity utilization in the face of the world recession in the late 1970s.

26. Gradual increases in the import liberalization rate were envisaged as the main instrument of the overall trade liberalization. The import liberalization rate was scheduled to rise, for example, from 76 percent in 1982 to 92 percent by 1986, and the gradual replacement of non-tariff protection by tariffs was granted for a limited time period. Korea has been under increasing international pressures to open its trade and finance market. Liberalization measures, however, will likely proceed gradually on the basis of reciprocity of the trading partners. Korean policymakers are well reminded of the disastrous experience of Chile in the late 1970s.

27. For an empirical work, see R. D. Norton and S. Y. Rhee, "A Macroeconometric Model of Inflation and Growth in South Korea," in W. R. Cline and S. Weintraub, eds., *Economic Stabilization in Developing Countries* (Washington, D.C.: Brookings Institution, 1981), pp. 407–463.

28. An estimate by Morgan Guaranty Trust Company.

29. For a fuller discussion, see D. Holden, "Korea's Debt Outlook," *Oriental Economist* (November 1983): pp. 26–28.

30. The year 1982 was a particularly good one for Korea, as it had a good harvest with the resulting reduction in grain imports by over 50 percent from the previous year's level.

31. For instance, exports and industrial production during the first four months of 1986 registered an increase of 12.3 percent and 22.9 percent, respectively, over the level of a year before. The jobless rate was 3.9 percent in April of 1986. Deputy Prime Minister's Office: *Monthly economic report to the President,* May 1986.

32. The current softness in the world oil market is projected to continue over the next two or three years after some temporary wild fluctuations. The more serious problem will be possibilities of domestic unrest as well as unprogrammed wage and price hikes preceding the presidential elections and the Summer Olympic Games in 1988.

33. *Business Asia* (September 29, 1986); p. 306.

34. According to Klaus Fertig's calculations (in "South Korea: Successful Large-scale International Borrower," *Intereconomics* [May-June 1983]: pp. 142–147), the marginal capital productivity for Korea was more than 20 percent which was well above real interest rates on borrowed funds. The World Bank cited in its annual report (*World Development Report,* 1981, p. 68) South Korea as the most efficient developing country.

35. The Confucian countries in East Asia have far less bureaucratic insubordination in comparison with other countries.

36. For a comparative analysis of country experiences on this issue, see P. Nunnenkamp, *The International Debt Crisis of the Third World,* pp. 70–91.

The Double Paradox of Conditionality

*PAUL P. STREETEN**

In analyzing conditionality, it is important to draw a distinction between conditionality that applies to creating the conditions for the repayment of the loan, and conditionality that applies to broader macropolicies which are supposed to be in the interest of the borrower for putting his house in order. Father Hesburgh quite rightly reminded us of the overzealous lenders. Nicolas Barletta told us that there may also be profligate borrowers. Even though the lender may be greedy, the loan must still be repaid. Promises should be kept.

In a commercial transaction, conditions beyond those required for capacity to repay are ruled out. If a loan is requested from a bank, the person's private life cannot be questioned, but the lender has a right to know how the loan will be repaid. However, when there is a concessional element, the lender may want to "buy" policies that improve the borrower. Thus, the conditions that are attached to the concessional or the non-commercial part of the loan from the International Monetary Fund or the World Bank may be criticized.

Now, if there were a visitor from Mars, he would be very puzzled by two features. First, multinational institutions such as the International Monetary Fund and the World Bank impose conditions on a borrower that are thought to be in his

*Paul P. Streeten is the director of the World Development Institute at Boston University. He has served as the special advisor to the policy planning and program review department of the World Bank, and director of the studies at the Overseas Development Council. He has published extensively on issues in world development and the role of transnational corporations in that process.

best interest. Second, the borrower is rewarded with more money for accepting what is deemed to be in his own best interest. Normally one would expect to pay for good advice, not be rewarded for accepting it.

This double paradox calls for some kind of explanation. Ten proposals are submitted for consideration.

1. The borrower is ignorant of economic analysis and has to be instructed.
2. The borrower's causal analysis differs (e.g. he believes devaluation will worsen the balance of payments, or direct quantitative controls are more effective).
3. The borrower's forecast of future states of the world is different (e.g. he believes the future price of oil will be high, while the lender thinks it will be low).
4. The borrower's objectives are different (e.g. staying in power or protecting the poor).
5. The borrower's objectives are the same but are given different weights (e.g. to income distribution compared with reducing inflation).
6. The borrower's basic philosophy or interest is different: "the government can do no wrong" versus "the government can do no right," or the lender's conditions are believed to impose the demands of international capital and imperialism.
7. The borrower's time horizon is different (more weight is given to short-term or to long-term growth).
8. The borrower's risk aversion to uncertain future outcomes is different.
9. Borrower and lender agree on everything, but the borrower likes to blame the foreigner (scapegoat).
10. Borrower and lender agree but adjustment calls for extra resources to ease the transition (but extra finance can also delay adjustments).

The principal remedy for many of these conflicts is humility, especially within dialogue. For other conflicts, the test should be to concentrate on *results* rather than *means* and design alternative packages. For still others, signaling without conditionality is needed—supporting "good" countries or potential improvers, but without imposing performance criteria. Cases such as wanting a scapegoat raise difficult questions as to whether outside support for the "good guys" inside a country is a help for good policies or the kiss of death.

The main principle is that a change from a set of "bad policies" to better policies is a costly transition and requires additional resources. It can be financed by the additional aid. The definition of aid analysis has changed from the 1950s and 1960s to the present. Aid is now thought of more as easing transitional difficulties or of adding flexibility, rather than filling gaps in savings or foreign exchange. In this light, the conditions that the institutions require are not always the most important: from import substitution to exports, from industry to agriculture, more food for domestic consumption, etc. Why not contribute to the transitional costs of land reform? Or tax reform? Or for educational reforms? Why not even transitional costs for certain types of radical or revolutionary reforms? Revolutionary Adjustment Loans (RALs) as well as Structural Adjustment Loans (SALs)?

If we accept the prescriptions of these institutions as being in the borrower's best interest, then the philosophy that Peter Bauer and the Heritage Foundation and the American Enterprise Institute propagate has to be reversed. They tell us that concessional loans are inefficient because they weaken the moral fiber of the borrower, and they do not apply hard commercial criteria to projects, resulting in lax standards and inefficiency. On the contrary, concessional loans with good macropolicy conditions would be *more* efficient than commercial loans. Commercial loans concentrate on the returns from the project. Concessional loans also look at the correct macropolicies—the exchange rate, the interest rates, the wage policy, trade policies. These are therefore *more* efficient types of loans than the commercial ones, where conditionality is confined to returns on the project, and the good yield may be undone by bad policies.

The move away from project aid to program aid has been justified by the argument that projects are fungible—the Bank may finance one splendid project and free domestic funds to finance a bad project. But the Fund and the Bank have forgotten that policies also are fungible. They can prescribe policies but a clever borrower can get around these conditions. They can prescribe devaluation but subsequent inflation can negate it. They prescribe one set of liberalization policies but, by a combination of taxes and subsidies, the borrower can evade them. It is terribly difficult in practice to prescribe a set of policies that closes every loophole. For those who disagree with the Fund, this is a sign of hope.

In the light of what Father Hesburgh has said, issues of human rights and morality must be included in conditionality. Most people are more certain that it is wrong to torture people than that the exchange rate is too high or the supply of money is excessive. It is known that the Bank and the Fund are not allowed to include such conditions because they are regarded as political. However the Bank and the Fund could be much more humble and diffident about the economic prescriptions while moving in the direction of paying some attention to human rights.

Further, Rose Spalding's point is well taken. The causes of maladjustments should be examined. The performance test should be the purpose of the exercise—for example, an improvement in the balance of payments, and not the instruments dear to the Fund, such as reduced budget deficits, restraint in the supply of money, exchange devaluation, or trade liberalization. Only in this way can the ideological element be removed from the dialogue which has caused so much friction. If a borrowing country wishes to improve its balance of payments by means other than trade liberalization, money restraint, and devaluation, why should it not be allowed to do so?

Interlocking Time Frames:
Adjustment, Structural Change,
and Strategies

GUILLERMO O. CHAPMAN, JR. *

In analyzing the impact of the debt crisis and searching for ways to move beyond it, it is necessary to look at three time frames which require different adjustment processes: the short term calls for stabilization; the structural adjustment programs make sense only in the medium term; and, for the long term a strategic approach is needed.

SHORT-TERM STABILIZATION PROGRAMS

A short-term stabilization program, as in a standard International Monetary Fund stand-by arrangement, concentrates typically on macroeconomic variables and aims to correct short-term imbalances with short-term tools. Such programs would include measures to correct balance-of-payments difficulties through devaluation of the national currency and the elimination of distortions affecting free trade. If the program is successful, the short-term results to be expected are obviously

---

*Guillermo O. Chapman, Jr. is the founder and chairman of the board of Investigación Y Desarrolo, S.A., a firm of economic and financial consultants. He has served as an economist in the planning office of the Presidency of the Republic of Panama and as a member of the Panamanian Canal Treaty Negotiating Mission.

a reduction of imports and ideally an increase in exports. The stabilization program would most likely include also measures to balance the public sector deficit or, at least, reduce it through revenue-enhancement measures and the reduction of expenditures, especially the subsidies on food and transportation prices so typical in Latin America.

It is not surprising therefore that these short-term tools have resulted in the deterioration in the lives of the poor since both the country's capacity to import is diminished in the short term and direct and indirect expenditure on the needy is curtailed. Stabilization programs are, of course, ineffective vis-à-vis the fundamental structural problems which characterize the present Latin American crisis since such short-term tinkering with a few macro-economic variables does not even aim to solve more fundamental situations that require other tools and longer time frames. Thus a first observation is that even though stabilization programs do very little for the poor or, worse still, tend to deteriorate their situation, it makes little sense to evaluate them in isolation for their effectiveness against poverty.

A short-term program would only make sense if it is part of a long-range, comprehensive, developmental perspective. Available historical evidence shows that in the majority of cases, economic growth, by itself alone, has not been able to solve the problems of poverty. A direct attack on poverty with new and innovative approaches is required since poverty will not disappear nor be ameliorated as an indirect consequence of promoting growth. Relying on the old trickle-down theory just will not work.

The Henriot-Jameson paper also points out that another problem with short-term stabilization programs is that they are dictated by one side only, that is, they are *imposed* on the debtor countries by institutions such as the IMF and the World Bank. Usually, when one finds instances of such imposition, there is also evidence of lack of initiative from the authorities of the debtor country, who have no consistent programs of their own other than surviving fiscally and politically in the short run through the use of the financial resources that are made available to them as part of the stabilization program.

Conditionality and the Poor

While there is little doubt that the situation has worsened for the poor, there are other factors in addition to conditionality to which one can attribute the observed deterioration. One such factor is the lack of a long-term strategy and of a medium-term adjustment program. There is also a crowding-out effect that works against expenditures on social programs within the framework of public sector finances by reason of the high level of interest payments on the external debt. This is especially acute in those Latin American countries whose governments are determined to service the debt. Independent of whether conditionality is present or not, the problem lies in good part in this crowding-out effect, which in essence means that no fresh resources are made available to the country in question as a counterpart to the adjustment measures included in the stabilization program. If conditionality could be structured in such a manner that it does not decrease the resources available to the public sector for its programs in favor of the poor, it would, at least, not be detrimental to their situation. In conclusion, there is a crying need for programs that provide for growth and for support to the poor at the same time that the macroeconomic variables are being brought under control.

The problem as it relates to the poor is serious, far greater than the conditionality, which at least in the International Monetary Fund variety—the very short-term—has proven to be unsuccessful in the present economic context of Latin America. This is a point well developed in the Foxley paper and is even accepted privately by some IMF officials.

Structural Adjustment

Structural adjustment programs deal fundamentally with changes in economic policies affecting the working of microeconomic variables which require a medium-term time frame for their effects to be felt. Some Latin American countries have adopted structural adjustment programs sponsored by the World Bank, which are supported with general purpose loans known as Structural Adjustment Loans (SAL), and include more reliance on market forces, freer trade, and development of new exports. Here, the Foxley admonition to avoid ideological preferences at both extremes (completely open markets or full-state intervention) is particularly well taken. As Foxley points out, and it is also well developed by Balassa, Bueno, Kuczynski, and Simonsen,[1] these adjustment programs make almost no mention of the possibilities of more efficient import substitution. Finally, the emphasis of the adjustment program is on microeconomic variables rather than on the macroeconomic variables contained in the typical IMF stand-by arrangement.

A brief comparison of various country groupings will highlight the need for a balanced structural adjustment. Let us look briefly at the twenty-year experience of five groups of nations: (1) the Asian newly industrializing nations (NICs), (2) the Latin American NICs, (3) the members of the Association of South-East Asian Nations (ASEAN), (4) the Nordic countries, and (5) three small Latin American countries which had relatively fast rates of economic growth in the 1970s up to 1982— Costa Rica, Chile, and Panama. With the exception of the Latin American NICs (Brazil and Mexico), all the countries considered can be classified as small economies. Four indicators were examined for each group of countries: the level of GNP or GDP per capita, the rate of growth of GNP/GDP per capita, inflation, and the rate of growth of exports. Table 1 summarizes the data examined.

Over the past twenty years, the *consistently* better performing economies of the world, and among the small economies, have been the Asian NICs (especially in the past fifteen years) and the Nordic countries. Asian or Nordic groups occupy the first two positions in all the selected performance categories, while the small Latin American countries and the Latin American NICs are either in the middle or at the bottom of the group in respect to all of the performance indicators.

Some of the possible explanations for such a difference in results may be found in the policies followed by the different groups of countries (see table 2 for a summary of policies). A few Asian countries have had relatively high levels of protection for local production in contrast with the low levels prescribed typically by the World Bank in its SAL programs. In the case of Taiwan and Korea, domestic production has been "selectively protected" at least for some periods, as Kim noted in his presentation, while Singapore and Hong Kong give no protection whatsoever to domestic production, which is almost totally for export. The Nordic countries, while not going to the extreme case of Singapore and Hong Kong, have had fairly low levels of tariff protection. On the other hand, the ASEAN countries have maintained intermediate to high protective tariffs on goods produced locally, while Latin American nations, both the NICs and the small countries, have protected their industries with high to very high tariff walls and have also resorted to non-tariff means of protection.

The general orientation of the national economies is another key policy component worth examining. The Asian NICs and the Nordic countries have an outward orientation, i.e., they have a set of policies stressing the development of exports as opposed to import substitution as the primary source of growth. The ASEAN countries also tend to favor exports as the mainstay of their economies but to a lesser degree than the first two groups. In Latin America the import-substitution approach sponsored by ECLA after World War II has dominated eco-

TABLE 1

Comparative Performance of Five Groups of Countries

Position	Growth in Per Capita GNP	Level of Per Capita GNP	Inflation*	Growth in Exports
1	N/A	NORD	N/A	N/A
2	ASEAN	N/A	NORD	ASEAN
3	N/L	N/L	ASEAN	N/L
4	NORD	P/L	N/L	NORD
5	P/L	ASEAN	P/L	P/L

*From lowest to highest
KEY

N/A = NICs Asia
N/L = NICs Latin America
ASEAN = ASEAN
NORD = Nordic countries
P/L = Costa Rica, Chile, and Panama

nomic thinking and policy in most of the countries, with Brazil being a major exception with a more eclectic approach—especially after the mid-1960s—in which exports and the substitution of imports were pushed simultaneously.

There are also important contrasts in the role played by the state as an economic agent. Government has acted primarily as a promoter of economic development in the Asian NICs and the Nordic countries through policies and programs to attract foreign investment, capture, adapt, and adopt external technology, reward gains in productivity, and foster exports in general. The state has not been a major actor as a producer in any of these two groups of countries and has not intervened to supplant the working of market forces. But, at the same time, very widespread systems of social security provide protection to almost all the population in the Nordic countries and the state has played a decisive role in both Korea and Singapore in selecting the industrial sectors chosen for development, providing financing to them, and authorizing specific investments.

TABLE 2

Policy Emphasis in Five Groups of Countries

	GROUPS				
POLICY	N/A	N/L (BRAZIL)	NORD	ASEAN	P/L
Orientation of the Economy	External	Internal/ External	External	External	Internal
Role of the State	Promoter/ Regulator	Promoter/ Regulator	Promoter	Regulator/ Promoter	Regulator/ Promoter
Financing of Investment	Savings + External Investment	Savings + External Debt	Savings + External Investment	Savings + External Investment	External Debt + Savings
Technology	Adoption + Adaptation	Same + Development	Same + Development	Adoption	Undefined
National Consensus	Explicit & Solid	Explicit	Explicit	Variable	Undefined

Still, in these two groups of countries the emphasis has been on promotion rather than regulation, while in Latin America in general the opposite has been the case. In all the Latin American countries included in our sample (with the exception of Chile after 1973), the public sector has invested massively in production facilities, especially in heavy industry, and at the same time has subjected private firms to extensive regulations, which in many cases have covered the setting of wages and prices and interest and exchange rates at levels not necessarily reflecting market forces as well as setting controls on foreign exchange transactions.

Another important differentiation can be found in the way investment has been financed. In the Asian NICs and the Nordic countries there has been in general a heavy reliance on domestic savings and direct foreign investment, while the Latin American countries have relied primarily on external debt to finance a level of investment in which the public sector has had very heavy participation.

The lessons that may be derived from LDC countries achieving high and sustained rates of growth and which would be applicable to the design of a medium-term structural adjustment program may be summarized as follows: 1) While some countries do have protective barriers, the thrust of their trade policies have been toward the development of exports rather than import substitution; 2) There is very little or no state intervention in the setting of prices; 3) The state is mainly a promoter of economic growth and not its regulator; and, 4) Investment has been financed primarily through a high rate of domestic savings and direct foreign investment rather than by resorting to external indebtedness.

THE LONG-TERM STRATEGY

Short-term adjustment and intermediate-term structural choice should be made within a long-term strategy. Foxley stressed the importance of having consistency between short-term or medium-term adjustment processes and a long-term view. He raised two additional points: the importance of a new strategy, and within that new strategy, relying on comparative advantages that are deliberately developed or "manmade" so to speak, in contrast with the traditional concept of god-given natural resources or even traditional advantages more attributable to the unique historical circumstances of a given country.

As Kim pointed out, in Asia one can observe a system geared toward a long-term strategy of capturing and adapting external technology and the deliberate development of a national consensus as a precondition to the elaboration of a long-term strategy. In my view, it is the national consensus more than the SAL-type structural adjustments that is really the key to the difference, or the fundamental package explaining the difference, in the performance of the successful Asian NICs vis-à-vis the general experience of Latin America. This difference seems to be explained by excellence in the educational systems, the emphasis on developing management capacities, effective technological policies, an attitude of constant adjustment to change, the development of comparative advantages vis-à-vis relying on an advantage in natural resource endowment, and a working partnership between government, business, labor, and the universities. Thus a fundamental requirement, not currently recognized by many in Latin America, is that the short- and medium-term adjustments have to be coordinated with the long-term strategy.

NOTE

1. See Bela Balassa, Gerardo M. Bueno, Pedro-Pablo Kuczynski, and Mario H. Simonsen, *Toward Renewed Economic Growth in Latin America* (Washington: Institute for International Economics, 1986).

The Problem Is Adjustment, Not Debt

RICHARD WEBB*

How would one view the financial crisis from a country like Peru? The issue of adjustment and the debt problem have gotten intertwined. The essential problem in Peru, both now and in recent years, is not debt, but adjustment. The issue is how Peru can adapt, *at minimum cost,* to a once-over, large, and lasting deterioration in the balance of payments.

A degree of impoverishment has been dealt by the international economic system. Our export prices in real terms today are 50 percent below what they were five years ago, with no prospect of improvement. Inflation has not, and will not, go away. While the world seems to have developed a keener awareness of the costs of inflation, it is obvious that the problem has been handled in an artificial way. The U.S. recovery and control of inflation was based on an overvalued exchange rate—which is showing up in the trade deficit—and on international borrowing. Developing countries are continually criticized by the international financial institutions for taking exactly the same steps. These policies will come home to roost for the United States, but more so for the rest of the world. All of us will face a lot more instability in the next few years. Peru must learn to live with this situation and, I stress again, learn to do so at minimum cost.

What has happened in Peru over the last few years? The crisis came very suddenly. The world recession had come and

*Richard Webb is a professor of economics at the Catholic University of Lima. Formerly the president of the Central Reserve Bank of Peru, and a research economist at the World Bank, he has been a visiting professor at Princeton University and the University of Toronto.

gone before the real damage began for Peru in 1983. The external crisis was pictured to us as one more minor recession. Rather than adjust, Peru continued to borrow during 1981–1982 with the blessing of the Fund, the World Bank, and, of course, commercial bankers. Everyone assumed that by 1982, mineral prices would be back up. This did not happen. The world recession came and went, but world prices for Peru's minerals and farm products continued to fall. Then, at the end of 1982—seemingly at the end of the recession—the international financial crisis started with Mexico's default. Moreover, Peru was hit by an extraordinary natural disaster in the form of a climate change in 1983. Floods damaged crops, roads, and other infrastructure; some regions suffered drought instead. The losses totaled four or five percent of the Gross Domestic Product (GDP) in 1983. Additional recession was produced by financial instability and by efforts to adjust. In all, GDP plummeted 11 percent that year, the worst recession Peru has suffered in its recorded history. The coincidence of climatic disaster and balance-of-payments shock was partly responsible for the severity of the recession, but much was surely a mishandling of the situation.

In retrospect, Peru failed to adapt quickly enough to the collapse during 1983. An emergency needs an emergency response. The good housekeeping rules for guiding healthy economies are no longer adequate, and may be very wrong. The situation called for increased intervention in the economy to minimize the loss of output, to prevent the increase in the rate of inflation, and to squelch capital flight, all of which multiplied during that year. Peru did not adopt an emergency program. Instead, she tried to solve the problem as if it were one requiring minor stabilization.

Why did Peru not respond? Part of it was an inability to foresee the extent of the climatic damage. It happened too gradually for us to see what was going on. The rains, the drought, accumulated throughout the year and no one realized the extent of the devastation. The lack of response was also due to mental and institutional rigidities. The Fund and the World Bank were incapable of adjusting mentally to the severity of changes in the real, rather than financial, aspects of the

Peruvian economy, and they dispensed medicine for curing a cold rather than pneumonia. In fact, Peru was being demolished. The country needed a war economy, meaning considerable direct intervention and mobilization. Prices were escalating because of food scarcities resulting from the rain and the drought. Measures were taken to slow inflation by tightening credit and money, but excess demand was not the problem. In a situation like that, it is not enough to devalue or to reduce the growth of money; controls must be applied. Imports must be reduced sharply and controls and social agreements used to reduce inflation quickly to minimize the extent of recession.

It is hard to blame the Fund. The Fund is not equipped to deal with major disruptions in production and the rate of inflation. Banks responded by gradually and quietly withdrawing about 700 or 800 million dollars of short-term credit in 1983, even though Peru was paying its debt punctually. That withdrawal, in itself, was a balance-of-payments shock as large as that of the fall in export prices over the previous two years.

Peru needed an emergency program to contain the cost. One result of her failure was that a year later, in the spring of 1984, Peru began to fall behind on debt payments. The unpaid interest was added to the debt at penalty rates. Another was that GDP failed to recover. Between the two, the ratio of debt to GDP jumped from about 50 to 100 percent over three years. Yet, the debt, measured in real dollars per person, was actually lower in 1985 than in 1970. In 1982, just before the collapse began, bankers were eager to lend to Peru. In its 1982 report, the Fund told Peru that it was following good borrowing practices. No one foresaw the escalation in the burden of the debt.

In 1985, with a change in government, an emergency program was finally initiated. Runaway inflation—monthly rates were exceeding 200 percent on an annual basis—was attacked with a price freeze and zero fiscal deficit. The balance of payments was supported by both devaluation and import controls. Initial effects were good but the policies of fiscal caution and an expensive dollar have been discarded, suggesting trouble ahead.

One thing is clear, an emergency program must be based on considerable political support. The drastic measures required in a crisis situation cannot be taken unless the program is sold to the people. The present Peruvian program is a political success; it does have broad-based support. Even though the first results have been good, it is still too early to judge whether the economic results will be as successful in the long run.

Against this promise of internal success, Peru is being attacked from the outside for wanting to "drop out." In spite of these charges, Peru is paying as much as borrowers who are functioning respectfully within the financial system. For instance, the *net* transfer of funds through Peruvian payments to its creditors is as large as it is in Chile. A senior official of that country, during the Annual Fund Bank meeting in 1985 was upset by Peru's position. He said, "But Chile is paying less than Peru. What is all the fuss about?" After netting out what Chile is getting in the form of new loans to pay interest, Chile really is not taking much out of her own pocket. That seems to be true with most debtors. The difference with Peru is that what she pays comes entirely out of her own pocket. Peru does not have the additional component of borrowing from banks to pay past interest.

The Peruvian scapegoat position is sheer theater, but it is part of the way the system works. Regulations force the banks to treat Peru, but not countries such as Chile, as defaults. Peru is being asked to subject herself to Fund programs to comply with that theatrical component. For example, it has been stated that Peru is endangering the world system. Surely there is some room for regulatory adaptation to make it unnecessary for a country like Peru to follow policies she does not believe in simply for the sake of theater. Peru is not dropping out of the system. Her policies are not radically different from those of most countries. In fact, the only problem with her policies is that they are not very effective for stimulating exports.

Like most people, Peruvians worry about future access to funds for development. Personally, however, it seems that not being able to borrow for another few years is the best thing that could happen to Peru. To some, that may be tantamount to dropping out—but not in the sense that Peru is failing to pay for a fair share. Peru would continue to pay on existing debt.

The government would like to continue borrowing—politicians always want to borrow. Again, most of the money would be borrowed by the government, rather than by the private sector, and most of it would be spent by ministers with one- or two-year personal time horizons. If an examination were made of how the bulk of what Peru borrowed in the last fifteen years was used, the conclusion would have to be that it is better if Peru does not continue to borrow.

It Is Time to Rethink Our Development Strategies

*CHANDRA HARDY**

I agree with the observed impact of recession and conditionality on the poor but I believe that our discussion of what to do about these problems is misguided. My argument is simple.[1] The poor are suffering from austerity but they had not done so well in the period of high growth before the debt crisis. Therefore, to focus only on the need for higher levels of capital inflows and a renewal of economic growth will not produce greater equity. Neither will slight modifications of the concept of conditionality.

The quarter century from 1950–1975 was a period of unprecedented growth of prosperity in the world economy[2] but its benefits did not trickle down. Growth bypassed both the poorer countries and the lower income groups within countries.[3] In 1980, there were an estimated 800 million people living in conditions of absolute poverty and their numbers have since grown.

The Henriot-Jameson analysis of Bolivia and Zambia can be generalized to Latin America and Africa as demonstrated in the Kim paper. These analyses are typical of the impact of austerity on poverty. In two recent studies by the World Bank and UNICEF,[4] the impact of recession was the same across many more countries.

---

*Chandra Hardy is a senior economist in the East Africa department of the World Bank. She is one of the earliest authorities to warn about the severity of the debt problem and to argue for comprehensive solutions.

Bolivia and Zambia are also typical in the structural causes of poverty, in the political instability/corruption index in the countries concerned, and in the factors leading up to the present crisis. Finally, the response of the International Monetary Fund and the international banking community to these countries was typical.

As we turn from analysis to solutions, we all agree on the need for lower interest rates, higher capital inflows, and new forms of conditionality as a means of stimulating exports and economic growth. There is agreement that the interest burden is too heavy, and that the creditors should bear some of it. Foxley called for a new interpretation of conditionality and a lot more money. To be skeptical, his new interpretation of conditionality is basically to allow the debtor countries to have their cake and eat it too by having greater autonomy to write their own adjustment programs. But I agree with the contention that conditionality imposed without commitment will not work.

Last year Secretary Baker introduced growth as a necessary condition for solving the debt crisis, but the global amount of funds needed to stimulate recovery is very large. The estimate for Latin America alone is $20–$30 billion; perhaps another $100 billion for the rest of the developing world. This is a very large poverty budget. However, it is perceived that this sum will lead to renewed growth.

The stifling of growth associated with the debt crisis has been a major theme of our seminar. But neither money nor growth will sufficiently help the poor. Both Brazil and Mexico had enjoyed high growth rates during the 1970s. Yet in both countries, social justice did not do very well in the period of high growth. The distribution of income worsened in both countries as did the poverty indicators—hunger, illiteracy, incidence of disease, infant mortality—and this conclusion can be generalized for most of Latin America. This was before the onset of the debt crisis and these problems were not caused by conditionality.

There is no question that the recession and the type of conditionality imposed have increased poverty. A more enlightened conditionality might have tried to close the doors to capital flight or to promote land reform and redistribute the assets of the rich. But we must ask at this time whether a more relaxed form of conditionality, higher levels of debt, or more growth is what the poor need, and unless these proposed strategies will reduce income disparities and poverty, it seems to me that we need to formulate an alternative developmental strategy.

The first component of a new strategy must be a complete change in our mindset. The issue of debt and development must go beyond the discussion of "conditionality" in the IMF and the World Bank—a discussion that has been circling unsuccessfully since the crisis of 1982. The developing countries must also change their mindset. They believe that the old conditionality was the problem and that a new conditionality will provide the answer. That is not going to work. In the recent Mexico debt restructuring, the conditionality was much less stringent. Neither is more debt the answer. The restructuring agreement also provided for higher capital inflows if the price of oil fell or if growth faltered during the program period. This settlement may alleviate current balance-of-payments problems but it will not address the structural causes of poverty in Mexico.

Second, any long-term developmental strategy must deal with the population explosion. Development has become a race against population. The particular events in the world economy over the past ten years set against the rapid growth of population have been especially damaging, wiping out the gains most countries had made in the previous twenty years. Chart 1 maps the age spread of the global population. The bulge at the bottom is the developing countries and the one on top is the industrial countries. Sixty-five percent of the population of most less-developed countries on any continent is under the age of 25 and the jobs are simply not there for these people. In Mexico, no new jobs have been created over the past four years, which means that four million young people have entered the work force and do not have jobs. More than a billion new jobs would have to be created in the developing coun-

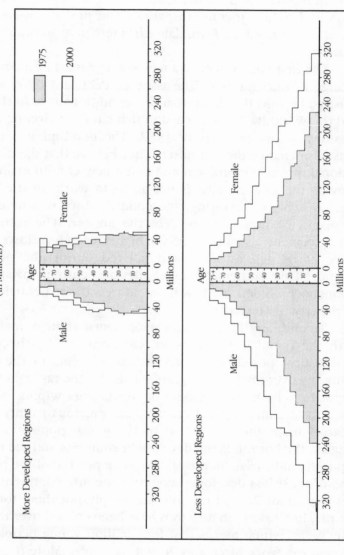

CHART 1

Age and Sex Composition of the Population, 1975 and 2000

(in Millions)

Source: *The Global 2000 Report to the President*, U.S. Government Printing Office, Washington, D.C., 1980.

tries in this decade simply to keep unemployment from rising. For Mexico and Brazil, that is one million a year; for Thailand, 700,000, and so it goes.

Unemployed youth are linked to what is called democratization. It is these young people who are calling for democracy, because they are refusing to accept the poverty in their lives that they see as imposed by governments that do not represent them.

Third, the new strategy must promote the kind of economic integration Foxley mentioned that people call "South–South" links. I agree with Foxley that the OECD growth will not be the familiar rising tide that lifts all the boats. A more likely scenario is for more protectionism and a continuation of low commodity prices and low levels of lending. Therefore, developing countries must search for new export markets among developing countries.

The debt crisis has provided an opportunity to rethink past developmental strategies—the focus on high growth and heavy borrowing produced neither social justice nor broad-based growth. To say that what Latin America now needs is a Korean or Japanese model is to opt for another easy solution that avoids the poverty issue. The path recommended by Foxley would produce a new coalition between unrepresentative governments, the middle classes who have been rapidly losing their recent income gains, and the ten percent of the population who control fifty percent of the income. It would result in a new social compact with these groups to produce for export but it is not going to produce equity.

A more poverty-focused developmental strategy would emphasize the need to promote *internal* sources of growth, create jobs, and expand trade among developing countries. Such an alternative developmental strategy would be directed at meeting the needs of the bulk of the population for housing and basic wage goods. It would require an increase in the purchasing power of the poor through some redistribution of assets. Hence, the need for broader political representation. Such a strategy would not ignore the need for increased exports but it would reduce the North-South focus of trade flows in favor of increased trade among developing countries. Finally, such an alternative developmental strategy would require lower levels of borrowing if it were accompanied by measures to increase domestic savings and shift to less capital intensive methods of production.

NOTES

1. In these comments, I will need to take off my hat as a World Bank economist if we are going to engage in a debate. We are all agreeing with each other far too much.

2. David Morawetz, "Twenty-Five Years of Economic Development 1950–1975," World Bank, 1977.

3. Ahluwalia Chenery et. al., "Growth and Poverty in Developing Countries," Working Paper no. 309, *World Bank*, 1978.

4. *Poverty in Latin America, Impact of Depression,* World Bank, September 1986; Richard Jolly and Giovanni Cornia, eds., "The Impact of World Recession on Children," *World Development,* March 1984.

Discussion Summary

Discussion of the papers and responses in this section centered on the issue of growth. Four questions were addressed: (1) How important is growth in the redevelopment process? (2) How can a country compete aggressively in the international markets through export promotion or efficient import substitution? (3) What are the implications for a country that adopts a policy stance of independence from the international financial system? (4) Is a return to the growth-oriented developmental strategies of the past a promising option for the future?

A headlong rush for growth as the key to national redevelopment strategies was viewed with suspicion. While growth was seen as a necessary precondition for renewed development, it was not viewed in itself as being sufficient for development.

There was a strong sense that export-oriented growth should be undertaken with caution. Streeten pointed out that the demand for Third World products may not be going to increase as rapidly in the future as in the past.

The rate of growth in the developed countries may well be much lower than in the 1950s and 1960s. There could also be an increasing reliance on trade protection in Europe, Japan, and the United States, as well as, with robotization, a relocation of more of the textile and electronic industries back to the United States.

A second concern with export-oriented growth was the possibility of missing the market trends. When a country concentrates on a few sectors as a point of growth or targets specific industries for exports, it commits resources for the long term while the global demand and supply for these products

161

can change in the short run. Barletta would minimize this danger by relying on more free market forces.

If the economies are freed and over-regulation avoided, if flexibility is allowed within the structure of government and private cooperation, there may be more success in developing the exports that will be successful in the long term, and the danger may be avoided of going in one direction when the world may just be changing in the opposite direction.

Foxley noted that Third World countries must still take the lead, relying on what they have learned in their move toward free-market policies.

For instance, exchange rate policy is very important and a high exchange rate is needed as a built-in incentive for export promotion and efficient import substitution. We have learned, however, that setting exchange rates is not enough, particularly when there is a problem of the magnitude facing Latin American countries. These countries have to make a deliberate effort to mobilize resources away from the non-traded toward the traded-goods sectors. The government must take the lead in increasing investments in those sectors in coordination with the private sector.

On balance, the importance of "governmental planning with the market, not against it" as Guillermo Chapman put it, was a uniform conclusion of the group.

Another point of the discussion centered on the acceptance of externally imposed conditionality. This discussion built upon the concern expressed in Part I, as to whether policies designed to enhance the balance of payments achieved their desired objectives. To avoid the impairment of conditionalities, a policy of national independence from the international system was advocated. Reporting on one of the small group discussions, Jameson advocated a "go it alone" policy for Latin American countries:

If a country were to service its debt on its own terms, rather than those dictated from the outside, two counteracting forces would occur. One component of independence would be the reduction of debt service. This would massively reduce the funds needed. The offsetting reaction would be no new money as in the case of Peru. The key issue, then, is how to raise domestic savings as a means of financing a country's own growth, its own development.

An associated point was how to keep the funds at home— how to discourage capital flight. John Caron posed the question, "One of the major problems in the debt crisis is the flight of capital. If there were no flight capital, there would be fewer problems."

Foxley responded:

The flight of capital was made possible by a certain conception of how financial markets should be run in the industrialized economies. In an environment in which international finances are very unstable, there is a tendency for capital flight. Over the past ten to fifteen years, instability has been due not only to domestic economic events in the Third World, but also in the international financial system. With the reinforcement between domestic instability and international instability, it is likely that there will be substantial capital flight unless the financial system is operated in a way in which there are some regulations vis-à-vis the movements of capital from the country toward the rest of the world.

In my judgment, we went too far, too quickly, in terms of an international financial reorganization, given the external and domestic instability. To return the money, it is said that the countries should produce conditions for people to find it attractive again to invest in the country. To accomplish that requires stable conditions and getting the prices right in order to have markets operating without governmental regulations. While the market solution might be effective in the long run, it will not have much of an impact on today's conditions. Why would people bring their money back to their countries when they have so many other more "attractive" opportunities in the United States, Asia, or in some European countries?

Of course, if bankers were to disclose whose money is lying in their banks, direct action could be taken. If governments were to know those who are steering money out of the country, they could devise policies for returning it. That, of course, is not feasible since it would violate confidence and trust in the banks.

While most of the discussion was founded on how to enhance growth, Goulet challenged the growth-oriented strategies of the past.

We should not only change the mindset of developing countries but also our own in defining what development is. In much of our discussion and even in the title, "Rekindling Development," we are assuming that we had genuine development before, we lost it, and we need to get it back. For every Chile that might possibly have an outside chance of developing new comparative advantages, there are ten or fifteen Haitis and Paraguays that cannot; for every Korea, there are ten or fifteen countries like the Papua New Guineas and the Nepals and the Bangladeshs that cannot. So instead of playing the game of trying to be competitive in the international market of the 168 or so countries that are less developed, there are only a few that are the privileged ones who even have outside chances (the Brazils and the Mexicos are the obvious ones). They have a demographic base and an industrial base, they have political clout to leverage the external resource transfer system. The vast majority of peoples in those countries cannot get a job, even if they successfully rekindle the old development. The old development took as its objectives economic growth, institutional modernizations, and harnessing technology, all with a competitive framework as the main instrument.

These countries need to discover new ways of defining different objectives of development that will harness their old networks of solidarity, their old institutions. It seems to me that we need to redefine development with different objectives, not rekindle it. This does not mean that there could not be some space for a small number of countries to be truly developmental with equity and respect for cultural differences and self-reliance. Thus, I would question not only the feasibility of rekindling development but also its desirability.

Chandra Hardy noted:

Governments everywhere in the developing world are far more responsive now to the needs of this marginalized population. The proportion of young people in the population of the developing world is at an unprecedentedly high figure. There is a phenomenally large number of young people under the age of twenty-four who know no other life but poverty. They owe allegiance to no one. They know what they are being deprived of and they know that they do not have to be deprived of it. They are a very radicalized group. We will either reach them or they will reach us.

PART III

The First World Financial System

Vulnerability in the Third World becomes the vulnerability of the First World through the international financial system—a system that is not in a particularly good position to withstand the shock of a repudiation by a major debtor country. The value of the dollar is plunging and surging on international markets, rising protectionism will disrupt trade and financial flows among industrialized countries as well as between First and Third World countries. U.S. bankers must keep a wary eye on the energy and agricultural components of their loan portfolios. This section explores the development and current state of the debt crisis from the viewpoint of the international financial system.

Christopher Korth traces the background of the crisis, documenting the shifts in funding sources and their current availability. He addresses two conditions of the debt overhang: (1) Its threat to the viability of the international financial system, and (2) the limits its existence is imposing on the ability of the Third World debtor countries to finance further developmental needs. The necessary characteristics of a "comprehensive, integrated, well-coordinated, and long-term program" to deal with these dual issues are outlined.

Two panelists respond to the Korth paper. Richard Webb supports the Korth separation of the problem into two parts— the threat to the lenders' financial system, and the need for new funds in the Third World. He sees major practical and ideological barriers in achieving Korth's comprehensive solution.

Blake Friscia believes that the international financial system is resilient. Noting the new innovations in the system since

1982, he points out that, with patience and a developing country focus on efficiency and productivity, the process of rescheduling–new money paralleled by a flow of small voluntary lending for the better credits will work out.

Four observers comment on specific aspects of the system. Michael Curtin outlines the role of international financial institutions. He traces the evolution of these institutions as they move from orthodox adjustment in debtor countries to the restoration of growth. Curtin concludes by describing the move of the Inter-American Development Bank into sectoral lending.

The vulnerability of U.S. commercial banks is analyzed by Henry Terrell. He points out the substantial decline since 1982 of the exposure of most major U.S. banks to Third World debt. As for future shocks, he presents a simulation model to assess the impact of individual country defaults on individual banks and analyzes the impact of lower nominal interest rates on the vulnerability of these banks.

Leonard (Ted) Marks views the debt problem from the banker's perspective. He analyzes the domestic opportunities and threats for U.S. banks resulting from deregulation set against their Third World debt exposure and the competition of foreign banks for U.S. business. Pointing out the severe restrictions these pose in decision alternatives, he calls for steps to reduce the commercial bank problems while permitting a reduction in interest and repayment schedules.

The muddling-through process of rescheduling is assaulted by William Glade. He argues that it has led to the subordination of real variables to financial variables. In comparing rescheduling to ritual, Glade explains why the rescheduling process has persisted in spite of the fact that it does not meet its instrumental objectives, and looks to the ritualistic dimension to suggest a way out of the current problem.

The Vulnerability in the International Financial System

CHRISTOPHER M. KORTH[*]

The international debt and lending crisis of the 1970s and 1980s has been very traumatic, not only for borrower/debtors but also for the private sector lenders as well. This paper will explore how vulnerable the international financial system, both the commercial banking and capital-market components, is to the shocks that it has received—and how well it is likely to weather future shocks.

THE INTERNATIONAL DEBT SITUATION IN THE 1960S AND EARLY 1970S

The watershed of the international debt crisis was the oil price hike in December 1973. Prior to that time, both the magnitude of the debt problem and the relations among the major lenders, regulators, and borrowing countries were very different from what they are today.

The borrowing needs of many less-developed countries (LDCs) often seemed large even prior to 1973. However, by recent standards, those needs and the total international debts of most LDCs were relatively small. For example, table 1 shows

[*]Christopher M. Korth is a professor of international finance and banking at the University of South Carolina. He has served as a senior Fulbright Fellow in Equador, as the director of research at the Institute of International Commerce of the University of Michigan, and as an assistant vice president and chief international economist with the First National Bank of Chicago.

that the total annual international funding needs for all of Latin America had only risen to $7.4 billion by 1973. Prior to 1969, it had not even exceeded $3 billion. In contrast, from 1978–1984, the international funding needs of Latin America exceeded $20 billion annually.

Chart 1 summarizes the total annual international funding needs for Latin America between 1961 and 1985. The chart also shows the contributions from the three major sources of international funds: official credits, bank credits, and private non-bank sources. In the 1960s and early 1970s official credits were the most important source of international funds for Latin America. From the early 1970s until the mid-1980s, bank credits predominated. However, by the mid-1980s, official credits had again assumed the major role for Latin America's international funding needs. The *relative* share of the three categories of funds is shown in chart 2.

In the earlier period, developing countries could not generally borrow heavily from commercial banks. Most of the international loans to LDCs came from foreign governments, international agencies such as the International Monetary Fund, the World Bank, and the Inter-American Development Bank, and from trade credits from suppliers. Private sector borrowers in developing countries fared no better than did their governments. Except for short-term, secured trade financing, private companies in the LDCs could generally only borrow internationally from agencies or foreign governments with the guarantee of their own government.

In addition to having more limited international funding needs, the developing countries in the late 1960s–early 1970s

TABLE 1

Annual International Funding Needs of Latin America: 1961–1973
($ Billions)

1961	$1.83
1964	1.54
1967	2.23
1970	3.49
1973	7.40

Source: *External Financing of the Latin American Countries* (Statistical Abstract), Inter-American Development Bank (December 1985), Chart 4.

also benefited from economic conditions which made their international debts, both the interest and the principal, easier to service. Interest rates were low and exports from many LDCs were strong. Also, the prices of most of the major commodity exports from the LDCs were high. In table 2 (column 5), it can be seen that major commodities rose an average of 83.6 percent between 1965 and 1975. As a result of these favorable conditions, serious financial problems at the time were infrequent, and the debt burden was generally manageable.

Loans from foreign governments (bilateral credits) and from international agencies, such as the International Monetary Fund and World Bank, (multilateral credits) were a major

CHART 1

Sources of Latin American Funding, 1961-85
(in Billions)

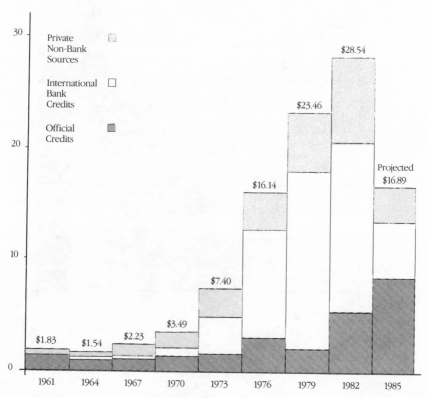

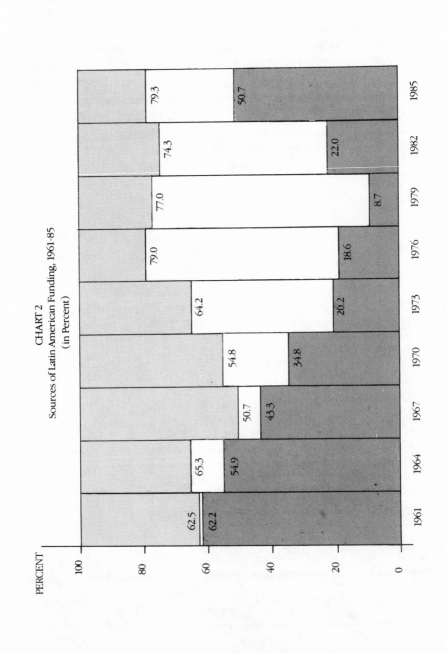

CHART 2
Sources of Latin American Funding, 1961-85
(in Percent)

source of international funds for the developing countries. During this period, bilateral credits were more important than multilateral credits. As can be seen in table 3, these sources together still accounted for more than 20 percent of international financing needs for Latin America in 1973. In the early 1960s, it had been three times as high. Official credits tend to be even more important for such groups of developing countries as Southeast Asia, Africa, and the Middle East than for Latin America.

Before 1973, the number of commercial banks that were actively involved in international lending was much smaller

TABLE 2

Index of Prices for Selected Major Commodity Exports from Developing Countries: 1965–75

	(1)	(2)	(3)	(4)	(5)
	Index (1965 = 100.0)			Percentage Change	
	1965	1970	1975	1970–75	1965–75
All Commodities	100.0	107.4	183.6	70.9	83.6
Cocoa Beans (Brazil)	100.0	214.8	413.3	92.4	313.3
Coffee	100.0	123.2	176.8	43.5	76.8
Bananas	100.0	104.0	153.8	47.9	53.8
Copper (US)	100.0	164.9	181.7	10.2	81.7
Tin	100.0	98.7	192.5	95.0	92.5

Source: Calculated from *International Financial Statistics*, 1986 Annual, pp. 172–3.

TABLE 3

Official Credits for Latin America: 1961–1973

	($ BILLIONS)			Portion of Total International Funding (%)
	Bilateral	Multilateral	Total Official	
1961	$0.79	$0.35	$1.14	62.2%
1964	0.52	0.32	0.84	54.9%
1967	0.59	0.37	0.96	43.3%
1970	0.78	0.43	1.22	34.8%
1973	0.76	0.73	1.49	20.2%

Source: *External Financing of the Latin American Countries* (Statistical Abstract), Inter-American Development Bank (December 1985), Chart 4 and Chart 5.

than it is today. Most of their international lending was extended to private sector corporations. Except for the extension of short-term trade credits to finance imports and exports, the commercial banks were generally not major lenders to the governments of developing countries. For example, even by 1970 (table 4), only 20 percent of the new external financing of Latin America came from commercial banks. As recently as 1968, commercial bank lending had provided less than 6 percent of all of the international funding needs for the Latin American countries.

Beginning in 1972, the relative importance of borrowing from international banks grew rapidly. In 1973 the banking share was 44.0 percent for Latin America as commercial banks started moving aggressively into international lending. Many more banks were getting involved, and the relative importance of the international activities for the banks was growing rapidly. The stage had been set for their critical role in helping to alleviate the oil crisis which came in 1974.

It is well to bear in mind though that even then there were (and still are) many developing countries which were too poor to qualify for much, if any, bank financing. Those are the so-called "non-commercial" or "official borrower" countries—especially in Africa, the Middle East, and Southeast Asia. For the "commercial" or "market borrower" countries, however, the oil crisis led to a major growth in their market borrowings. Even so, the total of *all* of the *international* loans of even the largest commercial banks was a much smaller share of their total loans than it became in the late 1970s and early 1980s, or

TABLE 4

International Bank Credits for Latin America: 1961–1973

	$ BILLIONS	%
1961	$0.00	0.3%
1964	0.16	10.4
1967	0.16	7.4
1970	0.70	20.0
1973	3.26	44.0

Source: *External Financing of the Latin American Countries* (Statistical Abstract); Inter-American Development Bank (December 1985), Tables 4 and 5.

is today. As a result, the banks had much more flexibility in being able to expand international lending than they do today.

International capital markets have two broad sectors: the domestic markets that are tapped by foreign institutions (for example, when a Latin government floats a bond in the United States) and the Euromarkets. The debt portion of those markets has been of very limited value to developing countries. Even more than with international bank credits, there are many LDCs that have had *no* access at all to those markets. Except for a two-year period in the late 1970s, the international bond markets have not provided more than 6 percent of Latin America's international funding needs (table 5).

A much more important source of funds for developing countries than the bond markets has been foreign direct investment (FDI). In the 1960s, when direct investment from the United States was especially prevalent, FDI accounted for as

TABLE 5

Private Non-Bank Sources of Foreign Capital for Latin America: 1961–1973

5-A: TOTAL VALUE ($ BILLIONS)

	Suppliers	Bonds	Foreign Direct Investment	Other	Total Private Non-Bank
1961	$0.19	$0.10	$0.41	($0.01)	$0.69
1964	0.07	0.05	0.42	(0.01)	0.53
1967	0.46	0.03	0.52	0.09	1.10
1970	0.40	0.06	1.07	0.05	1.58
1973	0.38	0.02	2.30	(0.05)	2.65

5-B: SHARE OF TOTAL INTERNATIONAL FUNDING (%)

	Suppliers	Bonds	Foreign Direct Investment	Other	Total Private Non-Bank
1961	10.3%	5.5%	22.4%	(0.7%)	37.5%
1964	4.5	3.1	27.5	(0.4)	34.7
1967	20.8	1.2	23.2	4.1	49.3
1970	11.5	1.6	30.7	1.4	45.2
1973	5.1	0.2	31.1	(0.6)	35.8

Source: *External Financing of the Latin American Countries* (Statistical Abstract), Inter-American Development Bank (December 1985), Charts 4 and 5.

much as 40 percent (1969) of Latin American international funding. Even in the early 1970s, its share remained above 30 percent. (table 5–b).

During the 1960s, trade financing (i.e., accounts payable) often accounted for more than 10 percent of the international funding needs of Latin America (table 5–b). After 1972, suppliers became relatively unimportant as sources of credit. However, it is important to bear in mind that most trade financing is short term: Substantial amounts of suppliers' credits are issued and retired within the course of a year.

In general, commercial banks are tightly regulated, especially in the United States. However, U.S. banks have much more freedom internationally than domestically. The danger to the lenders and to the world economy from international lending was much lower in the late 1960s and early 1970s than it is today. This was true whether the loans were made from a bank's home offices, from its local offices in foreign domestic markets, or from its Eurocurrency offices. (The Eurocurrency markets are banking markets that, like all Euromarkets, are free from most regulations.)

As a result, the regulators of the international banks—the Federal Reserve, the Office of the Comptroller of the Currency (OCC), and the Federal Deposit Insurance Corporation (FDIC) in the U.S., the Bank of England, and the Bank of Japan—were less aware of, less concerned with, and less capable of either analyzing or regulating the risks of the international loan portfolios of the banks which they supervise than they are now. For example, until the United States agencies finally began coordinating their regulatory efforts through the creation of the *Inter-Agency Country Exposure Review Committee* in 1978, the review procedures used by the three agencies varied greatly, and only the Federal Reserve had any meaningful capability of analyzing country lending risk. The regulations confronted by the commercial banks were thus not very restrictive, allowing the banks greater freedom of action.

The domestic bond and stock markets in most countries also tend to be tightly regulated. The strictness of the regulations were often sufficient to restrict LDC participation. In addition, the greater conservativeness and lack of international sophistication of the investors in the domestic capital markets greatly restricted the ability of most LDCs to access such markets. While the borrowers from some select countries such as Brazil and Mexico successfully tapped such markets, most LDCs were unable to do so.

The Eurobond market, which like the Eurocurrency market is mostly unregulated, waxed and waned during the late 1960s and early 1970s. Despite the lack of regulation and despite the international sophistication of most investors in the E robond market, however, relatively few LDCs were su ccessful in tapping the market.

THE INTERNATIONAL DEBT SITUATION IN THE MID-1970S AND EARLY 1980S

The decade of the 1970s was one of ambitious economic expansion in many developing countries causing a sharp increase in their imports. There was also rapid inflation in most industrialized countries, causing the prices of most of the manufactured products being imported by the LDCs to rise at the same time that the volume of imports was increasing. This, of course, caused sharp deteriorations in the balance of trade of most developing countries.

The prices of many nonindustrial imports also rose rapidly. The most important of those products was, of course, oil. However, oil was not the first major commodity to rise sharply in price—the prices of many other commodities had risen sharply even before the oil price hikes.

This was also a period in which most governments greatly increased their budget deficits. In many countries, subsidies on basic products (both domestically produced and imported) rose sharply—especially food and fuel. Rising interest rates on foreign debts exacerbated the problem. These deficits further aggravated the funding problems of these countries.

At the same time as the importing and international borrowing needs of most LDCs were rising rapidly, the ability of most of those countries to pay for those imports and loans declined. The end of the Vietnam War, widespread inflation, and other economic disruptions led to international recession. As a result, exports from the borrowing countries fell.

Commodity prices continued strong through the end of the 1970s (table 6, column 2). However, the prolonged recession of the early 1980s substantially weakened the prices of most commodities (column 4), and they generally remain weak today—although mostly at substantially higher prices than in 1975.

The need for international funding is increased in most developing countries because of the inadequacies of domestic funding options: inadequate systems of taxation, coupled with insufficient capital formation (savings) and inadequate local money and capital markets to mobilize what domestic capital does exist. This means that domestic funding is not going to be sufficient to finance the needs of those countries. As a result, when the funding crises hit, most LDCs needed to sharply increase their borrowing abroad.

Table 7 shows that the international funding needs of Latin America rose from $7 billion in 1973 to more than $17 billion in 1976. The annual total was above $20 billion every year in the 1978–1984 period with a peak of more than $28 billion in 1981–83. Initial 1985 estimates indicate a drop to less than $17 billion.

TABLE 6

Index of Prices for Selected Major Commodity Exports from Developing Countries: 1975–85

	(1)	(2)	(3)	(4)	(5)
	Index (1975 = 100.0)*			Percentage Change	
	1975	1980	1985	1980–85	1975–85
All Commodities	100.0	168.1	127.6	(24.1)	27.6
Cocoa Beans (Brazil)	100.0	189.0	167.7	(11.3)	67.7
Coffee	100.0	207.9	184.2	(11.4)	84.2
Bananas	100.0	152.7	154.5	1.2	54.5
Copper (US)	100.0	159.5	99.5	(37.6)	(0.5)
Tin	100.0	227.8	157.2	(31.0)	57.2

*Note change in base year from 1965 in Table 2.

Source: Calculated from *International Financial Statistics*, 1986 Annual, pp. 172–173.

The traditional source for foreign *borrowing* by developing countries had been international agencies and governments of industrialized countries. However, the international agencies, even though their lending resources were increased greatly in the 1970s and early 1980s, and the major industrial governments were unable or unwilling to finance the huge increase in demand which these developments created.

Table 8 (column 1) illustrates that bilateral official assistance, which had been $790 million in 1961, was at almost the same level in 1973. It rose above $2 billion in 1983, 1984, and 1985. Multilateral credits to Latin America, although low in the 1960s, rose much more rapidly than bilateral lending: from $350 million in 1961, there was an increase to only $730 mil-

TABLE 7

Annual International Funding Needs of Latin America: 1973–1985
($ Billions)

1973	7.40
1976	16.14
1979	23.46
1982	28.54
1985 (preliminary)	16.89

Source: *External Financing of the Latin American Countries* (Statistical Abstract), Inter-American Development Bank (December 1985), Chart 4. 1985 figure is unpublished IDB estimate.

TABLE 8

Official Credits for Latin America: 1973–1985
($ Billions)

	(1)	(2)	(3)	(4)
	Bilateral	Multilateral	Total Official	Portion of Total International Funding (%)
1973	0.76	0.73	1.49	20.2
1976	0.80	2.20	2.99	18.6
1979	0.21	1.82	2.03	8.7
1982	1.87	4.41	6.28	22.0
1985 (preliminary)	2.43	6.14	8.57	50.7

Source: *External Financing of the Latin American Countries* (Statistical Abstract), Inter-American Development Bank (December 1985), Chart 4 and Chart 5. 1985 figures are unpublished IDB estimates.

lion in 1970. Thereafter, it jumped to $2.20 billion in 1976 (column 2), and up to $6.14 billion in 1985. The peak level (not shown) was $9.53 billion in 1983.

For most of this period, even these totals provided only a fraction of the rapidly growing international funding needs of Latin America. Between 1975 and 1982, total official credits (column 3) never provided more than 22 percent of Latin America's total international funding needs (column 4). However in 1985, with the reduction in private-sector lending and with a hefty increase in multilateral lending, the share exceeded 50 percent.

Fortunately, by the time of the sharp increases in oil prices in 1973 and in the 1979–81 period, the number of internationally oriented commercial banks was expanding rapidly. Also, their willingness to lend on a large scale and the resources available to them had increased greatly. Thus, from 1972 the commercial banks began replacing the official agencies, governments, and FDI as the major source of external funds for developing countries.

After 1973, the OPEC governments, which had received such huge increases in revenues from their oil price increases, deposited most of the funds in the international banks. Seeking profitable ways to invest such receipts, the banks proved only too willing to service the borrowing requirements of the developing countries. For example, as was seen in table 4, the banks' share of the total international funding for Latin America jumped from 7 percent in 1967 to 20 percent in 1970 to 44 percent in 1973. It remained above 50 percent from 1974 to 1982—with a peak of 68 percent in 1979 (table 9). However, the commercial bank share of funding for Latin America dropped sharply in 1984 and 1985 to less than $5 billion, which represented less than 29 percent of the 1985 total.

The significance of FDI has fallen from its heyday prior to 1974 (table 10). However, only twice (1976 and 1983) has it been below 15 percent. Therefore, FDI continues to play an important role in international funding for Latin America. Recognizing this, a number of Latin American countries (e.g., Venezuela, Chile, and Argentina) have become much more interested in attracting foreign direct investment.

Table 10 (columns 1, 2, and 4) shows that private non-bank sources of international funds such as trade credits and the bond markets have become relatively unimportant for Latin America.

THE DEBT CRISIS OF THE 1980S

The international debt problem has thus been pyramiding since the mid-1970s. Despite widespread concern and despite many warnings about its seriousness, the problem continued to worsen for more than ten years. It remains very serious today.

Major defaults were generally averted until the early 1980s. This was not so much the result of the ability of borrowers to keep their loan payments current, as it was the result of the feeling by lenders as well as borrowers that a declaration of actual (*de jure*) default should be avoided as long as possible. *De facto* defaults, which are determined by the covenants of the loan and typically refer to loans that are more than 90 days in arrears, were common even in the 1970s; they became very common in the early 1980s.

Defaults would be much more common if mutually beneficial negotiations between lenders and borrowers had not succeeded in delaying the "day of reckoning." Unfortunately, these efforts have generally served as nothing more than short-term delays to any meaningful effort to actually resolve the

TABLE 9

International Bank Credits for Latin America: 1973–1985

	($ BILLIONS)	%
1973	3.26	44.0
1976	9.75	60.4
1979	16.02	68.3
1982	14.97	52.3
1985 (preliminary)	4.83	28.6

Source: *External Financing of the Latin American Countries* (Statistical Abstract), Inter-American Development Bank (December 1985), Chart 4 and Chart 5. 1985 figures are unpublished IDB estimates.

problem. The time gained has *not* been used very productively by most lenders and borrowers.

The debt crisis is not simply the worry that the existing loans will not be paid. Indeed, that concern is only part of one of the two basic worries regarding the debt problem. The first issue concerns the potential impact of the debt burden on the *vitality of the entire international financial system—* including the issue of the repayment of the loans. The second issue relates to the likely effects of the debt overhang upon the *future ability of developing countries to borrow* to help fi-

TABLE 10

Private Non-Bank Sources of Foreign Capital for Latin America:
1973–1985

	(1)	(2)	(3)	(4)	(5)
		10-A: TOTAL VALUE ($ BILLIONS)			
	Suppliers	Bonds	Foreign Direct Investment	Other	Total Private Non-Bank
1973	$0.38	$0.02	$2.30	($0.05)	$2.65
1976	0.33	0.65	1.55	0.87	3.39
1979	(0.07)	0.66	4.99	(0.16)	5.41
1982	1.48	0.24	5.68	(0.08)	7.32
1985p	0.33	(0.70)	3.89 (partial)	(0.03)	3.49

	10-B: SHARE OF TOTAL INTERNATIONAL FUNDING (%)				
	Suppliers	Bonds	Foreign Direct Investment	Other	Total Private Non-Bank
1973	5.1%	0.2%	31.1%	(0.6%)	35.8%
1976	2.0	4.0	9.6	5.4	21.0
1979	(0.3)	2.8	21.2	(0.7)	23.0
1982	5.2	0.9	19.0	(0.3)	25.7
1985p	2.0	(4.1)	23.0 (partial)	(0.2)	20.7

p: preliminary

Source: *External Financing of the Latin American Countries* (Statistical Abstract), Inter-American Development Bank (December 1985), Charts 4 and 5. 1985 figures are unpublished IDB estimates.

nance their development, rather than simply to refinance past borrowings.

Impact Upon the International Financial System

The international debt burden is a sword of Damocles overhanging the entire international financial system, the seriousness of which must *not* be underrated. In the past two years the acuteness of the threat from the LDC debt has lessened. However, unless major changes take place in the international financial system, we will remain hostages to this threat of chaos in the future or, at the very least, suffer a serious constraint upon both developing countries and the financial system.

One of the factors which has moderated the threat of the debt overhang over the past several years has been a marked decline in the new borrowings by the debtor countries—especially from the private financial markets. "Net borrowing from private creditors has fallen in every year since 1981, from $76 billion in 1981 to $4.5 billion in 1985."[1] Part of this has undoubtedly been the greater difficulty which most of the LDCs have experienced in trying to attract new loans. However, there has been a substantial decline in the absolute need for extra funds as well.

The balance-of-trade deficits of the debtor countries have fallen sharply. Much of the improvement in 1986 has resulted from the plunging oil prices of the past year. However, even prior to that development, there had been noticeable improvement in the trade balances of many LDCs. Under financial constraints, many countries trimmed government budgets, lowered exchange rates to more realistic levels, imposed import controls, and otherwise took steps to stem the demand for imports. Some countries such as South Korea, Taiwan, and Brazil have also been very successful in expanding exports. Of course, while the declining oil prices have helped most developing countries, they have hurt the oil-exporting LDCs such as, Venezuela, Mexico, Nigeria, and Indonesia.

Another very favorable development for the debtor countries over the past several years was, of course, the decline in interest rates. Table 11 shows the trend in the London Interbank Bid Rate (LIBID). This is the rate at which banks can fund their loans in the Eurocurrency market; and as such, it is one of the major components of the banks' cost of funds and a good reference for the trend of lending rates as well.

LIBID had traditionally remained below 8 percent prior to mid-1978. It rose to almost 20 percent two years later. Nominal interest rates were high from late 1978 until early 1985. From late in 1979 until mid-1982, LIBID rates were generally above 14 percent! Although these nominal interest rates have fallen substantially, greatly reducing the interest burden of borrowers, in *real* terms (i.e., when the nominal rates are adjusted for inflation) interest rates remain high even today.

Naturally, fluctuating interest rates affected various developing countries very differently. Ironically, the poorest countries were generally the *least* affected. They were too risky to qualify for loans from commercial sources. Thus, they had to rely primarily upon loans from development banks and foreign governments. Such loans are generally long-term and at concessionary (subsidized) *fixed* rates. As a result, rising market rates had relatively limited impact on them.

TABLE 11

London Interbank Bid Rate* (LIBID): 1976–85
(6-month deposits; end of month) (%)

	MARCH	JUNE	SEPT.	DEC.
1976	6.19%	6.81%	6.13%	5.38%
1977	5.56	6.06	7.12	7.50
1978	7.81	9.19	9.69	12.31
1979	10.56	10.50	12.75	14.44
1980	19.56	9.94	13.94	16.37
1981	14.81	17.25	18.06	14.81
1982	15.44	16.00	11.94	9.50
1983	9.75	9.94	9.69	10.06
1984	10.94	12.63	11.56	9.13
1985	9.44	7.88	8.31	7.88

*The rate quoted for interbank deposits of Eurodollars in London
Source: *World Financial Markets* (Morgan Guaranty Trust Co., various issues) table entitled "Eurocurrency Deposit Rates."

On the other hand, those developing countries which could qualify for private market credits, whether from commercial banks or from the capital markets, had to pay the prevailing, non-subsidized interest rates. In addition, of course, they had to pay a risk premium, which might vary from 0.25 percent to more than 2 percent above the base lending rate.

More and more of the loans to developing countries have been made at floating rates. Such rates vary with the changes in market rates over the entire life of the loan. For example, a loan which was tied to the six-month LIBID rate would have a different interest rate every six months. As was seen in table 11, that would have resulted in wild swings over the life of a medium-term loan. For example, a five-year loan issued in March 1978 at LIBID plus 1 percent would have cost the borrower 8.81 percent for the first six months (i.e., 7.81% + 1%), but would have risen to 20.56 percent for the six months beginning March 1980. It would then have fallen back to 12.94 percent during the final six months of the loan, beginning in September 1982.

Countries vary greatly in their exposure to such movements in interest rates. As can be seen in table 12, Western Hemisphere countries are especially sensitive to such swings since more than 70 percent of their loans are on a floating rate basis. This, of course, includes the largest LDC borrowers in the world: Brazil and Mexico, as well as other heavy debtors such as Argentina and Venezuela. Brazil has more than $50 billion of floating rate debt. For every 1 percent change in interest

TABLE 12

Share of Total Debt of Developing Countries at Floating Rates: 1973–1985

	1973–74	1975–78	1979–80	1981–82	1983–85*
All capital-importing developing countries	21.1%	34.7%	44.6%	51.1%	53.6%
Sub-Saharan Africa	9.4	15.4	17.8	20.6	19.1
Asia	8.1	21.9	31.3	38.1	45.2
Western Hemisphere	34.1	51.3	66.4	71.7	72.4

*The erratic spans of years were chosen by the IMF.
Source: *World Economic Outlook;* International Monetary Fund; April 1986; p. 88.

rates, the cost of the country's international debt rises or falls by $500 million annually.

Although there has not been any systematic, comprehensive program by the international commercial banks to confront the threat of the debt overhang, most major banks have made noticeable individual adjustments. This has served to reduce the seriousness of the international threat to the banks. However, the threat is still there and many of the banks are removing themselves as much as possible from any new financial ties with the developing world—a thrust that is part of the international financial dilemma.

Many international banks have enjoyed high profits during the past few years. As interest rates have declined, so has the cost of the banks' funding—more rapidly than the rates charged to borrowers. That large spread between funding and lending rates has brought high profits to many banks. In 1987 many banks, led by Citibank, sharply increased their international reserves. Some banks, such as Bank of Boston and NCNB, went a step further by writing down all or part of their exposure in certain countries or to certain borrowers.

However, banks that wish to keep profits and bank capital high have tried to forego this move. For example, banks that are anticipating merger or acquisition (as either the acquirer or acquiree) have tended to avoid any write-downs that are not mandated by either the bank regulators or auditors.

Governments in some major industrial countries have added strong pressure to encourage such write-downs. For example, in Canada and Japan, the bank regulators have *mandated* that a portion of all exposure to a large group of developing countries be written down: in Canada it is 10 percent of all of those loans. In the U.S., the regulators have targeted specific debtor countries and mandated specific write-downs. Table 13 lists the countries which were targeted through mid-1986. The mandates for Poland and Zaire occurred several years ago. The others were more recent. Peru has been targeted for two different mandates, each of 15 percent.

Other factors that have influenced the decisions of various banks have been tax considerations (German tax law is especially accommodating) and "hidden" reserves. It is common practice for banks in several European countries and Japan to maintain large reserves in the form of undervalued assets, such as real estate or gold. These hidden reserves have traditionally been used to absorb the impact of large losses (large foreign-exchange losses or the collapse of a major debtor). By writing *up* the value of those assets and then writing the assets back *down* to reflect the losses, the bank is able to absorb losses without any substantial impact upon its balance sheet or unduly worrying its shareholders or depositors.

Such reserves are not permitted in the United States. However, some banks (most notably the Bank of America) have sold off visible assets with capital gains boosting bank capital. For example, the Bank of America sold its financial subsidiary, FinanceAmerica, to Chrysler, and its headquarters building in San Francisco (it remains in the building as a tenant). It is also selling its profitable Italian subsidiary to Deutsche Bank.

Many banks have also increased their capital. This can be accomplished by keeping more retained earnings (when profits are high) or, even better, increasing loan-loss reserves with pre-tax money. The increase of capital can also be accomplished by the issue of either stock or bonds. However, most of the major U.S. commercial banks in the U.S. have common stock trading at a relatively low price and have seen their credit ratings drop (which increases the cost of borrowing). These conditions greatly reduce the attractiveness of either of these alternatives. Interestingly, many major *regional* banks are perceived much

TABLE 13

Mandatory Write-Offs for U.S. Banks of Loan Exposure
(by Country)

Liberia	15%
Peru	30%
Poland	45%
Bolivia	50%
Zaire	75%
Sudan	80%
Nicaragua	85%

Derived from banking contacts.

more favorably by the stock market. Indeed, several regional banks have higher market values than such major banks as Chemical and Bank of America.

Banks with financial problems, for example, many of the Texas banks which are suffering from the recession in the "oil patch," including bad oil, natural gas, and real-estate loans, may not be able to utilize such approaches as either the sale of stock or aggressive write-downs of poor quality loans.

A creative approach to reducing loan exposures has been the rapid development during the past year of a secondary market in LDC loans. In some cases, banks sell the loans outright (for example, the sale by First Wachovia of $15 million of its Chilean loans). Any asset can be sold if the price is right. The loans, of course, generally sell at a discount. Obviously, the quality of LDC loans varies greatly: Quality varies between countries and between different borrowers within a country. In countries with a significant amount of private sector international debt, the price will vary between government and the private sector.

Some of the discounts on LDC credits are very substantial. Table 14 shows some recent quotes. As shown, debts of coun-

TABLE 14

Discounts Quoted on the Bank Loans of Selected Developing Countries (Bid Rates, December 31, 1987)

Turkey	−3%
Algeria	−8
Colombia	−35
Chile	−39
Venezuela	−43
Mexico	−50
Philippines	−50
Yugoslavia	−51
Brazil	−54
Poland	−57
Ecuador	−63
Argentina	−66
Nigeria	−71
Dominican Republic	−77
Zaire	−81
Bolivia	−89
Peru	−93
Sudan	−98

Source: "International Loan Trading," Salomon Brothers Inc.

tries such as Peru and Sudan are selling at less than $0.10 on the dollar. Not surprisingly, there are some rumors of countries operating through intermediaries to buy their own debt at a discount. If they have the resources, this could be a very wise investment—a chance to retire part of their debt at bargain prices.

Much more debt, however, is being swapped or exchanged than is being sold. Several billion dollars of such transactions have occurred in the past year. Various motivations have prompted such exchanges. Some banks have simply swapped out of countries in which they have relatively small exposure. For example, First Interstate Bank exchanged its entire $5 million of South African debt for an equivalent amount of Mexican debt. The small amount of South African credits simply was not worth the expense and trouble, while the extra exposure in Mexico was a small addition to their overall exposure there and would not require much additional work.

There are some fairly characteristic patterns of many of the swaps. Much of it has involved the exchange by American banks of some of their Eastern European exposure for Latin American debt of European banks: The Americans are closer to and more comfortable with the Latin debt while the reverse is true of European banks. To a lesser extent, American banks have also been trading African debt with European banks— again in exchange for Latin debt. European countries with former African colonies are more familiar and comfortable with and have much larger exposures in Africa. Bankers Trust disposed of its Ivory Coast exposure in this way.

As in these examples, both banks may perceive that they are better off as a result of the exchange. However, swaps do not always work out well. First Union swapped much of its debt in other Latin American countries in exchange for other banks' debts of two major oil exporters, Mexico and Venezuela, shortly before oil prices began their precipitous decline in late 1985.

Most of the trading has been done by European banks and regional American banks. Japanese banks have not been active. Money-center U.S. banks are constrained by U.S. auditing requirements: If a bank sells or swaps a loan, it must write off any discount which was realized. In addition, it may also be required to write down *all other credits* to the same country. In cases where large money-center banks are eliminating their entire exposure in a country, this poses no problems since there are no other loans to write down. Similarly, large regional banks, whose exposure in LDCs is much less than that of the money-center banks, might opt to sell off or even write off all of their exposure in certain countries. The large positions of the money-center banks prevents them from doing the same.

If the regulators have already mandated write-downs, the problem of taking a "hit" on all unsold loans when other loans are discounted is lessened since much or all of the "hit" has already been absorbed. However, this accounting rule serves as a major barrier to banks with substantial additional exposure in that country.

A different type of swap has also begun to gain momentum—and with some degree of debtor-government approval. This form involves the exchange of debt for equity.

The country that has pioneered such debt-equity conversions is Chile. In the simplest form of swap, Bankers Trust exchanged its own holdings of Chilean debt for 40 percent of the equity in the pension-fund subsidiary of the Banco de Chile. It also acquired the largest life insurance company in Chile. In a similar transaction, a group of foreign banks represented by Manufacturers Hanover Trust accepted stock in Industrias Forestales, a Chilean company, in lieu of some of that company's overdue interest payments. Since these transactions take place at par, there is no discount; and thus, the bank can avoid the demand by its accountants to write down other Chilean debt.

The government of Chile is actively encouraging such exchanges. In fact, it often plays an active role and takes a commission for its permission and services. There are two different programs—one designed for Chilean companies and investors and one designed for foreign companies.

Bankers Trust and other commercial and merchant banks are also active in trying to find potential investors (either foreigners or Chilean citizens) who are interested in purchasing outstanding Chilean dollar debt at a discount. If Chilean debt were selling at about a 30 percent discount, for example, the seller would receive from the intermediary (the merchant or commercial bank) 70 percent of the face value of the note ($700,000 for $1,000,000 of Chilean debt). The purchaser would, of course, pay somewhat more ($725,000 or 72.5 percent of the face value) with the intermediary keeping the difference ($25,000).

The purchaser would exchange the dollar-denominated debt with the central bank in Chile for pesos at the free-market exchange rate. If the exchange rate is 195 pesos/dollar, the purchaser of the debt would receive Ps 195,000,000—far more than could be received from a straight purchase of $725,000 worth of pesos (the amount actually spent by the purchaser). However, the central bank charges its fee which, depending upon the priority which it assigns to the proposed investment, could range up to 15 percent. Assuming that it is 10 percent, the investor would receive Ps 175,500,000 (Ps 195 million minus the 10 percent commission). This is still a very favorable incentive: an effective exchange rate of 242 pesos/dollar rather than a market rate of 195 pesos/dollar.

This scheme offers advantages for many different people:

(1) The creditor, by selling its debt, is able to reduce its Chilean exposure, although at a 30 percent discount. If the creditor (as in the Bankers Trust case above) uses its own credits to sell to the Chilean government, it can reduce its exposure *without* selling at a discount, although the investment is more expensive.

(2) The government is able to retire $1 million of foreign debt, and not only does it pay in pesos but, as a result of the commission that it charges, it acquires the debt at a discount— the peso equivalent of $900,000 (Ps 175,500,000 at 195 pesos/ dollar).

(3) A foreign investor is brought into the economy, probably either strengthening the Chilean company in which it has invested or building new facilities.

(4) If the purchase is of a government-owned corporation, then the government accomplishes the further goal of reducing the number of nationalized companies.

(5) The investor is able to make the investment at a much lower price than the market exchange rate would dictate. The

Ps 175,500,000 which it invested would have cost $900,000 instead of $725,000. That higher market rate might have made the investment uneconomical.

Mexico, Brazil, and the Philippines are other countries with similar schemes. However, thus far, their programs have been much less ambitious or effective. One major transaction in Mexico involved the purchase by Nissan, the Japanese automobile manufacturer, of $20 million of Mexican foreign debt at a discount. The notes were then sold to the Mexican government for redemption in Mexican pesos at the market exchange rate less a commission (similar to the Chilean example).

In addition to adjustments in assets and equity, there has also been a strong shift among the major international banks in policies, priorities, and even financial activities. These adjustments have helped buffer most of the banks against the threats from their LDC debt portfolios.

One change has been a strong shift away from a willingness by banks to lend to LDCs. The banks have been burned by excessive exposure to the LDCs suffering large losses. Still, huge potential losses remain. The threat leads to much worry and additional work for the bankers.

The banks are being forced repeatedly to extend involuntary loans in order to keep old credits from going into default. These accommodations to the inability of countries to repay their international debts may take the form of a rescheduling (spreading the repayment over more years than originally scheduled) and refinancing (refunding the old loan with a new loan which may have not only a different repayment schedule but a different interest rate, and probably new fees as well).

Furthermore, the bankers are faced with chronic criticism from senior management, banking regulators, shareholders, and stock analysts. It has been a sobering and disillusioning experience. Most bankers now feel that new lending to most LDCs would be simply throwing good money after bad. As a result, many large banks have sharply reduced their international staffs—a trend that bodes ill for LDCs in the future.

At the same time as this lack of interest in LDC lending, banks are being drawn to other markets in response to deregulation and competition from other types of financial institutions, which are threatening to erode banks' markets. Deregulation of domestic banking systems is occurring in many different countries: Japan, the United Kingdom, and the United States most prominently. In France, the trend toward deregulation will involve the privatization of the government-owned commercial banks. Such deregulation offers new opportunities in these very important international and domestic markets. However, the increased competition which occurs will also bring risks to those banks that cannot fight to protect their current positions.

In the U.S., the advent of interstate banking, the rapid increase in competition from non-banks (savings and loans associations, credit unions, non-bank credit cards, brokerage houses, and even retailers), the shift of traditional customers to direct funding in the money and capital markets thus bypassing the commercial banks, and the progressive dismantling of the restrictions on investment banking activities of the Glass-Steagall Act are offering both opportunity and threat.

All of these developments pull bankers' attention away from the developing countries. So also do the domestic problem areas of commercial banks—oil and natural gas, real estate, agriculture, etc. This shift of focus and the interest in non-lending activities (advisory services such as mergers and acquisitions and underwriting of Eurobonds) which bring fees without adding assets (loans) to the books is not a passing fancy. It is a fundamental change in commercial banking. This means that debtor countries are going to have increasing difficulty in finding commercial (private-sector) sources of financing.

Impact Upon the Availability of Funds in the Future for LDCs

The second great worry concerning the debt overhang is the impact that this experience is going to have upon the availability of funds for *new* borrowing by the LDCs (not simply borrowing to repay the old loans).

Commercial banks generally are not interested in voluntarily satisfying demand for additional loans. Except for a few

LDCs which have avoided serious debt problems and which are showing strong adjustment (South Korea, with its strong export performance, and Taiwan, which is actually reducing its international debt), international commercial banks have shifted their focus elsewhere. Countries that encountered any serious debt problems in the past remain relatively "noncommercial" now—with the capital markets as well as commercial banks effectively closed to them for new loans. The commercial banks now know they made bad investing decisions—not just in their LDC portfolio but in a variety of domestic areas as well. And, they are being frequently reminded about the continued threat from those past LDC-loan decisions. Having been burned, they are reluctant to be drawn deeper into commitments to the same group of countries. Mark Twain once said that if a cat sits on a hot stove, it will never sit on a hot stove again. It may also never sit on a cold stove.

Commercial banks need to know they always have the option of "cashing out" of a loan at maturity. Since it is not their own money which they are lending, they depend upon the flexibility of being able to get all of their depositors' money back on schedule.

Banks may opt to roll over loans—but at their own discretion. Banks are well aware that many large borrowers, including most governments, will *never* pay off, or even substantially reduce, their total *net* debt: American Telephone and Telegraph, General Motors, other major corporations, and governments commonly pay off old debt with new. The net amount of the borrowing generally trends upward. However, in those examples, the lenders can be cashed out with cash infusions from other investors. The lenders are not generally *forced* to refinance old credits—they refinance at their own discretion. If lenders are forced to refinance or reschedule the loans of such companies as a result of the bankruptcy of the borrower, the banks will be averse to lending more to the same borrower.

Brazil, Mexico, and other LDC debtors are never going to substantially reduce their debts. In fact, under almost *any* scenario, their total international debt will continue to grow—if only from involuntary loans to capitalize unpaid interest. However, there are *no* alternative sources of financing which offer the lenders the promise of cashing out. As a result, the lenders find themselves "locked in"—forced to refinance and reschedule their own loans, and perhaps even to absorb the shares of smaller banks. Furthermore, they remain skeptical about the long-term commitment of LDC governments to sound structural adjustment. As a result, it is going to take time to rebuild lender confidence.

The private money and capital markets are no more receptive than are the commercial banks to lending to countries with poor credit histories and, especially, current repayment problems. Countries with a recent history of financial problems will find it difficult to obtain private-sector financing, except at very high cost: The price will reflect the risk.

Official sources of financing will, of necessity, continue to play a much greater role in the financing needs of most LDCs than was true in most of the 1970s. The borrowers will include many countries that were "commercial" in the 1970s, but are only marginally commercial now. Fortunately, the quantity of official funds available has risen in recent years. When coupled with the retreat of the commercial sources of financing, this has caused the relative and absolute importance of official sources of financing for LDCs to increase markedly.

For Latin American borrowers, the significance of official credits, which had been very important in the 1960s (62 percent of total external credits in 1961), had fallen to only 9 percent of total external financing needs by 1979 (table 8). Over the same period, bank lending grew from less than 1 percent to account for more than 68 percent of the financing needs (table 9). In 1985, bank lending was down to 29 percent and official lending had risen to over 50 percent of LDC financing needs.

The role of bilateral credits has not grown substantially in absolute terms. Most of the growth in official credits has been in the form of multilateral assistance, which has risen substantially in both relative and absolute terms. Capital infusions from member countries have helped, but the primary source of funds for institutions such as the World Bank and the Inter-American Development Bank is from their ability to borrow from the private markets at very favorable rates. At the present time, with limited new LDC funding needs, their resources are adequate. However, those resources will be wholly inadequate if developing countries' borrowing needs should again grow rapidly (for example, if oil prices or interest rates increase sharply once more).

The future availability of funding is the more severe crisis stemming from the continuing debt overhang. Means must be found to provide the future financing needs of the LDCs. If oil prices were to increase, the international banks would again receive substantial infusions of petrodollar deposits. However, as we have seen, they are unwilling to continue in the role of recycler of those funds to the oil-importing LDCs.

The private financial markets are the *only* source of funds that would be adequate. The commercial banks *must* be provided with the incentive to again lend to the LDCs, and the capital markets *must* be opened to the developing countries. However, few LDCs have access on their own merits. A comprehensive scheme for resolving the debt overhang problem must address this issue of future funding as well.

Summary and Recommendations

The international debt crisis is currently much less acute than during the first half of the 1980s. Nevertheless, the problem remains very severe. Temporary remission should not be interpreted as solution.

There are two major dimensions to the crisis:

(1) its impact upon the international financial system; and,
(2) its impact upon the ability of the developing countries to find financing for their future *developmental* needs (as opposed to simply refinancing their existing debts).

The seriousness of the first dimension has diminished. However, it remains a major threat to the international financial system because the fundamental problem has not been resolved. The world, including both the debtors and creditors, has benefited from both lower interest rates and lower oil prices (although, of course, the oil-exporting developing countries benefited from the former but have been hurt by the latter). Also, many banks have made adjustments which have reduced the extent of the threat of the debt overhang from their large LDC loans. Some countries too have made adjustments which, at least temporarily, have reduced their needs for extra funding.

Although the acuteness of the threat has declined, the international financial system remains allergic to further serious economic shocks—whether from rising oil prices, rising interest rates, default by a major borrower, or any of a variety of other potentially system-disrupting crises. Recovery remains too tenuous and the inaccessibility of the developing countries as a group to the private financial markets remains a serious threat.

The ability of the developing countries to find financing for their future development is the second dimension of the dual threat that overhangs the international financial system. Its seriousness cannot be overemphasized. As a result of the first dimension, the commercial banks and capital markets have generally lost interest in the developing countries. Yet those countries need substantial external financing. Their levels of social and economic development are not satisfactory to them. Furthermore, in many developing countries the per capita standard of living has been falling in recent years.

This is a potentially explosive situation. Both humanitarianism and the self-interest of the industrial countries dictate that serious efforts must be undertaken to ameliorate those conditions. However, without access to the private financial markets, there is not going to be sufficient funding for most of the countries.

What is needed is a comprehensive response to this dual threat. Short-term, *ad hoc* responses are wholly inadequate. Yet that is what has generally been occurring since the debt crisis began. We have successfully "muddled through" thus far. However, this respite has simply given us the opportunity, if we have the wisdom to use it, to attempt to design a solution without the threat of imminent collapse. We need a *comprehensive, integrated, well-coordinated and long-term* program to address these problems. If leaders of wisdom and statesmanship do not come forth to lead the way, then we are likely to be thrown back into the maelstrom.

The crisis is like a hurricane. We are currently in the eye of that storm experiencing a temporary peace while the tempest surrounds us. We will not forever remain in the eye, away from the ravages of the storm. While decisions reached with calm deliberation are generally preferable to those reached in the heart of a crisis, it is not at all clear that the statesmanship exists to resolve the problem under calm deliberation. Too often, the human race requires the gun of crisis at its head before the necessary negotiation and compromise occur. Hopefully, we will not need to await that condition in this situation.

A comprehensive response to the crisis of the debt overhang must attack both dimensions of the problem—the threat of the overhang to the debtors and creditors as well as the problem of access to future funding by the developing countries. The bottom line for the accomplishment of these two objectives is the protection and buttressing of the international financial system. Failing that, neither of the above is possible.

Solution of these problems requires the participation and cooperation of many different groups: the debtors, the private creditors, the creditor governments, the international agencies, and perhaps even new participants such as the insurance industry.

At the bottom of the task of resolving the crisis has been the reticence of any leader to initiate the process of comprehensive reform. Perhaps what is needed is a "Bretton-Woods" conference to bring all of the major parties together. The catalyst might be a major creditor government. It might be a major creditor bank. It could even be a critical debtor (most notably Mexico—although it is not at all clear that the lenders would respond to a comprehensive initiative by the debtors).

The most likely candidate for the role of catalyst is the IMF and/or the World Bank. Their roles will be critical in the success of any outcome. Lenders and borrowers are vocally seeking new initiatives and leadership from the two institutions. The IMF and World Bank have the credibility and resources to get the process moving.

Thus far, each group has been waiting for a significant concession from the other groups. Debtors are awaiting a willingness on the part of the banks to relieve their existing debt burdens. The banks are reluctant to set precedents by granting any major concessions to debtors. The international agencies are encouraging cooperation and innovation on the part of both debtors and creditors, and offering assistance. Basically, all groups are waiting for the others to move first, to make the first concessions. This is a sterile approach. Everyone is going to need to make concessions—big ones. A piecemeal process of solutions will not suffice. Both of the basic problems must be attacked simultaneously. The solutions can be, must be, a joint package. One of the key issues is that the banking system must gain increased confidence in the likelihood of having its loans repaid; The issue involves both principal and interest. The banks are generally not receptive to suggestions that principal be "forgiven."

The banks have reached a number of agreements with borrowing countries which provide for rescheduled payoffs and also capitalization of past-due interest. This type of procedure would be at the heart of a comprehensive package as well. However, the rescheduling period will need to be much longer for many debtors than the two to five years which are commonly used. Also, what is needed is a package for handling all of a country's foreign debts, not just those that are already in arrears or within twelve months of being due.

On their part, the debtors must be offered a package for repayment that brings their repayment schedule to a level which they can afford. Their chronic problem is too much repayment being scheduled over a short period of time. This part of the package is going to primarily require sacrifices from the creditors. Repayment schedules may need to be spread over five, seven, ten or even more years. Interest-only payments may be necessary. Much or all of the past-due interest will need to be capitalized, thus becoming part of the principal of the loan and the burden of bringing past-due interest current is simply impossible for many countries.

These concessions are basically mechanical. The lenders, however, will need to make additional concessions as well. A likely request will be that they reduce their lending spreads. There will still be some variation based upon risk, but the international agencies or major governments may need to subsidize the risk differential (just as the U.S. and other governments do for education loans, agricultural loans, etc.).

Many developing countries have paid very high interest spreads in the past. A *retroactive* reduction of some of the spreads would help relieve some of the debt burden; This could be made more acceptable if, in exchange, the banks were to receive a guarantee, from the World Bank or creditor governments for example, of part of the principal against which the high spreads were applied. Finally, rescheduling or refinancing fees would need to be foregone. The task is to help the banks get their loans repaid and to do it on a schedule that the LDCs can afford. Additional fees would be self-defeating.

The comprehensive package being proposed here incorporates a guarantee program, and such guarantees could come from either an international agency, such as the World Bank, or from governments, or perhaps a combination of the two (for example, a World Bank guarantee with reinsurance provided by the Group of Ten governments for losses beyond a certain level). The guarantee facility might be patterned on some of those which the IMF already makes available to certain countries under special conditions (e.g., the Compensatory Financing Fund or the Supplemental Financing Facility). However, in this particular case it would be clearly understood that these guarantees would be grants and not loans. The program might be financed in several ways: special contributions, IMF profits, gold sales, etc.

These institutions, agencies as well as governments, would also be the source of subsidies. Subsidies are tempting tools, but they need to be judiciously applied in order to prevent the debtors and creditors from becoming addicted to them. However, they may be necessary in some cases where guarantees are not used to help reduce the interest burden for the very poorest countries or those otherwise in the poorest position to repay. These guarantee and subsidy programs could be important ingredients in attacking the problem of the debt overhang. They may be indispensable in encouraging the private sector to help fund future borrowing for developmental purposes.

An additional source of guarantees for new loans might be feasible from the private sector through the insurance industry.

For example, insurance companies provide insurance for trade financing through the Foreign Credit Insurance Association in the United States. A similar type of private-sector insurance facility should be explored in the efforts to resolve the world debt crisis.

Insurance companies have considered some type of loan-insurance program in the past. Citibank has actively engaged in trying to arrange such a facility with insurance companies also. The discussions were unsuccessful, but the kernal of the idea remains. It would be useful to incorporate as many resources as possible in the resolution of this present crisis.

Another method for reducing the threat to individual banks would be for further development of the securitization of loans. The packaging of loans (either all from one country or a portfolio of loans from different countries) so that they could be sold to institutional investors in secondary markets would help to spread the risk more widely. This would be analogous to the packaging of groups of mortgages and automobile loans which are sold as securities in the United States.

By attracting new investors, this securitization of existing loans would ease some of the strain upon lenders and reduce the pressure upon the debtors as well. This is, of course, a variation on the sale on the secondary market of bank loans which was discussed before; it would reflect a maturing of the market.

Sale by banks of packages of loans would also be at a discount, which would require a write-down of the corresponding amount. However, because of the diversification provided by the package, the cost of the discount could well be less than would result from the individual discounts if each loan were to be sold separately.

The debtors would need to agree to pursue the type of adjustment programs which the IMF has been encouraging for many years. However, as was suggested in the Baker Plan, these recommendations might need to utilize longer time horizons. Also, it is not intended that this package of programs, which is designed to provide additional assistance to overcome the debt crisis, should eliminate some of the creative steps that countries such as Chile and Brazil have developed (such as the debt-equity exchange programs). Even under the best scenario, the levels of international debts for many countries will remain very high. Efforts to reduce the level of those debts are to be encouraged.

The policies and guidelines of both banking regulators and accounting groups must be considered in the final plans. As noted before, in the U.S. the auditors and regulators of commercial banks tend to take the attitude that discounts and some other concessions which are granted to borrowers can trigger mandatory write-downs of other loans to that country. Since the governments of the United States and other industrialized countries will be participating in the deliberations and since the discussions are directed toward reducing the risk to the banks, the regulators and auditors need to incorporate these changes into their policies and procedures. It would obviously be self-defeating for the banks to be penalized for cooperating in this generalized program of adjustment.

Even loans which were written off in the past would regain some or all of their value if an overall adjustment program is successful. That would please the banks and should soothe the regulators.

The future access of LDCs to external capital is a critical part of the comprehensive adjustment package. The role of the international agencies and perhaps even the creditor governments is two-fold. The first involves the continued direct loans to the borrowing countries (multilateral and bilateral official credits). An increase in the World Bank's capital and borrowing capacity should be a part of the overall adjustment package. This is especially important for the non-commercial countries such as Mali or Sudan. However, most developing countries, not just the poorest, have access to and make use of the resources of the World Bank. As was seen in the proposals above, the World Bank along with the IMF will need to continue to play a vital and expanded role through increased lending, plus guarantees and subsidies, for a wide range of even "commercial" countries.

It has been proposed by some commentators that the World Bank move away from its basic purpose of funding development projects toward "balance-of-payment" loans which are not tied directly to any project. In my view, this is not advisable, nor is it necessary within the context of the proposals made here. Indeed, it is precisely such non-project loans that are so highly criticized for having been wasted and stolen by corrupt politicians in the past. World Bank loans should continue to be tied to specific projects. Furthermore, the expertise of World Bank's advisers in support of these projects has often provided invaluable assistance to the borrowers or potential borrowers.

The IMF should also receive additional capital. However, in addition the IMF could also begin utilizing its very substantial borrowing capacity to tap the private markets. Even though the Fund has the statutory right under its Articles of Agreement to borrow in the private markets, it has chosen to abstain, ostensibly to avoid squeezing other international agencies and developing countries out of the private markets. However, the developing countries do not have much access on their own merits and the other major agencies should find adequate funding in an international market that has grown enormously since the IMF policy was adopted.

The Fund does make "balance-of-payment" loans. However, these loans tend to be short term and have strings attached. These practices should continue. In addition, the Fund and the Bank might each, or both jointly, issue guarantees to help developing countries tap the private markets. From a lender's point of view, a guaranteed or insured credit is the risk of the ultimate obligor. Thus, with an IMF or World Bank guarantee, from the banks' and regulators' and auditors' perspectives, it is not a country risk—even if it was issued by Sudan. It is a Fund or World Bank risk.

It might be argued that large-scale guarantees of specific project financings for LDCs is beyond the scope of the Bank and Fund. However, the Bank already issues a variety of guarantees of private-sector loans to LDCs. Also, the very function of the World Bank is to borrow under its own prime credit rating and itself lend to developing countries. This is not very different in function from its guarantee of a loan or bond taken out directly under the name of the borrowing country. With those guarantees, of course, the bonds and even the loans might be very marketable, which would also serve to broaden the market.

Again, the role of the private insurance industry in issuing guarantees should be carefully examined. Insurance companies are not only specialists in covering risk, but also represent vast sums of investment funds.

The basic reason for advocating guarantees and insurance programs into the comprehensive adjustments package is that the private financial markets *must* be reincorporated into the financing of economic and social development—not by coercion but through incentives. Only the private sector has the financial resources necessary to provide the vast sums that will be needed in the future as developmental programs again move forward after the consolidation of the past few years. In order to reattract the commercial banks and to open the capital markets, the risk of that lending must be reduced for the private lenders. *There is no shortage of capital.* It is simply being poorly distributed. What is needed are adjustments in the international financial system to get those resources flowing to where they are needed most.

Now is the time for vision and leadership. Too much time has been wasted already in wishful thinking and short-term, *ad hoc,* and myopic adjustment packages. The international financial system has the resiliency to survive and prosper, but, it needs help. No partial packages will suffice. The type of comprehensive program outlined here is mandatory, and the time is now.

NOTE

1. IMF, *World Economic Outlook* (April 1986): 68.

Comprehensive Solutions: Needed But Not Likely

RICHARD WEBB*

Korth's paper was instructive and a good review of the history, particularly of what has been going on within banks over the last few years. Korth makes an important point by separating the vulnerability issue into two parts—the threat to the lenders' financial system and the need for new development funds for Third World borrowers. From the point of view of the banks—the financial system—he states that the crisis has moderated, although at the end of his paper, he stresses the risks to the system. From the perspective of the borrower, he is pessimistic throughout. Besides the risk to the system itself, he sees reduced flows of repayment to the lender linked to difficulty in encouraging adequate future flows of new money to borrowing countries.

It is difficult for me to comment on the main point—the degree of risk in the system as a whole. I would make a point from the perspective of someone who, in a small country, has been dealing with the financial system intensively over the last few years: The system is really much less at peril than is often claimed. Banks and the financial system as a whole, by their very nature, are defensive. Bankers stress the fragility of the banking system—borrowers are told that if their 30–day loan is paid on the 31st day, they are endangering the entire financial

---

*Richard Webb is a professor of economics at the Catholic University of Lima. Formerly the president of the Central Reserve Bank of Peru, and a research economist at the World Bank, he has been a visiting professor at Princeton University and the University of Toronto.

system. This stress on fragility is understandable since the banking system is based on confidence; depositors must trust their banks, and bankers must trust borrowers. The subjective basis of the whole system needs a conservative ideology.

In fact, however, banks have a great capacity to defend themselves. They constantly face problems and absorb losses.

Korth, after reviewing the way the system has been evolving the last few years, concludes with a detailed, richly developed, specific proposal. He stresses the need for a comprehensive solution. He criticizes the muddling-through nature of the solutions of the last few years. To be complete, Korth needs to discuss how one can get the principal actors to accept a comprehensive solution. What are the political and ideological barriers?

This proposal reminded me of a visit with Mr. Volcker in 1983, when I cornered him at a bankers' meeting and pressed him on the need for a comprehensive solution. I took the liberty of doing this because I admired his sensitivity to the debt issue at a time when no one else in authority outside the less-developed countries appeared to be paying attention. I had discussed the Peruvian situation with him at length on more than one occasion. I was impressed that he took so much time to listen to people from a small country like Peru, and I knew that he was also listening to other countries. I thought, if there is going to be anything comprehensive, he is the only person in a position to take it on. I was quite disappointed in his reaction. He seemed to reject the concept and he was pessimistic about the willingness of world leaders. He said, "There is no way that we are going to get anything like that."

In his reply I sensed something more than just a judgment of political feasibility to the bankers and statesmen who are managing the world financial system today. A general or comprehensive solution runs counter to a practical rule that is close to ideology: Problem borrowers must be dealt with on a case-by-case or ad hoc basis. With general rules, a bank gets swamped. With an across-the-board solution, banks give up much more than they would by dealing with difficult debtors one by one.

Thus, the problem is both practical and ideological. It is also ethical, as has been stressed in our discussion. Much of the difficulty in accepting write-downs and other aspects of a real comprehensive solution is that people do not see the ethics of the situation—particularly people who are running governments and banks. This is a real stumbling block.

There is now greater acceptance of co-responsibility and bankruptcy, but these are seen as applying to strictly limited and specific cases. The moral thinking that has gone into dealing with the current situation has not been brought to bear on the overall problem. Ethicists have a lot to say. If there is going to be an unblocking of this mental problem, we need their help.

The System Is Resilient

*A. BLAKE FRISCIA**

While Korth has a good appreciation of the international debt problem and has provided a useful survey of the difficulties faced by the Latin American countries in particular, questions need to be asked about some of the points raised.

First, a distinction should be drawn between the differences in behavior of large and small banks. Korth says the banks are removing themselves from any new financial ties with the developing world. While this may be true of some smaller banks, the major bank lenders are still in the business with debt-to-equity swaps, local currency lending, "new money" provided as part of rescheduling exercises, and even "voluntary" new loans on a rebuilding basis for a limited number of creditworthy borrowers. The banks that have taken "hits" and written down all or part of their exposure have been the smaller banks. The "reserving" measures taken in 1987 by major banks—to increase their provisions for possible loan losses in developing country debt—were prudential actions and do not represent actual losses or write-downs. The outright sale of loans has been mainly a small bank phenomenon.

The charge that bankers are "throwing good money after bad" is a vernacular and commonplace saying, with vague ana-

---

*A. Blake Friscia is a vice president and head of the Western Hemisphere section in the Chase Manhattan Economics Group. In the Latin American external debt rescheduling programs, Dr. Friscia has participated actively as chairman of the economics subcommittee for the Venezuela and Equador bank advisory committees, and as a member of the Argentina subcommittee.

lytical implications. From the point of view of the debtor country, new lending reduces the outward resource transfer and does permit new investment. From the banker's point of view, the casual expression of "throwing money away" glosses over the considerable deliberations, credit and economic analysis, and finally senior management approvals that have to be secured in making new loans.

A corollary point is that banks are reducing their international staffs and this trend bodes ill for the less-developed countries in the future. What should be noted is that the larger international banks are adding to their staffs in the field of investment banking and other financial intermediary services and perhaps reducing in traditional sovereign lending. To say that this trend of staff reductions bodes ill for the less-developed countries is simply to ascribe too great an influence to banks as a force for economic development. Certainly banks have been recognized as facilitators and as good intermediaries for channeling funds from savers to investors, but there are many, and perhaps more important, causes of economic development.

Despite the assertion that banks are running away from debt, there is the question of the proper balance between external (bank) funds and internal savings. Economic development can be defined as the process of moving funds from capital-surplus to capital-deficient countries, but this cannot be a permanent movement because it would doom the developing countries to eternal underdevelopment. A vision of a country shifting from the capital-importing to capital-exporting stage must be part of economic development, and in this stage banks will naturally be lending less and the total external debt of the country would be reduced in absolute amounts. Korth's statement that the private financial markets are the *only* source of funds cannot become much of a rallying cry. The argument can be made that the multilateral and bilateral lenders (the World Bank, the Inter-American Development Bank, EXIMBANKs of the United States and Japan, etc.) should be the more important sources of net lending in the future. His further normative injunction that the commercial banks *must* be brought back to the less-developed countries raises questions of who is going to do the forcing. If the force comes from a national government of the creditor banks, then there is an implied guarantee.

Korth believes that the debt negotiations since 1982 have been a period of wasted time—the time gained has not been used productively by lenders and borrowers. This is not the case. The lenders—commercial banks, the International Monetary Fund, the World Bank, international agencies—have greatly refashioned themselves for a new world of structural change and limited debt growth. Borrowers have also had to examine their productive structures and to more carefully discern between external and internal sources of savings and between commercial and public sources of funds. The days of the billion-dollar jumbo loans of pre-1982 are gone, and the time since then has been used to devise new financing techniques (floating rate notes, on-lending, re-lending, interest, and foreign exchange hedges) as well as considering grand global ideas for "solving" the debt problem. A minor industry of these global notions has developed to the extent that catalogs of proposals have become standard reading for bankers and economists.

The Korth paper, of course, must be viewed in the context of the earlier (Part 1) discussion of the need for the debtor countries to undertake structural reforms to generate internal sources of capital, to limit capital flight, to develop attractive projects that would entice direct investment capital, to develop manufactured goods exports, and to build efficient import-competing industries. In isolation, the argument in this paper would be too one-sided on the deficiencies of the suppliers of external funds. The debtor country also has responsibilities, and the primary one is to produce an efficient, productive economy that can attract both loan and investment funds.

Further, Korth neglected some points. Related to the omission of structural change, Korth makes only brief mention of the Baker Initiative. Whether or not he is in agreement with this program, it has to be recognized that the Baker proposals are essentially for the return of voluntary bank lending and the resumption of economic growth—all in the context of structural improvements in the borrowing country. In terms of institutional innovations, Korth also failed to mention the Institute of International Finance, a Washington forum of the major creditor banks, involved in useful research and public policy analysis relative to debtor countries and the international financial system.

Hopefully these remarks will not be seen as mere caviling and detract from the good points and solid analysis Korth has incorporated in his paper. These observations are offered in an attempt to ask questions and cite points not mentioned.

It may be fair to ask how I would go about "solving" the international debt problem. I do not have a large, global vision of a new Bretton Woods; however, the system is resilient enough to provide a patient working out through the rescheduling/new money process for those countries that are not yet fully creditworthy, the menu of options approach for the more creditworthy, while a parallel flow of small voluntary lendings are beginning to appear for the better credits.

The flow of bank lending responds to perceived investment opportunities in the borrowing countries. If the flow of lending has been reduced, it is because policies and performance in the economies of the developing countries exhibit a downward shift in the investment schedule. What is needed to lift this schedule are appropriate policies on interest rates, the exchange rate, and the fiscal, wage, and financial sectors. Along with a better policy set and longer-term structural changes, the developing countries—particularly Latin America—could indeed become more creditworthy and attractive to bank lenders. There could be changes in policies and practices on the lending side, but the fundamental changes needed are in the market as expressed by economic policies and performance of the demanders of funds.

The Role of International
Institutions in the Debt Crisis

The debt crisis is surely challenging the mettle of the international financial institutions, particularly against their charge when founded at Bretton Woods in 1945. As the workout procedure moves from adjustment to growth, the international financial institutions must work with Third World governmental policy changes as well as financial flows.

In examining the role of international financial institutions in the debt crisis, remarks will be limited to a perception of three institutions: the International Monetary Fund, the International Bank for Reconstruction and Development (the World Bank), and the Inter-American Development Bank, which is the largest of the multinational regional development banks.

The Fund and the World Bank were created in a conference held in 1945 in Bretton Woods, New Hampshire, attended by the world's leading statesmen and economists of the time. Out of their endeavors emerged the concept that the world's financial system needed two institutions, linked by their common work within the world monetary and trade systems, to work together toward a more stable pattern of growth.

---

*Michael E. Curtin is the executive vice president of the Inter-American Development Bank. A manager with extensive corporate experience in Latin America, he is a member of the advisory council for the Helen Kellogg Institute for International Studies at Notre Dame.

As outlined in its articles of agreement, the purposes of the International Monetary Fund are:

(1) To promote international monetary cooperation through a permanent institution which provides the machinery for consultation and collaboration on international monetary problems.

(2) To facilitate the expansion anᵈ balanced growth of international trade, and to contribute thereby to the promotion and maintenance of high levels of employment and real income and to the development of the productive resources of all members as primary objectives of economic policy.

(3) To promote exchange stability, to maintain orderly exchange arrangements among members, and to avoid competitive exchange depreciation.

(4) To assist in the establishment of a multilateral system of payments in respect of current transactions between members and in the elimination of foreign exchange restrictions which hamper the growth of world trade.

(5) To give confidence to members by making the Fund's resources temporarily available to them under adequate safeguards, thus providing them with opportunity to correct maladjustments in their balance of payments without resorting to measures destructive of national or international prosperity.

(6) In accordance with the above, to shorten the duration and lessen the degree of disequilibrium in the international balances of payments of members.

As originally outlined in its articles of agreement, the purposes of the World Bank are:

(1) To assist in the reconstruction and development of territories of members by facilitating the investment of capital for productive purposes, including the restoration of economies destroyed or disrupted by war, the reconversion of productive facilities to peacetime needs, and the encour-

agement of the development of productive facilities and resources in less-developed countries.

(2) To promote private foreign investments by means of guarantees or participations in loans and other investment made by private investors; and when private capital is not available on reasonable terms, to supplement private investment by providing, on suitable conditions, finance for productive purposes out of its own capital, funds raised by it, and its other resources.

(3) To promote the long-range balanced growth of international trade and the maintenance of equilibrium in balances of payments by encouraging international investment for the development of the productive resources of members, thereby assisting in raising productivity, the standard of living, and conditions of labor in their territories.

(4) To arrange loans made or guaranteed by it in relation to international loans through other channels so that the most useful and urgent projects, large and small alike, will be dealt with first.

(5) To conduct its operations with due regard to the effect of international investment on business conditions in the territories of members and, in the immediate postwar years, to assist in bringing about a smooth transition from a wartime to a peacetime economy.

In brief, the International Monetary Fund (IMF) has as its basic objective the surveillance of the short-term economic problems of its member countries, focusing primarily on the imbalances which occur from time to time in the current account balances, adjustment in trade flows, and macroeconomic issues, primarily exchange rates and monetary and fiscal policies which impact on these areas. Receiving its funds through its member countries, the Fund makes resources available under various short-term mechanisms—after reaching agreement with the countries as to the adjustments which must be followed in order to bring the account balances into alignment with the basic economic variables.

The World Bank, in contrast to the IMF, is in essence a "development bank," which lends funds on significantly longer terms, traditionally to finance projects and investments of a productive nature. Its loans assure the availability of the foreign exchange resources necessary to carry out investment projects of high priority in the developing member countries.

At the end of the Bretton Woods Conference, John Maynard Keynes is reported to have said that, as time goes on, the Bank will act more like the Fund and the Fund will act more like the Bank. While the economic prophecy often attributed to Keynes is widely admired, there are at least two events that can be cited as having made this prophecy more likely.

When the United States, as a matter of its own economic policy, delinked its currency from the gold standard in 1972, the rules of the game, insofar as the world monetary system is concerned, were forced to change. Subsequently, the dramatic increase in the price of oil coupled with the emergence of the Eurodollar market, the increase in the ability of the financial system to generate means of payments not directly linked to national monetary constraints, and the communications revolution all joined in creating a growth in the means of payment which greatly outpaced the production of goods and services for which payments were being made.

Thus, the role of the IMF in monitoring the internal and external economic variables, current accounts, trade balances, flows and trade, etc., became increasingly complex during the 1970s and 1980s.

At the same time, the World Bank found that, inevitably, its role in assisting its borrowing member countries also underwent changes. The World Bank, created largely to finance the reconstruction of Europe, found that other regions of the world needed attention, and its traditional mode of specific project financing was less than suitable in confronting the obstacles to development present in its new borrowers.

EVOLUTION OF THE DEBT CRISIS

The debt crisis which erupted on the front pages of our newspapers in August 1982 was sudden in its appearance; however, its arrival was understood to be inevitable.

Most of the countries in Latin America had experienced substantial real rates of growth from the 1960s to the 1980s, a growth partially financed by enormous borrowings from foreign commercial banks as they recycled the petrodollars deposited by the oil exporting countries after 1983. If an "average debt profile" of a Latin American country could be constructed (which is a contradiction in itself), the profile in 1980 would be characterized by short-term, variable-rate commercial bank borrowings by both the public and private sector, most of which had been utilized to finance rising consumption or in long-term investment projects.

Since 1980, the economic models which have been followed by the countries in Latin America have ranged from rigid socialism to almost "laissez-faire" capitalism. However, the common denominator of their economic policy making has favored a very active role for the public sector in production of goods and services, often manifest by centralist planning through the creation of planning ministries and national development banks, often sector-driven.

The ideological and analytical basis for a predominant number of these economic models was set forth by the "structuralist" theorem expressed by the Economic Commission for Latin America (CEPAL) founded by Raul Prebisch. The structuralist model was based on an observation that, when the terms of trade in Latin America were worsening vis-à-vis those of the developed countries, the region had no choice but to begin to produce its own goods. This would decrease its need for imports and reduce its dependency on the developed countries, while internally generating its own dynamics of growth.

The idea of turning inward for growth through integration of the Latin American economic sphere appealed to the nationalistic feelings of Latin America, and the modernization of the economy became equated with the industrialization of the economy. As part of this strategy, important advantages were granted to the private sector in the form of over-valued exchange rates. In addition, the subsidizing of interest rates, which made capital fictitiously cheap in real economic terms, resulted in the suppression of private financial markets. This state of affairs created a situation in which access to credit became a function of influence, rather than of economic efficiency.

The centralization of control and economic planning had great appeal to the public sector, expanding its role in political/economic decision making while providing jobs for an ever-increasing bureaucracy driven by political influence.

Thus, when the debt crisis erupted, Latin America was faced with having to adjust both private and public structural rigidities which had evolved and become stationary for over two decades. During this time, Latin America had experienced a growth rate in real terms in excess of 5.5 percent per annum over the twenty-year continuum.

Working the Way Out

When the world economic milieu went through its recession adjustment in 1980–1981, characterized by dramatic drops in international trade, tightening of credit, lowering of worldwide inflation, etc., it was obvious that dramatic adjustments were in order.

The IMF took the lead for two basic reasons. First and foremost was a perception commonly held in 1982 that the crisis was one of liquidity. Second, the IMF was, in fact, the most appropriate institution to deal with short-term liquidity problems. Indeed, one of the basic economic treatises written in 1983 by the Institute of International Economics sustained in its model that, should OECD countries grow on an average of three to four percent, then under certain conditions the major debtor countries of Latin America could, in fact, work their way out of their debt problem by mid-1992. Unfortunately, it has not worked out that way. Now, there is a generally accepted realization that the debtor countries of Latin America cannot realistically depend upon the engine of OECD growth and debt rescheduling to work through the crisis.

The early rescheduling of Latin American debt, and, indeed, those today, follow a very similar pattern. The debtor country, finding its credit lines restricted and its external account balance in extreme disequilibrium, notifies the IMF that it wishes to enter into consultations in order to obtain credits. Concurrently, the country indicates to the commercial banks that, due to its foreign exchange shortage, it will be unable to service its commercial debt obligations in a timely manner. The IMF then sends a mission to the country to begin consultations with the economic authorities. The IMF technicians discuss those adjustments which they feel are necessary, in order that the country qualify for IMF funding. When these consultations have progressed to a sufficient level, the major commercial bank creditors form a committee to deal with the rescheduling of the commercial bank indebtedness. The economic advisory team, formed by the banking committee, then travels to Washington where it enters into conversations with the IMF, the World Bank, and in the case of Latin America, the Inter-American Development Bank.

These meetings, which generally take two to three days, are basically an interchange of views on the economic situation of the country, together with an estimation of the financing gap in the current accounts over the next two to three years. The net financial flows of the international financing institutions, based on present as well as probable future operations, are then calculated, the result of which leads to the discovery, inevitably, of a gap to be financed. After further analysis of the figures, a country presentation is generally scheduled before the full committee in New York.

These presentations follow a similar pattern. The committee meets to hear the report of its economic advisory committee in the morning of the first day. That afternoon, presentations are made by the IMF, then the World Bank, and then the Inter-American Development Bank. These presentations address the economic prospects for the country and the contribution of each one of the international financing institutions to help solve the problem. On the second morning, the economic team of the country makes its presentation to the commercial banks, and then, as the saying goes, "The fun begins."

The "fun" is the negotiation of how the package is to be structured, and who is going to finance what—the country, the international financial institutions, or the commercial banks.

The country in question, as is natural, tries to seek the maximum amount of funds possible, while the commercial banks, as is natural, try to restrict their commitments to a minimum. At this point in the process, official bilateral and export credit funding has not played a major role. Without going into further detail, the process culminates with a compromise which reflects what is "doable," not always what is optimal.

Many critics of this process have observed that it often results in the application of orthodox IMF prescriptions, based upon austerity, reduction of imports, cuts in fiscal budgets, and inflationary changes in the exchange rate, all of which lead to economic stagnation, which in turn, lowers economic and social welfare in the member countries. Others have observed that it has only been through such shock treatment that a government may regain control of its economy, present and future.

It is inappropriate at this time to make a value judgment as to the final result of the process. However, there is general agreement that, at least in the majority of the countries, a move has been made from Phase I, orthodox adjustment, and there is firm involvement in Phase II, restoration of growth.

Most observers have indicated that Secretary of the Treasury James A. Baker's proposal for a "Program for Sustained Growth," presented at the 1985 IMF–World Bank annual meeting in Seoul, Korea represented a dramatic change in the U.S. perception of the debt problem. Even though the announcement was dramatic, Secretary Baker's proposal was much more evolutionary than revolutionary. There is now the beginning of yet another evolutionary change in the perception of how the debt crisis will be handled in the future.

Most people do not understand and appreciate the tremendous and dramatic efforts which have been made by the Latin American countries in adjusting their economies. The steps which have been taken in country after country to change their basic economic models are considerable. For example, Ecuador's program to liberalize its economy, particularly with respect to tariffs, exchange rates, and the pricing mechanism, has done away with 56 years of monetary and financial rigidity. In Brazil, the adaptation of the "Plan Cruzado" has reversed the system of indexation which had been in place for almost 20 years. The dismantling of public sector enterprises in Chile has reversed a trend which began in the early 1960s with the creation of Corparacion de Fomento (CORFO), and most recently the utilization of debt-equity swaps has reduced the foreign exchange debt by almost one billion U.S. dollars. Mexico's recent agreement with the IMF and commercial banks, together with its becoming a member of the General Agreement on Tariffs and Trade (GATT), represents a dramatic change of historical political/economic practice.

With regard to the Inter-American Development Bank and its role in the coming years, it is important to review its historical role. Traditionally the Bank has maintained a specific project financing orientation similar to that of the World Bank. Since its inception 26 years ago, through specific project financing and through the modality of global loans, the Bank has loaned nearly 32.6 billion dollars to its member countries to finance approximately 106 billion dollars worth of investments. This means that borrowing member countries have contributed almost 73.5 billion dollars of their own funds as counterpart to the Bank's loans.

During the last two years, when the Latin American member countries were undergoing these dramatic adjustments, the rate of growth in lending, disbursements, and the rate at which member countries provided local counterpart funds slowed significantly.

At the current time, the Bank is engaged in negotiating with its member countries the Seventh General Increase in Resources, or Seventh Replenishment, as it is called. These negotiations will determine both the size and nature of the lending program during the years 1987 to 1990. While the negotiations have not yet been completed, it appears likely that the Bank will be able to significantly expand its lending operations, increasing them from approximately 12 billion dollars over the last four years to nearly 25 billion dollars during the next four years.

In addition, the member countries have indicated that the Bank should play a great role in encouraging the countries of the region to restore sustained economic growth and social progress. This will result in the Bank's expanding its activity in what are called "sector loans." These loans are designed to disburse more rapidly—over two to three years—than the traditional project loans which disburse over four to six years. In addition, sector loans are policy-related. This structure is dependent upon an analysis of the constraints and structural rigidities present in a given economic sector, and the type of reforms, including policy reforms, necessary to remove the bottlenecks and constraints to development.

The challenge facing the Bank and its member countries in entering into this new type of lending can only be met through a more candid dialogue between the Bank and its member countries.

The Bank's programming process with each member country has been evolving over recent years and will be further strengthened in order to fulfill the requirements of sector lending. While the member governments have not yet determined exactly how much of the lending program will be devoted to sector lending, it is anticipated that 20 to 25 percent will be utilized for this purpose during the next four years; that is, a range of 4 to 6 billion dollars.

The Bank is not abandoning its traditional role in financing investments of high priority which promote long-term economic development and social progress. The Bank's member governments are fully aware that this primary role should continue and grow. However, there is also the recognition that the Bank must address the pressing needs of renewed sustainable growth as part of its mission during the next four years.

Entering into sector lending on the scale previously indiated will not only require a closer coordination with borrowing member countries, but will also necessitate closer coordination with the other multilateral and bilateral financial institutions, as well as with the commercial banks.

The interdependency of policy changes and financial flows to borrowing member countries should not be viewed with alarm. Each of the Inter-American Development Bank's countries is unique, and each economy has its own characteristics and problems which must be addressed. Similarly, each of the financial institutions has a unique role to play in providing the funds necessary to renew sustainable growth. Thus, each country and each institution must work together, coherently and constructively, in order to meet the challenges that lie ahead. To do otherwise would only result in a continuance of the present unacceptable situation.

The Vulnerability of Multinational Banks to an International Shock

HENRY S. TERRELL[*]

> Crisis: An unstable condition in political, international, or economic affairs in which an abrupt or decisive change is impending.
>
> *The American Heritage Dictionary,*
> Second Edition, 1982

A Few Lessons from Recent History

The current debt difficulties of many developing countries first attracted attention in August 1982 when the government of Mexico announced it would be unable to make timely payment on its outstanding debts to commercial banks.[1] In a relatively short period of time a number of major borrowers indicated a need to restructure the contractual obligations on their external debt. In ensuing years the external situation of many indebted developing countries, and the broad exposures of multinational banks to these countries, has been referred to by observers as the international debt crisis.

The process of renegotiating and restructuring external debt of major developing countries has continued on a virtually non-stop basis since the late summer of 1982, hardly conforming to the dictionary definition of a "crisis." While

---

[*]Henry S. Terrell is a senior economist at the Federal Reserve Board. He has served as a visiting scholar at the Federal Reserve Bank of San Francisco and the Fletcher School of International Law and Diplomacy, and published widely on international banking and public issues.

semantic debates should not impede important efforts to implement effective policy measures, the inappropriate use of terminology and excessive hyperbole can impair the dialogue needed to solve the underlying problem. In particular it can lead to the search for short-term "quick fixes," which do not address the underlying fundamental problems and which may have long-term consequences that are not properly analyzed.

One lesson that has been learned in recent years is that the vulnerability of banks to shocks from their international exposures is a condition that will remain with us over a relatively long time horizon. The debt overhang for many countries is quite large, and it is unrealistic to expect that the need to negotiate and restructure debt for some group of countries will disappear in the near future. Therefore, it seems more appropriate and constructive to refer to this situation as a problem rather than as a crisis.

A second lesson from the recent period is that while many similarities exist among individual debtor countries, each country has its own unique circumstances in terms of external trade relations, debt, level of development, and dependence on imported oil or reliance on particular commodity or industrial exports. Therefore, uniform formulas or simple policy rules will probably not work to lessen instability and vulnerability in all cases. An important corollary to this lesson is that the external situation of individual countries can change very quickly. Therefore, in assessing bank vulnerability to international shocks, it is preferable to consider bank exposure to individual or small groups of countries rather than focusing on broad country aggregations. For example, data aggregates covering all developing countries include Taiwan and Korea whose external accounts are currently in reasonably good shape.

A third broad lesson from the recent experience is that countries that have followed outward-looking, export-oriented policies have tended to fare better than countries that followed inward oriented policies of import substitution, and thus have caused less systemic vulnerability. The appropriate policy mix includes the avoidance of overvalued exchange rates which retard export growth, stimulate imports, and can lead to problems of capital flight.[2]

A fourth lesson is that the gains from cooperative behavior appear to outweigh any possible gains from unilateral action in mitigating vulnerability. The Baker Plan, which is more a set of principles to guide the negotiations than a detailed plan, is based on these gains from cooperative behavior. Under the Baker Plan each of the three major participants—banks, borrowing countries, and official agencies—would pursue a course of action that might not appear to be directly in its own perceived self-interest. Banks would lend more, expanded official credits would be forthcoming, primarily from the World Bank, and indebted countries would pursue policies they might not otherwise undertake. The cumulative effect of these three actions would be growth oriented, and hopefully in the collective interests of all parties.

Finally, a fifth and very important lesson in assessing bank vulnerability to international shocks is that the value of a bank's assets seldom goes from par to zero in any one year. As any borrower's condition deteriorates, a bank might have to write off (or reserve) some proportion of its exposure to that borrower. Conversely, and not infrequently, as a borrower's condition improves, the bank may actually recover some of the value of its outstanding loan. The need to consider fractional changes in the value of bank assets is particularly important in considering bank exposure to major developing countries with many private nonbank and bank subborrowers, some of whom have assets outside the country to service their indebtedness.

THE EXPOSURE OF MAJOR U.S. BANKS

Against this broad backdrop it is useful to review the historical record of the exposure of major American money center banks to developing countries. These major money center banks tend to be the most exposed of all U.S. banks, and thus the most vulnerable to any shocks to the system. In addition, the most comprehensive data are readily available for these banks.

Table 1 provides a historical perspective on the exposure of major U.S. money center banks to the aggregate of all non-

TABLE 1

Cross-Border Exposure of Nine U.S. Money Center Banks to Non-OPEC Developing Countries
($ Billions)

Date	Total Exposure to Non-OPEC Developing Countries[a]	TOTAL CAPITAL		EXPOSURE AS PERCENT OF CAPITAL	
		Accounting	Adjusted to Market Valuation[b]	Accounting Capital	Capital Adjusted to Market Valuation
1977 December	28.7	18.4	15.1	156	190
1978 December	31.7	20.0	15.3	159	208
1979 December	38.6	21.9	15.8	176	244
1980 December	49.0	24.0	17.9	204	274
1981 December	58.4	26.1	18.6	224	314
1982 December	66.4	29.0	20.1	229	330
1983 December	65.9	31.5	22.8	209	289
1984 December	66.4	36.9	26.6	180	250
1985 December	62.4	42.3	38.0	148	164
1986 March	61.3	43.6	46.2	141	133
June	59.3	44.2	46.1	134	129

[a]Exposure equals gross claims adjusted for external guarantees.

[b]Adjusts accounting capital (equity, loan-loss reserves, and debentures) to ratio of market price of stock to book value as reported by Salomon Brothers. Adjustment excludes Continental Illinois.

Source: Country Exposure Lending Survey.

OPEC developing countries. Exposure is defined as the banks' total claims on these countries adjusted for any external guarantees. Between year-end 1977 and year-end 1982 total exposure of these banks to developing countries increased more than 130 percent while their reported capital increased by about 50 percent. Therefore, exposure relative to the banks' reported capital increased by over 50 percent. By any reasonable measure this increased exposure relative to capital dramatically increased the vulnerability of these U.S. banks to any financial shock emanating from developing countries during that period.

Between year-end 1982 and mid-year 1986 the pattern changed dramatically. Absolute exposure of these banks to the aggregate of all developing countries declined by $7 billion, or 11 percent, while their aggregate reported capital increased by about one half. Therefore, the exposure ratio declined to 134 percent of capital by mid-year 1986, considerably less than the exposure ratio at year-end 1977. The reported decline in absolute exposure of these banks has not resulted entirely from a payback of loans by these developing countries. Some proportion (perhaps $1–2 billion) has resulted in loan writeoffs; some may have resulted from sales of assets to other investors as part of debt-equity swaps in Chile, Brazil, Mexico, and the Philippines; and a small proportion may have resulted from the exercise of guarantees by official agencies such as the U.S. Export–Import Bank.

The trend in large U.S. bank exposure to individual major developing countries has followed the pattern for the aggregate noted in table 1. Large U.S. bank exposure to Mexico increased from 32 percent of capital in December 1977 to 45 percent at year-end 1982, and then declined to 31 percent by mid-year 1986. For Brazil, the ratio rose from 40 percent of capital at year-end 1977 to 49 percent in 1982, and subsequently declined to 36 percent at mid-year 1986.

The calculations noted above are based on one measure of bank capital, an accounting estimate of the net worth of the banks based upon the accounting value of the banks' assets and non-capital liabilities. However, an alternative measure of the net worth of these institutions is provided by the price that investors are willing to pay to hold the shares of these banking corporations. Equity prices reflect a number of variables in addition to an estimate of the true value of a company's domestic and international assets minus the value of its non-equity liabilities. The viability of the firm as a going concern, its future prospects for profitability, and the discount factor equity investors place on expected future earnings are also important considerations.

Despite these conceptual issues, the equity markets are making an alternative evaluation of the "net worth" of these banking institutions. In table 1 this evaluation is explicitly taken into account by adjusting the accounting estimate of the banks' capital by the ratio of the market price of the banks' stock to "book value." (Book value is essentially the accounting estimate of the per share value of the bank). As shown implicitly in table 1, the equity market discounted the book value of bank equity by about one-sixth in December 1977, that discount widened to an average of about one-third between December 1979 and December 1984, and the recent rally in the market for bank stocks (as well as all stocks) has raised that ratio to about unity as of June 1986.

The adjustment to a market evaluation of bank capital allows an alternative estimate of the record of U.S. bank exposure relative to adjusted bank capital. As shown in the last column, the path of that ratio followed the general path of the unadjusted ratio, except that the adjusted ratio exhibited much wider fluctuations. Both ratios peaked at year-end 1982. However, on that date the adjusted exposure ratio was one and one-half times as great as the accounting ratio because of the equity market's relatively low evaluation of bank stocks. Because of the rise of the price of bank equities in early 1986, as well as reduced absolute exposure, the adjusted ratio has declined precipitously since 1982 to only about two-thirds of its level in December 1977.

No single measure of bank vulnerability to developing countries or any other exposure is, of course, completely adequate. Nevertheless, according to the conventional measures of aggregate exposure and the exposure to most major borrowers, vulnerability has declined substantially for money center U.S.

banks since December 1982. Alternative estimates based on the equity market's evaluation of bank capital suggests an even more pronounced decline in exposure ratios and vulnerability.

Assessing the Vulnerability of Banks to Shocks

The previous section attempted to quantify the general trend in total exposure of major U.S. money center banks to developing countries. As noted in the first section, however, the situation in individual countries can vary considerably. Therefore, it is more appropriate to develop a general methodology to estimate the impact of specific shocks on specific banks to determine which factors really influence banking vulnerability.

In assessing the vulnerability of banks to a particular shock from international lending, it is important to recall two lessons noted earlier. First, despite the fact that many observers refer to developing countries as a monolithic bloc, experience to date has shown that each country is unique and should be analyzed separately. Second, it is indeed exceptional for the value of any bank asset to go from par to zero in one year. This second lesson holds for the value of a loan to any domestic or international borrower.

To develop a methodology to analyze bank vulnerability, table 2A presents a simplified balance sheet of a hypothetical large banking institution called Bancorp. That bank has capital equal to 6 percent of its total assets, and loans to country X equal to one-third of its capital, or, alternatively, 2 percent of its assets. This would represent a very large exposure for a

TABLE 2A

Bancorp Balance Sheet

Assets		Liabilities	
Loans to X	$ 20	Deposits	$ 940
Other Loans	980	Capital	60
Total	$1,000		$1,000

bank to a single country. Table 2B provides an income statement for Bancorp. It pays 6 percent interest on deposit liabilities and earns sufficient interest on its loans to post a 12 percent after-tax return on capital after paying income taxes of 35 percent, which implies an after-tax return on its total assets of 0.72 percent. These figures are reasonable approximations for major U.S. banking companies.

In table 2C it is assumed that in one year Bancorp is subject to a major shock of receiving no interest on its exposure to country X and is also required to write down its exposure to country X by 10 percent. It was noted earlier that this sort of partial writedown in one calendar year would represent a major change in the status of country X. As shown in table 2C, interest paid on deposits remains the same, but interest earned on loans declines, leaving a reduced net interest income to the bank. The requirement to write off 10 percent of exposure to country X further reduces Bancorp's pre-tax income. After paying appropriate income taxes, the after-tax return to Bancorp on assets is 0.50 percent, a reduction of almost one-third from the no-shock case in table 2B.

How badly has Bancorp been hit by the shock? That is surely a matter of judgment, but the methodology developed above suggests that the bank could take that major shock from these actions by a single country and remain profitable. That bank might well have to reduce or eliminate its dividend, and would have a reduced flow of retained earnings to support fu-

TABLE 2B

Income Statement: Bancorp[a]

Interest on Loans	$67.48
–Interest on Deposits	56.40
Net Interest Income	11.08
–Writeoffs	—
Taxable Income	11.08
–Income Taxes	3.88
Post-tax Earnings	$ 7.20

[a]Assumes interest rate on deposits of 6 percent, after-tax return on capital of 12 percent, and effective income tax rate of 35 percent.

ture capital and asset growth, but the bank would remain profitable in response to that shock. Since the entire shock would be absorbed from the earnings flow, the stock of accounting capital of the bank would not be impaired except to the extent that there would be less in retained earnings for capital growth. Of course, equity markets might place other evaluations on the impact of that shock on the bank.

Table 2D examines the impact on Bancorp of that shock under certain alternative assumptions to help assess which factors are important in evaluating bank vulnerability. The alternative assumptions are: (1) an initially higher level of nominal interest rates on deposit liabilities of 12 percent, and (2) a higher effective rate of income taxation of 50 percent. The effect of the second alternative, higher income tax rates, is estimated under the assumption that interest rates charged on bank loans prior to the shock will be high enough such that the bank continues to earn a 12 percent after-tax return on capital. In the long run this is necessary for capital to be retained in the banking system.

The results of these simulations in table 2D are interesting. Higher nominal interest rates, everything else being equal, mean that the banks are indeed more vulnerable to shocks. It is more expensive for banks not to get interest on loans funded by 12 percent deposits than on loans funded by 6 percent deposits. Second, if the equilibrium conditions suggested above concerning bank earnings on capital hold, then lower income tax rates actually make banks more vulnerable to shocks. The

TABLE 2C

Income Statement of Bancorp if it Receives No Interest and Writes off 10 Percent of Exposure to X

Interest on Loans	$66.13
−Interest on Deposits	56.40
Net Interest Income	9.73
−Writeoffs	2.00
Taxable Income	7.73
−Income Taxes	2.71
Post-tax Earnings	$ 5.02

intuitive explanation is that higher income tax rates mean that a larger share of the impact of any negative shock is borne by the public sector. Therefore, a side effect of the recent tax reform, which lowered corporate income taxes, may well have been to increase bank vulnerability to international or domestic shocks.[3]

In summary, in any simulation of the vulnerability of individual or groups of banks to an international shock, the important parameters would appear to be: (1) the magnitude of the shock, that is, what actually happens; (2) the extent of individual bank exposure to the troubled borrower; (3) the earnings and capital of the banks; (4) the level of nominal interest rates if the shock includes deferred or omitted payment of interest; and (5) the tax rate and tax position of the banks in question.

LOWER NOMINAL INTEREST RATES: SOME ADDITIONAL CONSIDERATIONS

The previous section has noted why lower nominal interest rates may reduce the vulnerability of banks to an interna-

TABLE 2D

Impact of Alternative Assumptions on Bancorp Earnings

Assumption	Bancorp Earnings	Return on Capital
1. No shock	$7.20	12.00%
2. Shock of no interest for one year and requirement to writeoff 10 percent of exposure.	$5.02	8.37%
3. Same shock as #2, except deposit interest rate of 12 percent.	$4.29	7.15%
4. Same shock as #2, except tax rate of 50 percent.	$5.49	9.15%

tional shock. This section will further analyze the interest rate issue.

In theory, nominal interest rates contain two components. First, they contain a real component that is often considered a cost of utilizing borrowed capital, or, alternatively, a return to lenders for postponing consumption. The second component of nominal interest rates is some expectation for the future rate of inflation. When borrowers expect inflation, they are willing to pay higher nominal interest rates because inflation is reducing the real value of their debts. Lenders anticipating inflation will demand an interest premium to compensate them for the decline in the real value of their asset. In the real world these two components of interest rates are not directly observable and there is considerable debate among economists about how they should be measured if ideal data were available. Most economists agree that most of the variability in nominal interest rates reflects changes in expectations about future inflation.

In the previous section it was noted that it was less serious for banks not to be paid 6 percent interest than not to be paid 12 percent interest. The reason is that the difference in these nominal interest rates in large part reflects a changed expectation of future inflation. In the case of the 12 percent interest rates the lenders are being paid approximately 6 percent more to offset the decline in the real value of their assets expected to be caused by inflation.

According to data collected by the World Bank, approximately two-thirds of the external public debt of upper middle-income developing countries is on a floating rate basis. Interest rates on these credits are adjusted periodically as the market interest rates that lenders pay to attract funds change. The adjustment to interest rates means that the nominal cost of funds to the borrower, and nominal earnings to the banks, will follow changes in the expected rate of inflation with very little lag.

The use of floating rate borrowing instruments means that when nominal interest rates on loans increase because of higher expected inflation, the borrower's requirement to amortize the real value of that loan will be accelerated. The higher nominal interest payments are in fact compensating the lender *immediately* for the expected decline in the real value of the loan caused by inflation. The borrower can, of course, offset this *de facto* accelerated amortization in the real value of debt by going back to the market and borrowing additional funds. Such new borrowing requires that the borrower remain continuously creditworthy.

The rapid rise in nominal interest rates that occurred in the late 1970s and early 1980s had the effect of accelerating the real amortization schedule of the debts of many developing countries through the requirement that they pay higher nominal interest rates to compensate immediately for the erosion of the real value of their debts.

This concept can be made clearer by comparing the expected real amortization path of a standard Eurodollar bank loan contract under two alternative interest rate structures. A standard Eurodollar loan contract might involve a spread of about 1 percent over the Eurodollar deposit rate, a three-year grace period where only interest payments are made, and ten semiannual installments over the subsequent five years where interest is paid and nominal principal is amortized. If inflation were zero the entire real amortization of the loan would occur in the five years of the scheduled amortization. However, some amortization of real principal will occur in the three years of the grace period if high nominal interest rates result from expectations about inflation.

To estimate the expected time flow of real amortization of a loan, we need some estimate of the expected future course of inflation to deflate the nominal principal outstanding on the existing loan. A very rough estimate of the expected future course of inflation over the life of the loan can be derived by using the term structure of interest rates to estimate the course of future nominal short-term interest rates, and then subtracting an estimate of the real component.

The expected path of future interest rates to be paid by a borrower on floating rate debt can be estimated by using the expectations model where current observed rates on long-term instruments are the product of interest rates on short-term instruments over the life of the loan. For example, the one-period interest rate in time period $t + 1$ which is expected at time t can be estimated as:

$$E_t(1 + r_{1t+1}) = \frac{(1 + r_{2t})^2}{(1 + r_{1t})} - 1, \text{ where,}$$

r_{2t} = the observed interest rate on assets of two period maturity at time t, and,

r_{1t} = the observed interest rate on assets of one period maturity at time t.

Data for Eurodollar deposits for maturities of up to one year are available in *World Financial Markets* published by Morgan Guaranty. Interest rate data for Eurodollar deposits of longer maturities were estimated from the yield curve for U.S. Treasury securities, adjusted upward by the differential between Eurodollar deposits and Treasury securities of one-year maturity. To determine interest rates paid by the borrower a spread of 1 percent was added to the banks' cost of funds. Expected nominal rates paid by the borrower were converted into estimates of future inflation by subtracting a constant 3 percent component to represent the real cost of using borrowed capital which is unassociated with inflation.

Chart 1 compares the time path of expected amortization for a standard Eurocurrency loan under the interest rate structure that existed in December 1977, and the structure in effect four years later in December 1981. Clearly the much higher rates of nominal interest prevailing at the latter date accelerated the real amortization of debt for many countries borrowing at floating rates. At rates prevailing in December 1977 about 13.5 percent of debt would have been effectively amortized during the three-year grace period, by year-end 1981 that proportion had risen to 27.4 percent. Clearly the rise in nominal interest rates that occurred during the late 1970s and early 1980s accelerated the amortization of international debt beyond the expectations of either borrowers or lenders and contributed to the vulnerability of the system.

Chart 2 repeats similar calculations for two more recent dates, September 1983 and September 1986, when nominal interest rates declined sharply. As shown in chart 2 during this period there was a *de facto* lengthening of the expected amortization of real debt, with the share of expected amortization

CHART 1

Expected Amortization of a Standard Eurodollar Bank Loan
Under Alternative Interest Rates: 1977 vs. 1981

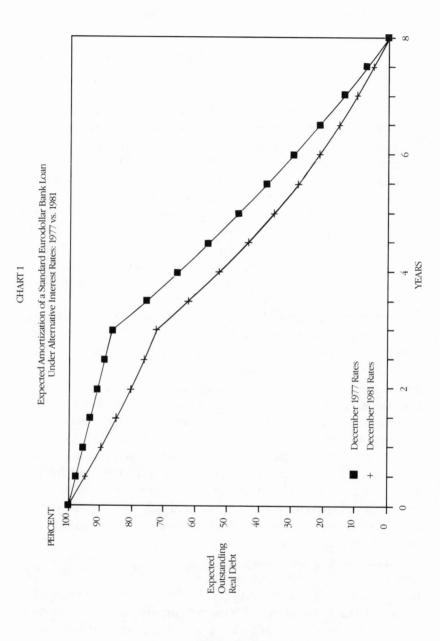

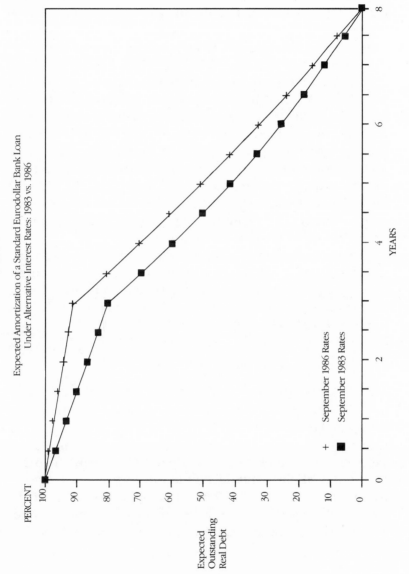

CHART 2

Expected Amortization of a Standard Eurodollar Bank Loan
Under Alternative Interest Rates: 1983 vs. 1986

PERCENT

Expected
Outstanding
Real Debt

+   September 1986 Rates
■   September 1983 Rates

YEARS

during the grace period of a standard Eurodollar loan declining from 19.7 percent to 9.1 percent. Everything else being equal, this reduces the need for borrowers to come to the market to seek financing to avoid having to amortize the real value of their outstanding debts. Thus lower nominal interest rates, if sustained, should reduce the vulnerability of the system to problems by reducing this hidden acceleration of the amortization of real debt.

The calculations underlying charts 1 and 2 are, of course, hypothetical. They involve a number of unresolved technical issues about the validity of using information in the term structure of current interest rates to predict future interest rates, problems of disaggregating nominal rates into real and inflationary components, the reliability of using *ex ante* nominal interest rates to predict future inflation, and the simplifying assumption about a constant real rate of interest on external debt. The calculations underlying charts 1 and 2 abstract from these important technical issues to focus on one simple result. The important conclusion derived from these two charts is that the reduction in nominal interest rates that has occurred in recent years, everything else being equal, has had the impact of lengthening the effective maturity of the floating rate debts of the developing countries.

Conclusion

This paper has reviewed some of the factors that have influenced the vulnerability of banks to international shocks. For major money center U.S. banks the reduction in their absolute exposures has combined with their capital growth to reduce their vulnerability. The decline in nominal interest rates in recent years has also had an important impact on systemic fragility by reducing the cash flow burden on borrowing countries associated with amortization of their real indebtedness.

NOTES

This paper represents the views of the author and should not be interpreted as reflecting those of the Board of Governors of the Federal Reserve

System or other members of its staff. An earlier version of this paper was presented to a session of the annual meeting of the Financial Management Association in New York on October 17, 1986. I am indebted to Robert S. Dohner of The Fletcher School for analysis and graphics in the section, "Lower Nominal Interest Rates."

1. Actually Poland and several other smaller debtors had been unable to service their obligations prior to August 1982, but the announcement by Mexico changed the focus from individual isolated cases to a potential systemic problem.

2. For a detailed consideration of these issues, see Jeffrey D. Sachs, "External Debt and Macro-Economic Performance in Latin American and East Asia," *Brookings Papers on Economic Activity,* 2 (1985), pp. 524–573.

3. Other more technical aspects of the tax reform bill, such as the repeal of the provisions allowing banks to establish tax-deductible loan-loss reserves against expected future losses, the requirement that past loan-loss reserves be recaptured in taxable income, the requirement that interest on deposits used to finance state and local securities acquired after August 7, 1986, no longer be counted as a deduction against taxable income, and the reduction from 10 years to 3 years for the period in which operating losses at banks may be carried *back* against operating profits, all limit the flexibility of banks to adjust the timing of their losses against their taxable income. These changes will reduce the share of any shocks that are borne by the public sector, and thus will increase the vulnerability of the banking system to such shocks.

The Retrenchment of Multinational Banks

LEONARD MARKS JR. *

In attempting to describe the strategic implications of the horrendous international debt situation for commercial banks, I will neither apologize for the commercial banks nor make them the whipping boy. They have already suffered enough in this country from the loan problems of the "oil patch" and the farm belt institutions that have had implications throughout the Central and Eastern banks as well.

Commercial banks are multinationals too—not just because they have offices throughout the world, not just because their normal function is to provide some of the fluid for trade, but because they are large international organizations that train people in various countries and have significant influence beyond the purely financial aspects.

More than a third of the international debt is owed to U.S. commercial banks. It is not important how the banks got into this problem, the fact is that they are there, and the issue is how to get out of it. The Bretton Woods Institutions are neither representative nor capable of dealing adequately with current problems. The debt problem is systemic, and systemic change is needed to avoid recurrences.

---

*Leonard Marks Jr. has recently retired as executive vice president of Castle & Cooke, Inc. Previously a professor of finance at Stanford University, he has served as the assistant secretary of the United States Air Force and been associated with the Times Mirror Company and Wells Fargo & Company.

The environment in which banks operate in this country has not only presented opportunities for these banks, as John Caron noted, but much more intense competition than ever before. Foreign banks such as the Bank of Japan own, either entirely or substantially, many large banks in California and on the East Coast. Moreover, competition is no longer just among banks. Savings and loans have been given greater authority, and deregulation has allowed credit unions to invade what used to be the province—almost the monopoly—of the banks. Investment bankers, by their dealing in commercial paper, can more efficiently transfer credit from a corporate provider to a corporate borrower. These other financial intermediaries have substantially reduced the role of commercial banks in normal consumer, trade, and working-capital financing in this country. This has resulted in a major structural change in commercial banks.

At the same time these changes were taking place, the banks were recycling petro dollars and lending money for what should have been perceived as long-term financing of development—not the normal short-term trade or working-capital loan—but with funds that were short term or at most intermediate term. This violated a fundamental principle: Do not borrow short to invest or lend long. Savings and loans still suffer from the time deposits, which they thought would continue at certain rates and encouraged them to lend long-term based on those rates before the cost of their money skyrocketed. Some lessons must be learned, and relearned.

What, then, might be the strategy to get out of—or, at least, to alleviate—the international debt problem?

Some have suggested that banks declare these loans nonperforming and suspend interest payments, arguing that such compromises have been made in the past under similar circumstances. They cite, for example, real estate loans made by banks and bank-sponsored Real Estate Investment Trusts (REITs). This alternative would be possible if these loans were a smaller proportion of the total and were distributed among more banks, as were the real estate loans. But these loans are larger and they are concentrated in a very few institutions. Writing them off could wipe out equity, or at least significantly reduce it, at a time when the regulatory authorities are saying commercial banks must increase their capital ratios. The required ratio of capital to risk assets or to deposits (the liabilities) was 4.5 percent. Now it is 6 percent and it will be increased to 8 percent, which will pose a significant problem for the banks.

Real estate loans were made by individual institutions to groups of individual borrowers or to companies in this country. It was possible to negotiate the use of equity in land or buildings, knowing that inflation and a resurgence of real estate values would enable eventual repayment even though opportunity costs would be high. In some small communities, properties actually were taken over by financial institutions. Obviously, this is not possible with sovereign nations and, besides, there is not that much "equity" available.

Commercial bankers do need to be imaginative in pursuing opportunities such as the Bankers Trust arrangement in Chile. Hopefully, they would not be too aggressive in seeking deep discounts. Such action could result in discrim nation later when those assets and investments increase in value and the government and host country business people realize they have given away a "piece of the store" in these deep discounts. But this is a matter of relative negotiating strength, and countries have proven to be much more skillful in their negotiations now than in the past.

What might happen that would alleviate the debt problem on both sides? This global problem requires multilateral intervention by governments and supranational financial institutions. Replacing individual loans with transferable debt securities could be one step. Initially, the security may be no more transferable or salable than a loan, but it provides a mechanism which, over time, could provide some liquidity—admittedly at a price. Obviously, there must be some value behind such securities other than the relatively poor credit of the individual debtor nation. Determining that value will take statesmanship on the part of governments and the multilateral financial institutions. If, for example, the supranationals and the developed nation governments were to provide guarantees for a portion of the debt, then the full loans would not be classified. This would help solve the problem, at least for the

U.S. commercial banks, by acknowledging that there is some value guaranteed. This would avoid the fiction that, as Glade cautioned, commercial banks are just playing a game in not writing off these loans. The problem with writing them off is that they are so large.

Some steps could be taken, however, to alleviate the commercial bank problems and, at the same time, permit a reduction or elimination of interest rates. A compromise on some of the principal payment, even if difficult to swallow for multilateral financial institutions and developed nation governments, would indicate an intention to help.

But repayment, scheduled over a long period of time, will depend on economic growth in the developing nations, which will require additional funds. The commercial banks should be in the business of short-term trade financing. If they are to be involved in the long-term financing of development, it should be through domestically based transnational corporations, by providing them with funds, which then can be invested and/or loaned in the foreign nation in ways that will benefit both the nation and the company. The company, with the protection of its capital, would provide protection for the loan that is beyond the normal trade financing of commercial banks.

This can be accomplished in other, more imaginative ways, but it will require a tremendous amount of flexibility and cooperation among supranationals, commercial banks, and sovereign nations.

Rescheduling as Ritual

*WILLIAM P. GLADE**

Academics cannot help but be mindful, as the academic year begins each fall, of the eventual days of reckoning that lie ahead. Hence, the high holy days of Rosh Hashana and Yom Kippur find a special resonance on university and college campuses. Our concern here, however, is not with these ancient rites, but with a much newer series of ceremonies, ceremonies that follow what by traditional reckoning is an especially odd calendric system. To be sure, a loose secular equivalent to the Day of Atonement comes around annually in the great gathering of the World Bank and the International Monetary Fund, where impecunious LDCs congregate to see if they are still inscribed in the Book of Life. But the debt rescheduling conferences that constitute the heart of the matter today come at irregular intervals scattered across the months and years, with borrowers and lenders coming together to discover whether each such occasion is a movable feast or a movable famine.

By referring to these occasions as rites and rituals, I do not mean to be either disrespectful or dismissive of the seriousness of these solemn assemblies of financial experts. After all, ministers of finance, prelates from central banks, and money-center monsignori all are there to attend to a practical, day-to-day business that they consider to be the essence of reality. To an increasing number of outside observers, however, the "real-

*William P. Glade is a professor of economics and past director of the Institute of Latin American Studies at the University of Texas at Austin. A recognized authority on economic development, he is a member of Notre Dame's Helen Kellogg Institute for International Studies Advisory Council.

244

ism" of the realm with which these pecuniary *peritos* grapple has features that resemble the magical realism of Borges. Richard Webb suggested as much when he spoke to us of the theatrical elements that abound in rescheduling conferences. Ritual lies also behind the stated necessity of maintaining the fiction of the debt and repayment obligations, though the purposes served thereby may escape the down-to-earth logic of the world in which most of us operate.

We can, however, catch much of the functioning and significance of the rescheduling exercises and bring together many of the instructive insights made in this volume if we fall back on a tradition of critical scholarship that owes much to the work of Thorstein Veblen and has since been fleshed out by anthropologists and other social scientists. At the center of this approach is recognition of the dual, almost schizoid, character of modern economic organization, which, in capitalist societies, derives its dynamics from an interplay between two quite different sets of phenomena: the pecuniary and the real. Together, these make up the two circular flows that appear near the beginning of almost every economic principles textbook. One is almost tempted to reach back to the analogy of Plato's cave, with monetary variables serving as the shadows of the more substantive real variables of land, labor, capital, and entrepreneurship. Relations between the two sets of phenomena are, however, more complexly interactive than the Platonic metaphor suggests. As Keynes made clear in his analysis of the Great Depression, the monetary shadows that flit across the market wall of a capitalist economy are not merely projected images of the real but are quite capable, if left to their own devices, of exercising a devastating control over the realm of real resources—a relationship that would have seemed bizarre or even perverse to Plato.

If the world learned anything from the experiences of the 1930s, the lesson might be summed up as the primacy of the real. That is, the participants in the national economy need not always subordinate the organization of the real factors of production to the peculiarities of monetary dynamics. On the contrary, contemporary macroeconomic management turns the historical experience of capitalism on its head and has, increas-

ingly in our century, learned to subordinate the realm of finance to the social orchestration of the real resources. The
same lesson was brought home by the remarkable post-war recovery of Germany and Japan, where financial systems—and a
great deal else—lay in ruins, but where the primary policy targets were set on real variables and financial requisites were
then mobilized accordingly. The great social inventiveness of
the post-World War II period also included the Bretton Woods
Conference, establishment of the International Bank for Reconstruction and Development and other multilateral lending institutions, and the Marshall Plan and bilateral aid programs. All of
these aimed at putting in center stage the real variables for
economic development, and accommodating these variables
with the financial arrangements that were judged necessary for
accomplishing the tasks at hand.

Despite the experience of the 1930s–1950s, we have not
yet begun to apply the same insight, at the international level,
to Third World debt. One cannot avoid noting that where the
U.S. economy and its foreign debt are concerned, Mr. Baker
has, in fact, tried to emancipate real growth factors from the
inhibitions of monetary variables by asking Japan and Germany
to lower interest rates and deflate their systems. At present,
however, there is markedly less enthusiasm for relaxing the financial constraints on LDC growth, no doubt partly out of a
fear that Third World regimes would in the end prove themselves unworthy and return to their wastrel ways of yore.

Why then are we trying so hard to preserve in one corner
of the international arena the very primacy of financial variables that has proved so unworkable elsewhere? Why are we
striving to maintain intact the social conventions of banking
when we are dealing with the management of the Third
World's external debt? On the one hand, the exercise would
appear to involve a continuous piling up of debts, the value of
which becomes ever more problematic and even partly illu-
sory, all the while maintaining the fiction that something important is happening and that it will all work out in the end.
On the other hand, the subordination of the real to the financial in this instance has entailed an enormous immediate social
opportunity cost in the form of idle production capacity and

the forfeiting of considerable growth in material output, to say nothing of immense human suffering. It seems likely, moreover, that the stresses of today's deteriorating social and economic conditions will produce a far more unstable and inhospitable investment environment in the future. To the extent that this happens, maintaining the volume of international financial flows will be increasingly difficult—the revenge of the real on the financial.

So far the cost-benefit assessments used in rescheduling exercises have emphasized the punitive risk to borrowers of reduced access to future financing should they fall delinquent, along with the lowered financial returns to lenders that would result from defaulting and write-offs. In its preoccupation with financial variables, however, this willingness to ignore the costs being shouldered by virtually all other participants in the system, including the multinational corporations, betrays a frame of reference for policy making that has long since been discarded at the national level and has even, in the late 1940s and the early 1950s, been judged not very useful at the international level so far as the industrially advanced countries were concerned.

To account for this curiosity, the continuing subordination of real to financial variables in the case of LDC external debt, the metaphor of ritual is especially helpful, for if we look at the nature of ritual, we can at least begin to see where the problems lie and glimpse some of the ways out. This is so because the rituals of restructuring are simply not very satisfactory from a ritualistic point of view.

The first aspect of ritual to keep in mind is that all rites and ceremonies are, in some respects, a reenactment of the past. This comes through quite clearly in the accusatory aspects of rescheduling discussions, starting with their recitation of (past) contractual obligations and the actions that gave rise to the contractual relationships and continuing with what is usually an implicit recital of the misdeeds of the past. In the *et tu quoque* political discussion that both reveals and shapes popular understanding of the rescheduling situation, the moral dimension comes prominently to the fore, bankerly greed and incaution being weighed against the profligacy of governments that mismanaged borrowed resources. As a result, the rescheduling exercise has come to resemble an act of expiation. Of both parties is demanded some atonement for past sins. The bankers, according to the widespread public view, ought not to be bailed out of their mistakes by, in effect, socializing their losses. By the same token, there is a disinclination to reward inept (or corrupt) planners and other government officials in the borrowing countries by wiping the slate clean or formally lightening their burden. We can talk, as Anglicans and as Romans, about forgiving others their trespasses (though in practice we seem not to want to let people get away without paying for them). Perhaps, however, it is now time to take a more Presbyterian view of things and speak, with Scottish forthrightness about what really counts, of forgiving debts. Be that as it may, what would seem to matter today is less the review of conscience that mutual recrimination entails than the contrition of conditionality wherein the debtors, at least, resolve to mend their ways for the future.

A second relevant aspect of ceremony is that rituals nearly always reaffirm authority relationships. In this we may be coming quite close to ascertaining why the parties to the debt persist in these ultimately futile exercises—exercises that are futile both in terms of actually getting the money back and in terms of repairing the damage done by the past mishandling of transferred resources. On examination, the debt renegotiating sessions, whatever their instrumental outcome, can be seen to serve an important function in reasserting who holds and wields the authority of management in the world's monetary system. Though on a national level the goals of monetary authorities have been generally subordinated to the determination of other policy objectives, the international flow of funds constitutes a residual sphere of authority in which control of money is still the fundamental unit of economic power in commanding resources and shaping other policies, absent any overarching public authority. It is, in other words, a last redoubt of finance capital, whose power, on the domestic front, has been progressively trimmed by the correlation of social forces that dominates the modern state. Indeed, it is precisely this development that makes this residual exercise of financial authority at once so gratifying to the ritually empowered, the bankers, and so galling to the debtors, whose faith in the primacy of the pecuniary has long since begun to ebb.

A third, and often overlooked, element of ritual, however, is the one that may ultimately lead to a way out of the present predicament. Besides reenacting the past and reaffirming (and symbolically ratifying) authority relationships, rituals are, at the same time, a forward-looking celebration of community and of solidarity, a ceremonial expression, as it were, of the fact that the parties thereto are all in the same boat. It is precisely here that the rescheduling mechanism breaks down and fails as ritual. Let us reflect on this facet of the problem for a moment.

This is not the first time that there have been problems of overborrowing and default in Latin America. Since at least 1820, Latin America has over-borrowed—or, put a different way, bankers have over-lent—time and time again. Miscalculations have been made repeatedly and no one ever thought it strange that when this happened, debts would go into default and crisis would ensue. (This is not, as it happens, even the first time that people have thought of using debt-equity swaps as a solution. In the nineteenth century the Peruvian Bondholders Corporation took over the management and operation of the Peruvian railways when that country went into default on its foreign debt.) Always there was an expectation, confirmed by subsequent developments, that once lenders and borrowers had been sufficiently discomfited mutually profitable business relations could be resumed.

Nevertheless, although today's crisis is the same as these antecedents in some respects, it has managed to evoke very different sentiments. As never before, there is a feeling that things cannot simply be left to take their natural course. There is a sense that something special must be done this time to prevent the crisis from being resolved in the traditional way.

Why then, is this crisis different from all other crises, to paraphrase the question posed in one of the oldest rites still practiced? There is, I think, a major difference, one that clarifies why the current rescheduling mechanism fails, both as ritual and in its instrumental objectives. In the past, the major

Latin American financial crisis linked capital-exporting economies in which the investible surplus was not widely held with
the borrowing enclave economies. The repercussions were not,
for all their high drama, really widespread. Not many people
were involved in the lending exercise on the capital supply
side. Not many were beneficiaries on the borrowing side.
Thus, the implications on either side of the market were fairly
limited or confined. Further, most of the connections between
lending and borrowing countries were trade connections, to
which the investment connections were distinctly subsidiary.
In large measure, it was possible to carry on the trade connections notwithstanding temporary interruptions of the investment connections. Hence, crises could come and go. Some
people were hurt here and there and now and then. But it was,
all things considered, relatively easy to recover. The recupera-
tive powers of the real economy were, in fact, remarkable.

What has changed today is that both national and global
economic systems have grown much more highly articulated
and integrated, so that the consequences of miscalculation and
failure, of disrupted flows of transactions, are far more widespread than they ever were in the past. What is more, the processes of production and trade have become so interrelated on
a global scale that it is not just those who did the actual lending
and those who did the actual borrowing who feel the cost of
breakdown. Indeed, on both sides of the equation the primary
parties to the transaction are probably those most able to shelter themselves from the larger repercussions of failure. As the
notion of a failed ritual suggests, present-day economic realities have structured a common bonding that has run quite a bit
ahead of our current social sensibilities and political solutions.

If this is not a fantasized view of reality, then the only way
out for the countries of the developed and developing worlds
is to move toward what is in effect a compact that must include
not only groups, interests, and classes within countries but also
those that span the global economic system such as the multinational corporations and multilateral financial institutions on
whose operations the welfare of the developing countries depends so much. The rescheduling exercises that have taken
place so far have tended to understate the broad range of exter-

nalities that are involved, thanks to which the international debt is, in important respects, now a quasi-public good—like ritual itself. The present crisis has illustrated, for example, how closely tied are the interests of multinational corporations and the countries in which they operate. For better or for worse, since the former can neither readily extricate nor afford to write off their investments in the latter, they necessarily have a strong and direct interest in long-term reactivation of the debtor economies that is far from congruent with the narrower interests of creditor institutions. So, too, have millions of ordinary citizens in both lending and borrowing countries, people who had no voice at all in the financial transactions that originated the crisis. Furthermore, the appropriate time horizon for maximizing and optimizing decisions has changed considerably as a result of the breakdown of the early 1980s. Ineluctably, short-term commercial decisions have been transmuted into a time frame that is linked directly into the long-term viability of developmental programs in the Third World countries.

We cannot, in other words, afford to ignore what happens to current output and production levels, to overlook the drastic declines in the per capita income, to be blind to the chronic unemployment that has been intensified and aggravated by the present crisis. Neither can we be oblivious to long-term adverse repercussions on the global investment environment if this state of affairs continues. We need to remind ourselves that by their nature rituals are evocations of shared meaning and destiny, mechanisms for expressing a social compact, a recognition of common long-term interest. With this reminder, we can surely set about finding a new set of social conventions that will finally free the international developmental process from the thralldom of financial variables just as we have in large measure succeeded in doing domestically. If we are all, in fact, beneficiaries of the externalities that would flow from a settlement that reactivates development in the Third World countries, it should not be impossible to devise a means of distributing and absorbing the corresponding costs at an international level. A considerable amount of learning may be involved, however, in reaching a new decision-making framework that internalizes these externalities. Those, the lenders, who have worshiped at the altar of the market are now surrounded, abroad, by the debris of market failure, just as they are, at home, by the fallout from collapsing real estate markets in a good many urban areas. Those, the borrowers, who worshiped before the shrine of governmental intervention are likewise chastened by the all too abundant evidence of public-sector failure. With both idols dethroned, perhaps we can all begin to face the world with that uncomfortable clarity of vision that has always been the hallmark of our best prophets.

Discussion Summary

The seminar discussions of the international financial system reflected the same full spectrum of views as were expressed by those presenting and responding to papers.
Nicolas Barletta framed the quantitative dimensions:

Most studies indicate that in order to regain the needed growth with adjustment, Latin America needs about $20 billion per year of additional capital over at least the next three years. It is difficult to speak of a horizon beyond three to four years, but at that point we would expect solvency to be regained and those countries to be in a better position to service their debt. Within that period, if these countries cannot grow again and increase their savings, maintaining their consumption a little below the growth in gross domestic product in order that the savings can go into capital investment as well as servicing the debt, there really can be no future. If we accept that these countries will do their part in adjustment, then they will still need about $20 billion in new capital.

What will be the source of these funds? It is estimated that the multilateral institutions—the World Bank, the International Monetary Fund, and the Inter-American Development Bank— could at best provide $7 billion per year for these Latin American needs. Add perhaps another billion dollars a year of flight capital that could be repatriated, and another billion in multinational investments (an enthusiastic estimate since multinational investments have dropped significantly over the last five years), we are left with a shortfall of $11 billion.

253

ALTERNATIVES DISCUSSED

A number of alternatives designed to deal with the present debt overhang in a way that would assure the needed funds, not only to Latin America but to Africa and Asia as well, were discussed. Each is flawed in some way.

On rescheduling debt repayments, Ted Marks stated:

At this point, we have experience with the restructuring of debt, an experience that has become organized and has maintained the confidence in the international banking system in spite of the massive debt. Other approaches could well create confusion and lead to a loss of confidence in the system.

Gerard Keeley argued that banks should have an opportunity to be compensated in the long run for what they lose through restructuring in the short run.

One of the ingredients that is used domestically in many workout situations is a mechanism that, as things get better, banks that have cut interest rates, rescheduled, and capitalized past-due interest (at least informally), can capture some of these give-ups as the debtor countries work their way out of the problem. This makes rescheduling more palatable for the banks. It is both legally and technically possible on domestic loans and should work internationally.

The pressure for rescheduling existing debt could be relieved if funds could be recycled from surplus countries— particularly Germany and Japan. Paul Streeten commented:

If we total the surpluses across the world, there would be at least $100 billion a year that could be made available to the Third World. If these funds were recycled through an international investment trust with multilateral guarantees against devaluation and perhaps inflation, rather than being invested in instruments such as U.S. Treasury bills, there would be immediate benefits: (1) The surplus countries would be investing in something safe that does not depreciate with the dollar and inflation, (2) The Third World would receive the needed capital, (3) OECD countries would earn more foreign exchange, and even the United States would benefit because some of the money would be spent on American goods, (4) The world economy would benefit because growth could be resumed and inflation would be avoided.

Now, assuming that we were imaginative enough to mobilize these surplus country savings and recycle them, should we use them to bail out the profligate borrowers and the greedy lenders to relieve debt, or should we mobilize them for the benefit of, say, India or Pakistan, who have been much more careful in their expenditures and thus deserving of consideration. This would not brew a debt crisis in these countries in fifteen years because the interest rates would be moderate and the projects carefully selected. An interest-subsidy scheme could be grafted on to it.

Chandra Hardy was skeptical about recycling for a different reason.

While we in the United States see the debt crisis in global terms, to the rest of the world it is essentially a "neighborly" problem of the Western Hemisphere—U.S. deficits and Latin American debt. The Japanese have their "prosperity" sphere which is doing quite well. The United States' prosperity sphere is not. Europe and Japan are not likely to vote a good deal of money to the United States in order to deal with our essentially local problem. U.S. banks, Latin American countries, and the United States' economy with its deficits—budget and trade— and its large internal market will have to come to grips with the crisis.

Alejandro Foxley evaluated the effectiveness of debt-equity swaps as they relate to the Chilean experience.

In Chile, there are two windows involved in debt-equity swaps—one for Chilean nationals, the other for foreigners.

The one for Chilean nationals is being used in the following way. Suppose, a decade ago, you were the owner of a bank and you had succeeded in forming a large conglomerate based on external loans during the period of the boom, and used those monies to purchase industrial assets in the Chilean economy. When things went sour, you then used the firms that you had purchased as cash cows to pay back the loans, and to de-capitalize the firms with the monies moved abroad. As these firms went bankrupt, they had to be supported by the government, with additional capital investments to keep them in operation. For those companies that recovered, the government then offered options to purchase the shares. At that precise moment the window was opened.

The same people who had taken their money out of the country along with that of their depositors—through capital flight—now had the opportunity to buy that government-guaranteed debt at $.70 on the dollar. After paying a commission to the government, they converted this debt to equity at 100 percent. In this way, those who liquidated at a high price were buying back at a double discount—buying the debt at a deep discount, and converting to local shares which were underpriced since these firms were just recovering from a prolonged period of losses.

The other window is for the international banks that have an exposure in Chile. Some of these banks are selling Chilean credits in the international market. Foreign investors, often banks, then buy these credits at the discounted price and follow the same procedure for converting them to equity.

These swaps do not lead to new investment in firms that will increase the capacity of the country, nor to generate foreign exchange, nor even to generate more employment. There is no real contribution to the economy through these strictly financial transactions. There is a significant question as to their legitimacy.

Still, in the short run the debt-equity swaps are an interesting, ingenious operation that everyone seems to approve, certainly the Chilean government. In terms of political legitimacy for the Chilean population, they lead to damage in the longer run.

International guarantee programs were also discussed. Chris Korth stated:

If the member nations that sponsor and finance the multilateral institutions are unwilling to increase the capital of those institutions or if these institutions are unwilling to guarantee

Third World debt obligations, we will find that the private lenders within the developed world are going to tell their governments, "You have a great deal more clout than we do as well as much more capital. We cannot resolve this debt crisis alone. However, if you would guarantee a portion of these obligations, at least the new obligations, there would be an opportunity to exchange them in the market." Developed government guarantees would enhance the creditworthiness and value of these obligations, as well as assure their liquidity.

There was a good deal of discussion about the need to move formally to debt repayment, to the ability to repay. Dennis McCann stated:

Common sense indicates that repayment should be based on ability to pay. If you are looking for a principle here, we are not Kantian deontologists thinking that everybody must pay their debts. It does not happen in the real world.

One way to stipulate repayment based on ability to pay would be to tie debt service to exports. In good years, you accelerate repayments and retire more of the debt, in bad years there would be flexibility and room to maneuver simply because the funds for repayment are not there.

A creative form of tying repayment to the ability to repay could be through a form of income bonds. In his report of one of the small group meetings, Howard Harris stressed the need to deal with existing debt as a prelude to new funds.

If the solution to the present outstanding debt is any good, it will certainly facilitate the raising of new capital for development. A first inclination may be to say that maybe it is not so bad after all to write off all of the debt, although one would like to preserve some kind of a fiction that it is not really being written off. A debt instrument that would formally extend the maturities and tie debt service to the ability to repay while preserving this fiction would be a type of income bond.

Roy Crum outlined the advantages of income bonds.

On the one hand, we realistically do not expect that most of the debtor countries in the Third World will ever pay back their debt and that they will ever be considered as performing loans. On the other hand, to the extent that some of these countries will generate foreign exchange, they should be paying something. A financial instrument that would meet both criteria would be a perpetual fixed-rate income bond. Since nation states are assured to exist forever, the perpetuity is not a problem. Interest would be tied to the country's ability to generate foreign exchange. In case the country does not have foreign exchange in a given period, it would be foregone at that time and accumulate as principle. In this way, many of the problems could be finessed and a nasty default situation sidestepped.

Lee Tavis commented on the income bond alternative.

Income bonds would be an informal means of forgiving the debt. Debtor country exports, to which debt service would be tied, are a function of debtor country policies and global competitiveness. There would be no conditionality forced on the debtor government. Banks would give up their payment timing assurance and, if interest accumulates significantly, perhaps the assurance of ever receiving the capitalized interest. Still, for the banker, there is no possibility of default or danger of required loan markdowns, and a market would develop for these bonds, providing a liquid investment for the bank.

Ted Marks noted the danger of any formal forgiving of loans.

Forgiving even a portion of the debt would cause banks to be subjected to the same requests from domestic borrowers. This could drive a bank out of business. Even though the securities market could survive the share price impact, the confusion of restructuring the banking industry as other banks accept the business of their failed competitors, probably would collapse the public confidence in the financial system.

What to Do

As point and counterpoint of the various approaches to "solving" the debt crisis are discussed (in the seminar and

*in the daily media), we realize that a time is reached where
tradeoffs must be established. Many participants believe
that the point of action is rapidly approaching. One uniform
observation was that banks could not act alone. Chris
Korth stated:*

Bank officers are under tremendous pressure from depositors and shareholders who believe that bank management has
done a lousy job in this international area. The banks are likely
to encounter very strong resistance to the voluntary extension
of new money.

Moreover, as was noted, American banks are turning toward other markets. It is not just a "push" situation—the push
from the international debt crisis to redirect the banks' efforts
away from international lending. There is also a "pull," a very
strong pull in the United States from the dismantling of interstate banking rules, the lowering of obstacles to investment
banking, the competition from institutions like American Express, Sears, and others, and the extension by banks of debt
and credit cards across state lines. The banks in the United
States are faced with a very significant pull to focus much more
of their energies and capital on securing their domestic base
and taking advantage of the new rules which give them added
flexibility.

Ted Marks noted:

There must be standstill agreements reached on a total,
across-the-board basis. These must be engendered or sponsored by the Federal Reserve Bank, the multilateral organizations which create the give-and-take among the borrowers,
borrowing nations or corporations, government and quasi-
governmental institutions. Even then, the provision of additional loans to foster the essential growth will have to come on
a multilateral basis simply because of the risk involved and the
lack of available funds from commercial banks.

We need coordination and the participation of regulations
even in the capitalization of past-due interest. Interest cannot
be capitalized without a major change in regulation. The equity
component of U.S. banks is very fragile, it represents a small
percent of the deposits and assets. If the assets are increased by

increasing the size of the loan due to capitalized interest, the ratio of equity to assets is decreased. It is this ratio that the U.S. regulators believe is already too low. The regulatory authorities are watching the fragile equity of the banks in the United States and trying to buy time.

Any capitalization of interest must be a collective action. If banks do not operate collectively, or if the regulatory authorities do not agree, there will be chaos.

A number of participants, accepting the need for coordinated action, viewed the problem as one of political will rather than of insufficient alternatives or the ability to decide which is the most preferred. Howard Harris put it well:

The massive problems of debt and development are truly disheartening. An enormous change is needed which in turn requires a good deal of time. Politics, in many cases, does not permit this kind of time. Political institutions are very tender and highly short-term oriented. Those who feel cheated or believe that they have been underprivileged, whether consumers or investors, have the power to upset the political institutions of a country.

Ken Jameson reporting on one of the small group meetings presented the following scenario.

Although our group was strongly split, a number of people believe simply that the banks should "take the hit." This could be accomplished through a number of mechanisms, preferably with a minimum cost to the United States' taxpayer.

By whatever mechanism, if the banks take the hit there will be no new loans to Latin America. What are the real implications of this?

First, perhaps the private banking system is not the appropriate mechanism for transfers of funds for development. Development is simply not the role of a commercial bank.

Second, there would be a reduction and the elimination of the funds needed. For the residual need, however, the key issue is how a country can increase domestic savings as a means of financing its own development. This would necessarily require a redistribution of assets. Clearly, there would be a reduction in some kinds of expenditures, such as military.

The larger countries, such as Brazil, could turn to the international bond market as a source of funds. Those bond markets, then, could impose conditions on the debt, with restraints varying according to the market's perception of the risk associated with the various conditions.

Throughout the seminar discussions, a number of us have concluded that a policy of "going it alone" may be the desired direction. Richard Webb argued convincingly that new credit, or capitalized interest, would not serve Peru well in the long run.

At the end of the discussion, Andy McCollough remained unconvinced that we had dealt with the fundamental issue.

One of the things that I have observed here is something that I have observed in my study of finance over the years—a continuing ambivalence, or schizophrenic attitude toward financial institutions. On the one hand, we see them as representatives of the free market, on the other we continually impose other objectives. When Paul Streeten indicated that we should not bail out the greedy bankers, it was a clear free-market statement. It is not self-evident why the shareholders in a commercial bank should be entitled to protection from the risks that they assumed when they purchased the shares of that bank. If in fact the market were allowed to play out without interjecting governmental policy and ideas, then this question of what should happen to these debts that are now classified as questionable, or uncollectable, would not be an issue.

But we apparently do not want that. We would like these financial institutions, which we view as instruments of private enterprise, to act as instruments of social and political policy, which raise dimensions much different from business decisions. Rather than rationalize their process in terms of return on equity, it must be rationalized in some other way. We try to take this instrument, a bank, with its business foundation and use it across the larger dimension. It is not surprising that we find ourselves continuously confused about the results. Until we are able to get our paradigm redirected, we are constantly going to debate these issues without a clear picture of our desired resolution.

PART IV

Reinvigorating Development: Multinational Corporate Contributions

As we approach the potential contribution of multinational agribusinesses, manufacturers, resource firms, and service corporations to reinvigorating development, the critical need for this contribution is abundantly clear. Multinational corporations have the technology and managerial skills to enhance the greatly needed productivity in the debtor developing countries. While their potential capital contribution is small relative to the credit flow of the 1970s and the more recent loans from international financial institutions, these investments are channeled directly to productive uses. Moreover, multinationals can provide the access to developed-country markets so needed by Third World debtors.

The papers and responses in Part 4 discuss the conditions under which these contributions can be maximized within the other constraints on corporate action.

Theodore Moran analyzes the impact of foreign direct investment on development in the Third World, how that climate has been changed by the debt crisis and how it can be improved. He calls for a relatively free, open, and competitive international economic order supported by developed countries as well as Third World host governments. Moran discusses the difficult tradeoff between the host government use of market exclusivity, which has been demonstrated to be a strong attraction for foreign direct investment, set against the negative

263

impact that market exclusivity will have on host country development.

Two participants responded to the Moran paper. Thomas Bausch would harness the free markets espoused by Moran. He argues that governments should control markets in order to achieve their non-economic goals, and be willing to pay the price, but they should do so without regulatory nuisances.

The flexibility of the multinational corporation and the creativity of its management are critical considerations according to Roy Crum. He discusses the objectives of the host country and those of the multinational corporation, pointing out that the essence of regulation is to ensure that both sets of objectives are served.

In the second paper, Paul Streeten calls on us to exercise our institutional imaginations to create new forms for multinational corporate participation in the Third World. Noting the new forms of direct investment that have emerged over the past two decades, he analyzes why they have appeared and what contributions, positive and negative, they bring to the host country and the multinational corporation. Streeten's own institutional imagination is demonstrated in this paper.

Responding to Streeten, Louis Wilking focuses on technology transfer, recognizing its interconnections and complexity as well as the many kinds of ownership and control mechanisms through which that technology flows. He argues that technology will be transferred as the firm pursues business opportunities, but that the transfer of technology is not the direct objective of the firm. John Gilligan challenges the basic assertion that multinationals enhance development. Citing the experience of the United States in the transfer of corporate resources from the North to the South, he argues that the devastating impact on the Rust Belt was not offset by an appreciable improvement in the Sun Belt. Based on this, Gilligan underscores Streeten's need for institutional imagination and calls for more of a global corporate vision.

Pointing out that entrepreneurs go where the opportunities are, John Caron sees considerable corporate opportunity in the Third World if the governments demonstrate a willingness to correct their past excesses in borrowing and the misallocation of resources.

A discussion summary concludes Part 4. The participants considered what should properly be expected of multinational corporations in Third World development, how that contribution is best guided, and how it is worked out between multinationals and host governments.

Multinational Corporations and North-South Relations: Old Threats and New Opportunities in the Coming Decade

*THEODORE H. MORAN**

The initial response of the multinational corporate community when the debt crisis hit the Third World was to cut the level of annual investment by more than 25 percent. At the same time there was flourishing rhetoric concerning the contribution such corporations could make if only investment flows were restimulated. Today there is unprecedented support, in North and South alike, for a larger role for multinational firms. Perhaps it is an appropriate moment, therefore, to reexamine the part that direct foreign investment may play in the developmental process, and how the positive contribution from that investment can be improved and the negative effects minimized or eliminated.

*Theodore H. Moran is the Landegger Professor and director of the Program in International Business Diplomacy at Georgetown University. Formerly a member of the policy planning staff of the Department of State, he has been on the faculties of Harvard, Vanderbilt, and the Johns Hopkins School of Advanced International Studies.

The Impact of Foreign Direct Investment
on Development

To begin this reexamination, Dennis Encarnation and Louis Wells of the Harvard Business School attempted to cut through more than a decade of controversy about transnational corporations with a simple methodology in order to ascertain whether the net impact of foreign direct investment on domestic economic activity has been positive or negative.[1] They drew on two previous studies—one with a critical perspective on foreign investment by Sanjaya Lall and Paul Streeten, completed for UNCTAD (the U.N. Conference on Trade and Development); a second, more sympathetic toward foreign investment, by a group headed by Grant Reuber for the OECD (Organization for Economic Cooperation and Development).[2] The study by Lall and Streeten included 133 foreign and locally owned operations in six countries with the national income effects calculated for 88 of the projects. The Reuber analysis covered 45 foreign-owned projects from thirty countries, with an approach that allowed a rough translation into the impact on national income, using world market price assumptions. In addition Encarnation and Wells contributed their own intensive examination of 50 manufacturing project proposals in one country and used a more sophisticated cost-benefit analysis.[3] Surveying all of these cases, Encarnation and Wells attempted to measure the benefits of each project in terms of goods and services produced minus the costs to the national economy in terms of resources expended, with both costs and benefits measured in world market prices.

This approach was deficient (as they knew) in many respects. It left some of the most important economic questions (Do the projects use appropriate technology?), political questions (Do the foreign corporations have undue local influence?), and social questions (Does the investment worsen the distribution of income?) to one side. But it gave a clear and important first cut at the debate over the impact of foreign direct investment on development.

In the resulting survey of between 150 and 183 manufacturing projects in at least thirty countries over a period of more than ten years, the evidence split into two distinct categories, good and bad. Between 55 and 75 percent of the projects did produce a positive net contribution to economic development. This finding constitutes a solid argument in favor of the contribution of foreign direct investment.

The bad news, however, was equally apparent: between 25 and 45 percent of the projects had a negative impact on economic activity. The costs to the host country in terms of inefficient use of scarce local resources outweighed the benefits. The split in the evidence between positive and negative projects was not close. Projects tended to cluster at either end—either greatly positive or greatly negative.

Most striking was the discovery that the difference between the positive and the negative cases was not related to the foreignness of the investor, but rather to the degree to which the projects were sheltered from competition. Protection from competition led to trade distortions, the use of inappropriate technology, oligopoly profits, and the creation of a small, privileged labor elite.

This negative impact on the host society was unambiguous despite the fact that *the treatment of the foreign investors was quite good and the private profit rate was quite high.*

The negative findings are most clear in the case of trade protection, especially when some form of quotas was used to insulate the foreign investor from competition. But the impact is similar in the case of preferential purchase agreements, guaranteed market shares, or other sheltered arrangements. The result is not only inefficiency in the allocation of resources in some abstract sense, but in the elimination of local producers and local workers who otherwise could have survived and prospered. The negative effects go still deeper.

Consider, for example, the difficult question of "appropriate technology."[4] The evidence shows that international corporations develop production processes in response to the ratio between capital costs and labor costs in their home markets. Furthermore, they tend to carry these same production processes with them when they move their operations abroad. (There are some offshore operations designed specifically to take advantage of cheap labor, but these are still a minority of investment projects.) The result is an "inappropriate" use of technology, employing too much capital and too little labor even in countries where labor is abundant.

This observed result is difficult to reconcile with profit-maximizing behavior on the part of the international firms. One hypothesis is that "engineering man" predominates over "economic man" in these large corporations, leading to the adoption of the most scientifically advanced processes even when less automation would generate greater revenues.[5] A second hypothesis is that the firm compares the total costs of developing a new labor-intensive technology with the marginal costs of continuing with what it already uses at home and chooses the latter.[6]

Whatever the explanation for the utilization of "inappropriate" technology, one thing is certain: Competition acts as the greatest spur to change the more familiar and comfortable conventional patterns. Wayne Yeoman, for example, has found that the greater the price competition faced by the multinational company in the host country, the more likely it was to modify procedures used in the home country to make them more responsive to local factor proportions in the host market.[7] Protection from competition, in contrast, generated a greater propensity to use home country production techniques in the host country without modification. Other studies have come to the same conclusion.

A number of variables are important in coming to grips with the complex issue of appropriate technology. Many host governments subsidize the use of capital by holding interest rates artificially low. Some governments prohibit foreigners from bringing in the most plentiful source of labor-intensive technology, namely second-hand equipment. (This is changing as more governments realize that second-hand is not necessarily second best.) While there are many ways host authorities can try to attack the problem of inappropriate technology, the presence (and promotion) of competition has proven to be a strong ally in the hands of Third World policymakers.[8]

The evidence does not provide a justification for pointing the finger of blame at either host officials or at foreign investors to account for the sheltering from competition. Whether foreign investors sought market exclusivity or host officials offered it, the outcome was uniformly negative for the country. This has important implications for the policies of Third World governments, for the policies of the developed countries, and for the strategies of the multinational corporations themselves.

IMPROVING THE UTILIZATION OF FOREIGN DIRECT INVESTMENT ON DEVELOPMENT

How can host countries improve the utilization of multinational corporate investment in the coming decade to avoid the negative impact and accentuate the positive?

Prior to the debt crisis, there was evidence of a growing ability on the part of some Third World governments, especially the governments of the newly industrializing countries (NICs), to bargain effectively with multinational corporations in the effort to harness them to the developmental effort. This thrust began in the extractive industries, including oil, copper, coal, iron ore, nickel, and other natural resources, and spread to manufacturing projects as well. At the same time, from 1973 to 1982, there was a gradual transformation of host country objectives in the bargaining process, from zero sum struggles over ownership and tax rates to non-zero sum negotiations about more domestic content and greater exports. Finally, there has been a shift over the past ten years from an insistence on stiff entry conditions to the exercise of the "obsolescing bargain," in Raymond Vernon's famous phrase, or the renegotiation of investment agreements after the foreign investment is in place. This latter process has proven to be the way in which the more effective Third World negotiators extract greater and greater benefits from the operations of transnational corporations.

To summarize work reported elsewhere,[9] foreign corporate investors whose projects are composed of large fixed investments, stable technology, low advertising intensity, and many alternative suppliers tend to find themselves quite vulnerable to a squeezing of their initial investment agreements six to eight years after their operations come on-line. The sectors in which there are foreign firms with these characteristics include a broad spectrum of natural resources, chemicals and petrochemicals, automobiles and automotive parts, industrial equipment, and (some) consumer electronics. It is in these sectors that there has been evidence of a growing ability of Third World authorities to impose performance requirements requiring greater local processing and greater foreign exchange receipts.

To be sure, many countries have not been touched by these improving bargaining possibilities, so it is misleading to represent such developments as taking place across the Third World. The cases of more effective negotiations are most apparent in (but not limited to) the NICs. Circumscribing the entire foreign investor-host government relationship is the fact that in the past fifteen years five countries (Brazil, Indonesia, Malaysia, Mexico, and Singapore) have received fifty percent of all foreign direct investment, while the lowest forty-one LDCs (excluding China and India) have received only two percent.[10]

How has the debt crisis affected the relationship between multinational corporations and host governments in the Third World?

Since 1982 there has been a burst of eagerness to attract new flows of private foreign capital with whatever generous treatment is needed to get the companies to make the commitment. This is leaving the Third World with a subtle new problem to replace the previous concern about exploitation and dependency. The countries of the South must now face the possibility that multinational companies may indeed come to help them out of the debt crisis but that they will come for the wrong reasons.

The enthusiastic welcome that host authorities are now offering to multinational corporations has to be scrutinized in the light of the findings in the previous section. Third World governments are being urged by the governments of many developed countries, led by the Reagan Administration in the United States, as well as by the International Monetary Fund and the World Bank, to provide a "good investment climate" to encourage the maximum foreign direct investment possible.

While there is nothing wrong with this advice in principle, in practice market exclusivity is one of the easiest, and most frequent, concessions used to create a "good investment climate." From the investor's point of view, trade protectionism, preferential purchase agreements, or a guaranteed market share ensure a high profit even if he is relatively inefficient. From the host government's point of view, trade protectionism, preferential purchase agreements, or a guaranteed market share are off-budget; they do not appear to cost anything the way subsidies, grants, or tax concessions do. Moreover, they are less likely to expose the public official who authorizes them to domestic criticism the way tax breaks and rebates do. Two and a half decades of research have shown that market exclusivity is the greatest stimulus Third World countries can provide to increase flows of direct foreign investment. It has been the centerpiece of most LDC efforts to create the proverbial "good investment climate."

But, as we have seen, the results are consistently damaging to Third World economies. The controversial but incontrovertible fact is that the kind of "good investment climate" that many foreign investors want most is not good for the countries where they are located.

What would constitute a genuine "good investment climate"—one that offers a high probability of nurturing projects that benefit the host country as well as providing adequate compensation to the foreign investor? The task is more complex than is conventionally assumed.

The first principle for host country authorities to acknowledge is that most international firms are, in fact, risk-averse. They are more strongly motivated by fear of loss (including loss of market share) than by desire for gain. This puts a great premium on attracting the first firm to invest in any given sector or subsector. It requires an active search, focusing on smaller and less well-known companies, who must be pursued with a diligence considered unseemly by nationalistic negotiators and attracted with an array of financial concessions that will probably be unpopular at home.

Once the first investor has committed himself, however, other investors tend to follow each other with what has been called a "burst phenomenon."[11] This process is well known in the petroleum industry, where the attraction of an independent impels the majors to rush in to guard their own market shares.[12] It has been documented in manufacturing industries as well.[13]

The competition among firms then can be used to ensure that the multinational investors make a contribution to the local economy that is non-distortionary. It can also be used to improve the terms on which all investors (including the first one) participate in the host country. In sum, key ingredients in building a genuine "good investment climate" in Third World economies include aggressive efforts to attract the initial investors in each sector or subsector, financial rather than market-exclusive incentives to persuade them to come, and the encouragement of subsequent competition.

INVESTMENT PROTECTION AND THE ROLE OF THE WORLD BANK

The task of building a genuine "good investment climate" involves another major, controversial step. Multinational corporations are likely to stay away from many of the most valuable long-term projects because of their past experiences of political risk. Their fear is that, as they become more exposed to the squeezes of economic nationalism six to eight years after they have invested, their projects will become unprofitable and/or will be nationalized altogether. To attract many of the largest investments, therefore, a warm welcome is not enough. Rather, the challenge is to provide credible reassurance that the terms of their investment agreements will not be so arbitrarily abrogated as to destroy the possibilities for successful operation. What these foreign investors require is an umbrella of protection against political risk that remains in place throughout an extensive payback period.

The most widely discussed initiative to provide an umbrella of protection that may allow such large projects to be approved is the Multilateral Investment Guarantee Agency (MIGA), which will operate under the auspices of the World Bank. It will offer political risk insurance against expropriation, breach of contract, inconvertibility, and war or civil disturbance.

As structured today, the MIGA has some features that will lessen its appeal to the investors who will have to decide whether to buy its coverage. The unfavorable features include voting procedures that could block the claims of foreign companies in a dispute and subrogation procedures that leave in doubt the ability of the MIGA to pursue the claims with host states.[14] To stiffen these procedures will be a controversial undertaking from the point of view of some LDC governments, but movement in this direction will be needed to persuade multinational corporate investors to pay MIGA's insurance premiums.

There are other initiatives, also controversial, that may be even more promising.[15] The first centers on the use of the remedies clause in World Bank loans to foreign investment-related projects. Here the Bank provides credits for the infrastructure surrounding the private sector operation, while negotiating within its own loan agreement a commitment on the part of the local government not to take any actions (including tax increases or other contract changes) that will impair the functioning of the project.

A second initiative, building on the one above, involves co-financing "B" loans, in which the World Bank participates in the later maturities of the project's long-term debt. This extends the umbrella of protection against political risk into the period of vulnerability when an investment with a long payback period might be squeezed by the forces of economic nationalism.

A third initiative consists of parallel loans made by the World Bank simultaneously to the host government and to a foreign private investor to cover the same project. On one side, the Bank negotiates an agreement with the host not to engage in certain detrimental practices; on the other side, the Bank inserts a political *force majeure* clause absolving the foreigner of his obligation to repay if the host does engage in such detrimental practices. As in the first two cases, a change in the terms of treatment of the investor could trigger a default to the World Bank.

There is no doubt that these initiatives involve momentous public policy issues, even philosophical issues, for host authorities since their thrust is to allow a Third World government to undertake obligations that may bind the hands of its successors. Some governments have dealt with this by requiring extraordinary majorities in their parliaments or congresses to approve such obligations; others have proposed constitutional amendments.

The issue should be thoroughly debated, but the implications not exaggerated. The actual terms are, of course, the subject of negotiation, and it is unlikely that the interpretation of these covenants will be so stringent as to prevent any change in the investment agreements whatsoever. Indeed one possibility might be to include a graduated tax rate if the project proves to be quite profitable (and in point of fact most international companies are not obdurate on this issue). In all cases the World Bank maintains some flexibility about whether it would actually declare a country to be in default or would actually stop disbursement of loans or halt access to further Bank credit, even if the original investment agreement were drastically changed.

Moreover, as Thomas Schelling points out with regard to other kinds of strategic negotiations, the side that can make credible commitments about its own future actions begins in a very strong bargaining position.[16] Precisely for this reason such commitments are very appealing to foreign investors fearful of being damaged by the inevitable pressures of economic nationalism. The investors will be willing to pay for such commitments in other areas of the negotiation. In the case of many of the largest and most important projects over the next decade, such commitments may allow investments to come to fruition which would otherwise never be undertaken.

FOREIGN DIRECT INVESTMENT AND AMERICAN JOBS

But is stimulating greater flows of multinational corporate investment to the Third World in the economic interest of the home country? A growing number of interest groups in the developed nations of the North are arguing that it is not. Instead of stimulus, they want the reverse.

The principal impetus for new restraints on foreign direct investment comes from organized labor and from import-competing firms who feel that their positions are being threatened by multinational corporations that "export jobs not products."[17] Their major focus is the *performance requirements* that Third World governments are using to enmesh international companies more directly in their own developmental process. They contend that these performance requirements constitute a distortion of trade, and they have pushed the developed country governments, led by the United States, to place an attack on performance requirements high on the agenda for the new GATT round.

The problem with this approach lies in measuring the extent to which performance requirements actually do distort trade, as opposed to merely pushing multinational corporations to explore new avenues of comparative advantage more vigorously. In a careful and sophisticated study, Stephen Guisinger has found that only four of seventy-four investments that he surveyed would actually have been located elsewhere except for the locational requirements imposed by the host governments.[18] Even in the automobile industry, where the charges of distortion on the part of the UAW (United Auto Workers) are most strongly asserted, there is evidence that the location of production for many parts and subcomponents is taking place in a pattern that is economically rational.[19]

Moreover, trade-related performance requirements seldom stand alone. Rather they are only one component of a much more diverse package of investment policies (tax holidays, grants, accelerated depreciation, infrastructure and training expenditures). As Guisinger describes them, performance requirements act like "turbochargers," directing the rents generated by incentive policies in certain prescribed directions. In terms of impact on corporate profitability, the assorted elements of investment policies are largely fungible, meaning that an attempt to proscribe LDC trade-related performance requirements through the GATT will probably not hit the target. At best the pieces that make up the package of incentives and obligations in any less-developed state that bows to pressure from the North are likely to become more opaque and subject to private negotiations between individual ministries and individual investors, without a major change in outcome.

But is not the attempt to put together an investment package of incentives and requirements in some sense unfair play on the part of those who want to get investors to locate within their jurisdictions? In general, the answer is yes. Yet twenty-four U.S. states and all twelve members of the European Community offer investment promotion programs that are not dissimilar in impact. Consequently, although the Senators from Michigan and Pennsylvania complain bitterly about LDC investment laws, the Governors of Michigan and Pennsylvania offer industrial development bonds, publicly financed job training, property tax, and other fiscal inducements that represent an approach equivalent to that of Mexico or Brazil. In the same vein, the members of the European Community, led by Ireland, offer both subsidies and direct cash grants with greater impact than India or Argentina.

Thus, the idea of pointing the finger in the new GATT round only at the investment policies of the LDCs is patently unfair. And the effort is likely to be counterproductive.

A much better and fairer approach would be for all parties to use what clout they have to push for general trade liberalization in both North and South. To this they might add a common ceiling on locational incentives. In this way they can minimize or eliminate the distortional impact of investment promotion policies in the developed and developing worlds.

FOREIGN DIRECT INVESTMENT AND THE DEBT CRISIS

The greatest contribution that foreign direct investment can make to Third World development comes through the generation of local economic activity and the jobs and exports that result directly and indirectly from it. What has commanded increasing attention, however, has been a much more narrow preoccupation, the contribution of foreign direct investment as a flow of capital helping to support the balance of payments. There is a hope in some quarters that multinational corporations can help relieve the pressure on commercial banks who feel they are already overexposed in the Third World.

On the one hand, there is reason to be optimistic about the response of the international corporate community as the Third World attempts to grow out of the debt crisis. Multinational firms have a record of coming back strong after downturns in business activity in the past (rising 34 percent in 1973 after a plunge of 16 percent in 1972, and 19 percent in 1977–78 following a decline of 21 percent in 1976). This leads David Goldsbrough of the International Monetary Fund to project a rise of nearly 40 percent by 1987–88 from the lows hit in 1982–83.[20] This upbeat appraisal is supported by survey data from fifty-two of the largest international corporate investors.[21]

On the other hand, the magnitude of this corporate response in relation to the "gap" that is preoccupying both LDC governments and developed country governments alike is very small indeed. The notion of a "gap" arises from the paradox that private commercial banks feel that they are overexposed in the less-developed countries in relation to the debtors' ability to repay their hard currency commitments; yet to produce greater hard currency earnings, the debtors need new capital and new hard currency loans to restore their domestic growth. The Baker Plan estimated the "gap" to be approximately $9 billion per year. More recent calculations indicate it may be substantially larger, requiring $15–30 billion per year in net new lending to allow the LDCs to grow out of the debt crisis. In this setting, Goldsbrough's relatively optimistic analysis indicates an aggregate level of foreign direct investment of $13 billion per year by 1987–88. But this represents only $2 billion per year in net new capital inflows. In short, under even the best of circumstances, foreign direct investment can fill only a very modest portion of what may be a $30 billion gap.

The previous section examined some innovative programs the World Bank has been considering to expand foreign investment flows to the Third World. Under even the best of circumstances, however, these will augment capital flows by only a very small amount. With regard to MIGA, for example, the World Bank's investment guarantee agency could cover a total of $2 billion of investor's assets by the late 1980s, with new projects equaling $500 million per year. Based on past studies of "additionality" generated by investment guarantees, a reasonable estimate is that $200 million of these might be projects that would not have taken place in the absence of MIGA. With regard to the expansion of other World Bank initiatives, remedies clauses and co-financed "B" loans that limit the potential for host country renegotiation of investment contracts might spread the umbrella against political risk over $600 million of investor's assets, of which approximately $300 million might be net new projects. This total ($200 million plus $300 million) is an impressive addition of half a billion dollars per year in foreign investment, but it is still quite small in relation to the $30 billion gap.

Finally, it should be emphasized that Goldsbrough's basic calculation of foreign investment flows, however modest, is based on crucial assumptions about macroeconomic behavior in the North: an average real growth of at least 3 percent per year; a reduction of government deficits by 1 percent of GNP, and a standstill in the growing pressures for trade protectionism. These measures are the responsibility of the North if foreign corporate investment is to play a greater role in the growth of the South; without them, foreign direct investment will fall rather than rise.

CONCLUSION AND POLICY IMPLICATIONS

The analysis presented here suggests that foreign direct investment can indeed play a valuable role in Third World development. But to utilize it most effectively host governments will have to avoid what has been, in the past, the strongest magnet to attract it—the promise of market exclusivity. Instead, competition should be used as a vehicle not only for efficient allocation of resources but also to promote the adoption of appropriate technologies and the widest possible job creation. It will be necessary, therefore, to make generous use of incentives other than protection from competition to secure the multinational investment. Even more controversial, host authorities will have to consider making commitments that limit the margins within which the investment contracts can be renegotiated well into the life cycle of the projects.

For multinational corporate investors, the analysis presented here underscores the diverse constituencies that will contend not merely (as in the past) for a share of the profits but also for jobs and exports. Within this context, the next decade is likely to push corporate strategies in the direction of being truly a-national, choosing the sites for their operations in terms not of special advantage but rather global comparative advantage. The argument made in this paper highlights the need for the promise of profits to motivate corporate investment, but it emphasizes that those profits should not come from seeking protection from market forces but from superior performance and efficiency. Comparative cost calculations must play an even more central role in investment strategy in the future than they have in the past.

For home governments in the developed countries, the analysis presented here reaffirms that the goal of expanding international flows of trade and capital continues to be in the interest of the North as well as the South. To manage the debt crisis successfully will require special efforts on the part of the North, probably much more extensive than those originally envisioned in the Baker Plan, to increase the liquidity available to Third World debtors. At the same time, it will require sustained resistance to trade protectionism directed against goods produced in the less-developed countries. Within the new GATT round, tariff and non-tariff barriers in both North and South should be the focus of concerted action, but the concern about "distortions" resulting from multinational corporate investment should lead to negotiating a common ceiling on locational incentives rather than singling out LDC performance requirements *per se* for prohibition.

Overall the role that foreign direct investment can play in Third World development is positive and valuable, but the full benefits can be realized only if authorities in both North and South take seriously their responsibilities to maintain a relatively free, open, and competitive international economic order.

NOTES

1. "Evaluating Foreign Investment," in *Investing in Development: What Role for International Corporations?*

2. Sanjaya Lall and Paul Streeten, *Foreign Investment, Transnationals and Development,* (Boulder, Colo.: Westview Press, 1977); Grant L. Reuber et al., *Private Foreign Investment in Development* (Oxford: Clarendon Press, 1973).

3. Their analysis followed the methodology of Michael Roemer and Joseph J. Stern, *The Appraisal of Development Projects* (New York: Praeger, 1975).

4. For a review of the issues in the "appropriate technology debate," see *Multinational Corporations: The Political Economy of Foreign Direct Investment,* ed. Theodore H. Moran (Lexington, Mass.: Lexington Books, 1985), pp. 17–19.

5. Louis T. Wells, "Economic Man and Engineering Man: Choice in a Low-Wage Country," *Public Policy* 21 (Summer 1973).

6. See Theodore H. Moran, "Multinational Corporations and Dependency: A Dialogue for Dependentistas and Non-Dependentistas," *International Organization* 32, no. 1 (Winter 1978).

7. Wayne A. Yeoman, *Selection of Production Processes for the Manufacturing Subsidiaries of U.S.-Based Multinational Corporations* (New York: Arno Press, 1976).

8. If the foreign investor uses appropriate technology in a relatively competitive setting, his operations are much more likely to improve the local distribution of income rather than worsen it. See Moran, "Multinational Corporations and Dependency."

9. Theodore H. Moran, "Multinational Corporations and Third World Investment," in Michael Novak and Michael P. Jackson, eds., *Latin America: Dependency or Interdependence?* (Washington, D.C.: American Enterprise Institute, 1985).

10. See Vincent Cable and Bishakha Mukherjee, "Foreign Investment in Low-Income Developing Countries," in *Investing in Development: New Roles for Private Capital?* (New Brunswick, N.J.: Transaction Books, 1985).

11. Fred T. Knickerbocker, *Oligopolistic Reaction and Multinational Enterprise* (Boston: Harvard Business School, 1973).

12. For the dynamics between independents and majors in oil and minerals, see Theodore H. Moran, "The International Political Economy of Cuban Nickel Development," in Cole Blasier and Carmelo Mesa-Lago, eds., *Cuba in the World* (Pittsburgh: University of Pittsburgh Press, 1979).

13. For the debate about competition among multinationals, see Raymond Vernon, *Storm over the Multinationals: The Real Issues* (Cambridge, Mass.: Harvard University Press, 1977) and Richard Newfarmer, ed., *Profits, Progress and Poverty: Case Studies of International Industries in Latin America* (Notre Dame, Ind.: University of Notre Dame Press, 1985).

14. See "Overview: The Future of Foreign Direct Investment in the Third World," in *Investing in Development: New Roles for Private Capital?*

15. *Investing in Development,* op. cit.; "International Political Risk Assessment, Corporate Planning, and Strategies to Offset Political Risk," in *Multinational Corporations: The Political Economy of Foreign Direct Investment;* Christian Walser, "Multilateral Institutions and Political Risk: Deterrence, Co-Financing and Compensation," in Fariborz Ghadar et al., *Managing International Political Risk: Strategies and Techniques* (Washington, D.C.: Georgetown School of Foreign Service, 1983); and Srilal Perrera, "Techniques in Protecting Foreign Investment Against Political Risk," Georgetown University Department of Government, PhD thesis, November 1985.

16. Thomas C. Schelling, *The Strategy of Conflict* (New York: Oxford University Press, 1963).

17. See *Resolution on International Trade and Investment,* adopted by the 16th Constitutional Convention of the AFL-CIO, October 1985.

18. "Host Country Policies to Attract and Control Foreign Investment," in *Investing in Development: What Role for International Corporations?*

19. Douglas C. Bennett and Kenneth E. Sharpe, *Transnational Corporations Versus the State: The Political Economy of the Mexican Auto Industry,* (Princeton, N.J.: Princeton University Press, 1985).

20. "Past Trends and Prospects for Foreign Direct Investment in Developing Countries: The Link with Bank Lending," in *Investing in Development: What Role for International Corporations?*

21. Council of the Americas, *Debt, Economic Crisis and United States Companies in Latin America* (New York: Council of the Americas, September 1984).

Harnessing Competition

The Moran emphasis on competition is well placed. As we encourage competition in the Third World, however, it must be
harnessed. There are four aspects that we should consider as
less-developed countries attempt to gain the advantages and
mitigate the dangers of competition.

1. Market exclusivity
2. The use of up-front subsidies
3. Minimization of regulatory nuisances
4. The need to create certainty in the environment

When we talk about the allocation of resources under
competition, we immediately conclude that resources are being allocated inefficiently in the Third World. I have trouble
with any analysis that suggests that scarce resources are being
used inefficiently. We are talking about another society. Their
analyses and values may be different from our own. We have to
be very careful that our assumptions, and the models that lie
behind these assumptions, do not interfere with the overall
analysis that we make. We must be more aware of their opportunity costs. The value judgment on what a society is attempting to accomplish with its resources is extremely complex for
the multinational. This point was brought home to me in the
years I spent in Venezuela through a study being done at a

*Thomas A. Bausch is the dean of the College of Business Administra-
tion at Marquette University and the president of the American Assembly of
Collegiate Schools of Business. Dean Bausch's scholarly interests are in business strategy and corporate social responsibility.

central university at that time. They were attempting to determine what it meant to be a Venezuelan, what the common values and characteristics were. They found very little consensus. This tells us that multinationals and governmental policy makers are dealing with a very volatile situation.

The strength of Moran's analysis is his point on the protection of competition. Indeed, this is often used as a strategy for economic development. But again, we have to ask the question, what is the society attempting to accomplish? What are the values we are attempting to maximize? There is a major issue here of economic rent but some countries are willing to pay a high price for noneconomic goals.

The economic technology argument is a long-standing one in the economic development literature. It is fascinating, extremely complex, and worthy of extensive evaluation. When competition is allowed to work, the end result is eventually a focus on the most appropriate technology. But what are the implications in terms of appropriate technology when markets beyond national borders are being considered? In the countries that we hold up as models today—Korea, Taiwan, Japan—very sophisticated technology has been used at some point. One of the analyses that I read recently of automobiles imported into the United States from Japan indicated that only ten percent of the cost differential is labor costs. If you are starting from the analysis that the resource which you want to utilize in a developing country is labor, then sophisticated technology may not be the answer.

The real issue is how to harness competition. How can the laws of supply and demand be harnessed in the developing context? Moran outlined the concept of the obsolescing bargaining—renegotiation—and changing bargaining positions. As a country tries to formulate sensible strategies for attracting foreign private investment, this issue must be examined creatively. What are some of the other tools that can be used? How many sliding scales or flexible scales can be built in up front? Rather than depending on the performance of the investment over the full time of the relationship—the relative dividing of the benefits between the host country and the foreign investor—this might be done before the fact. Initially including a number of "if" statements could possibly diffuse some of the political pressures that are inevitably going to come, particularly if the performance is successful. The need to renegotiate could be decreased by carefully thinking through some of these possibilities before the fact and building them into a contract.

Moran's comments on investment planning are well taken. There is a great danger early in local developmental efforts of giving away the shop. This can be seen right here in the United States today. A number of states and localities have given away a great deal in order to attract firms. It has been suggested that corporations that move within the United States decide on the new location before entering negotiations. Then they go to that location and bargain to get the best deal they can. They overlook the possibility of going elsewhere. The recognition of this corporate strategy does not sit well with local officials or voters, and may be a very costly way to go about business. If a long-term sustainable economic advantage is not there, the corporation is in dangerous territory. This has been repeatedly demonstrated in my work in Wisconsin.

Thus, up-front subsidies may make judicious sense. Subsidies are a way of modifying supply and demand but there is also the danger of economic rent. They may be necessary but must be approached with caution.

A third aspect of creating a favorable investment climate is the elimination of regulatory nuisances. Many regulations make business more difficult without accomplishing any other objective. They may affect profitability without having any impact on the accomplishment of the overall goals of the local society. Nuisance requirements must not be confused with regulation that serves social goals such as pollution control.

A fourth point that gets to the heart of a good investment climate is to create an environment of certainty. Here I purposefully use the term "certainty" rather than "risk aversion." "Risk aversion" or intelligent risk assumption is more appropriate in describing the behavior of small entrepreneurial firms rather than the large multinational. Entrepreneurs drive 60 or 61 when the speed limit is 55 miles per hour. They are assuming some risk, an intelligent risk in terms of their value of time. Large corporations, however, are obsessed with certainty. Multinational corporate managers drive 55 miles per hour because they are certain they will not get arrested and it will not be on their record. Within the dynamics of bureaucratic organization, when a manager does something wrong, it stands out, but when he misses an opportunity, no one ever notices it. This certainty seeking is clearly at work in large corporations. They will attempt to make the environment more certain, seeking assurance that the rules of the game will not change. Given the changes in their political landscapes, host governments may be unable to convincingly provide this long-term certainty.

But, this assurance lies at the heart of a favorable investment chart. This is where multilateral organizations—the World Bank, the International Monetary Fund—come into the picture. They can help to provide credible commitments.

Meeting Joint Objectives

The flexibility of multinational corporations and the skill of their managers were brought home to me about eleven years ago in a study with the Treasury Department.[1] The study was concerned with how multinationals might respond to particular modifications in certain tax laws and other regulations dealing with these corporations. Several distinguished economists had been commissioned to explore these issues and had made predictions based on very elaborate econometric models.

We decided to take a radically different view. Since the proposed changes would more or less alter the rules of the game, we felt that the use of econometric models, which assume constant or predictably evolving relationships, was ill-advised. Instead we adopted the viewpoint of multinational managers by analyzing ways to get around the new rules in order to maintain multinational objectives. We built a series of optimization models to simulate the decision environment and the managerial response. An integral part of the models was an assumption that the companies would take whatever steps were called for to maintain their consolidated worldwide profitability. Our models demonstrated that multinational corporations would respond to the changes suggested by the Treasury by altering the basic strategy of their operations, and, further,

*Roy L. Crum is a professor of finance and director of the Center for International Economics and Business Studies at the University of Florida in Gainesville. He has published extensively on the topics of multinational corporate management and the impact of multinational corporate operations on both host nations and the firm.

that the changes in the tax laws would not only be ineffective, they would be counterproductive.

Although our arguments did not convince the regulators, they found that the multinational response to their new requirements was reasonably close to what we had predicted. The moral of this story is the need to understand how multinational corporations make decisions in order to predict their actions or constrain their operations effectively. These firms have a clear idea of their objectives drawn from the market realities of the developed countries. The regulatory key is to channel their energies, their creativity, in a direction such that when they take a particular action to achieve their own objectives, it simultaneously achieves whatever the host country objectives may be. Simply to criticize the actions of multinational corporations is to miss the point. Enlightened self-interest is a very powerful motivating factor, and host governments must learn to focus this energy in the right direction.

If we do not start with a solid sense of objectives, we should not be surprised if they are not met. The objectives of the host country are different from those of the multinational corporation.[2] There are also other stakeholders within a local economy, including the poor, and each group has its own objectives. What is often overlooked is that the objectives of the host government do not necessarily coincide with what is best for all members of the society. In fact, the objectives of various groups within a country may well conflict with each other, though not in all cases. A careful enumeration of objectives would also include a timeframe—long term, short term, medium term. These again are not the same, with different actors and dissimilar dimensions.

A host government must know its own objectives and those of its constituent groups before it can ask how the multinational corporation can contribute to those objectives. An incentive scheme that allows the multinational to achieve its objective and simultaneously moves all the other parties in the correct direction can then be designed that would have the likelihood of producing effective results.

Moran argues that the monopoly incentive for attracting multinationals into a country does not benefit the country. It does, however, benefit multinational corporations, and naturally, they would prefer to continue with this incentive program. If we examine why, it may be possible to discover a more effective alternative.

The first fundamental theorem in finance is never to take a risk unless there is adequate compensation. The capital markets operate on this concept and reward or penalize companies accordingly. Multinational corporations have many investment opportunities available, each with different risk and return characteristics. One of the ways in which a multinational has a competitive advantage over purely domestic firms is this access to a much greater range of projects. This means that for any given level of risk, it can achieve a higher return than the domestic competitor or, conversely, it can achieve any given level of return at a lower risk. This is a very distinct advantage.

In selecting projects, multinationals are risk adverse. Moran points out that they are more interested in preventing losses than in achieving gains, a phenomenon we observe again and again. If a multinational corporation can reduce the risk of an involvement in a country, particularly in cases where return is not affected, it will. A monopoly position reduces competitive risk. Borrowing in local capital markets can also reduce risk. Multinationals have been criticized for siphoning off local savings rather than relying on their access to the international capital markets, but local borrowing makes good sense when viewed as a means of reducing foreign exchange risks and political risks. If the multinational assets are expropriated, the corporation can default on the local loans.

In dealing with the differences in objectives between the multinational and host groups, we need to realize that this interaction can—and must—be a positive sum game. If it is not, the investment makes no sense. If the multinational cannot win, it is not going to make the investment. If the country cannot win, the investment should not be allowed in the first place. Cooperation is needed. Both parties must try to find areas of commonality where, with give and take, they can achieve this positive sum game.

Obsolescing bargaining, as noted by Moran, does not make sense. It is a very pernicious form of behavior. The companies know that countries have sovereignty and that they can regulate in any way they see fit, unless actively prevented by some mechanism such as the World Bank. The multinationals, being risk averse, will naturally take steps to prevent future cases of obsolescing bargains from doing them harm. This usually means that they will look for ways to get their investment back very quickly. Such reactions are rational from the perspective of a value-maximizing corporation, but they may not be optimal for the country or its stakeholder groups. In fact, they may not be optimal for the company either if the business climate could be changed to one characterized by cooperation rather than suspicion and mistrust.

In structuring the involvement of multinationals in the Third World we are in particular need of creativity. We can draw on the experience of the developed countries to find new mechanisms for multinational participation. In the United States, for example, there is an acquisition strategy called an earn-out. While not exactly appropriate in this context, the idea behind the earn-out may be helpful. Consider the case of a corporation that would like to take over a smaller company whose profitability is in question. The owner of the small firm would like to get as much money as he can, while the acquiring company would like to pay as little as possible. An earn-out structures the deal before the acquisition is made, but the exact price to be paid is subject to future performance. The owner continues to run the smaller company for a number of years, and the price he will finally receive is a function of how well he does. He has the incentive to do as well as possible, and, if high profits are achieved, the acquiring company will be happy to pay the larger amount for the acquisition because it will see that the assets are worth it.

This type of innovative thinking might be applied to host country regulation. The initial arrangement for multinationals entering the country might be structured so that if the multinational is able to make a major contribution to the local stakeholders—both in the external sense as in the balance of payments effect, and in internal contributions such as employment—it is rewarded. If the multinational comes in and cannot perform as expected or promised, the profitability will be much lower. This "contingent reward" structure gives an incentive to cooperate in both directions.

Moran is correct in his prescription of how to achieve a good investment climate. I have always been rather uncomfortable with established rules and regulations which distort market mechanisms. Although financial rewards can also be distorted, they are less pernicious.

However, I am uncomfortable with the implications that the developing countries need to be like hustlers in a Middle Eastern bazaar in order to attract the first multinational to come, and then that everything else is going to follow automatically. Incentives are needed, but all parties must be able to gain from them. Perhaps giving a little bit extra for the first one or two who come into the sector and start the growth phenomenon is reasonable, but it should not be taken too far. It is not realistic to think that some of the poorest countries have much to offer to most multinational corporations, and I am not optimistic that this will be an important element of their development, even in the short run.

Small countries might do better in improving their investment climates by banding together. The Caribbean nations are a good example. While these small islands are not exactly the same, to a multinational they are probably perfect substitutes for each other. Why would a multinational go there? Why should it set up an assembly facility on Dominica rather than having it in Pusan, Korea? In terms of transportation costs, it is cheaper to ship from Pusan to New York through the Panama Canal than it is from Dominica to New York because of volume. If the Caribbean countries could join together to increase the transportation facilities and develop some infrastructure, they would be in a better position to compete with the rest of the world in attracting multinationals and in using them effectively to stimulate development.

Finally, the most effective host country strategies should focus on the ends themselves or the objectives to be achieved. Let the creativity of the multinational managers select the means. With properly structured bargains, there would be increases in creativity, and, if properly done, it would work out as a positive sum game.

NOTES

1. Abraham Charnes, Roy L. Crum, David Karney, Darwin D. Klingman, "Large-Scale Models of Multinational Companies," Analysis, Research, and Computation, Inc. report to the Office of the Assistant Secretary of the Treasury for International Affairs, March 1976.

2. For an extended discussion of the differences of objectives between multinationals and host governments, see Lee A. Tavis and Roy L. Crum, "Performance-Based Strategies for MNC Portfolio Balancing," *The Columbia Journal of World Business* 19, no. 2 (Summer 1984), pp. 85–94.

"New" Directions for Private
Resource Transfers

*PAUL P. STREETEN**

The traditional contrast in the area of private resource transfers has been between a package of resources in the form of a 100 percent equity investment by the parent company with continuing full control of the firm, and an arm's length market transaction between entirely independent agents where control completely ceases at the point of transfer. Since the 1960s there has been a growing tendency to add other arrangements to these two traditional forms.

There are cases where ownership has been diluted, control shared in varying degrees, and forms of control confined to specified areas. Moreover, these arrangements might be changed in a previously agreed manner over time. Sometimes called "new forms of foreign investment," these arrangements have been most evident in the petroleum and metals industries, but also in manufacturing, particularly for host country markets and in industries with mature technologies. And there is, of course, considerable variation in the experiences of different countries and sectors.[1]

While these "new forms of direct investment" are neither new nor in the strictest sense investment, they imply a compo-

*Paul P. Streeten is the director of the World Development Institute at Boston University. He has served as the special advisor to the policy planning and program review department of the World Bank, and director of the studies at the Overseas Development Council. He has published extensively on issues in world development and the role of transnational corporations in that process.

nent that forms part of the investment. They cannot be understood as simply arm's length sales of goods or services that are part of the old package—a whole factory in the case of a turnkey project, technology in the case of a license, or management for a management contract. They are part of investment in that they imply the creation of assets and a degree of continuing control.

It is for this reason that these "new" forms are lumped together under a single heading rather than regarded as simply ordinary sales and purchases.[2]

The trend toward these "new" forms is partly dependent on host country policies and partly due to changes in organization and business practices relating to technology transfer, risk-taking, and management. There is a tendency for the multinational corporate-producing enterprise to concentrate on the provision of technology, while the host countries retain ownership of assets and some managerial tasks, such as labor relations. In order to understand the growing trend of "new" forms and in order to formulate proposals for future directions, it is useful to identify certain factors which help explain these tendencies.

HOST COUNTRY CONSIDERATIONS

From the earliest days of direct private foreign investment, host governments have thought to gain from "unbundling" the package of capital, technology, management, and access to markets that the multinational corporation brings with it. It was thought that to buy the components of the package separately would be cheaper, would reduce foreign control, would avoid restrictions by multinational corporations such as those on local dissemination or use for export, and would allow for greater adaptability to local conditions. The "new" forms are partly an application of the unbundling technique that resulted from stronger bargaining power of the host countries, greater availability of capital, and of alternative supplies of technology and management.

One of the most important and controversial components of the package is technology. In seeking the benefits of science and technology, the question for the developing country seemed to be whether the knowledge is transferable from one country to another, or whether it is tied to a particular place. Where knowledge is transferable, the best way to transfer it must be determined, and to what extent different methods of transfer are substitutes or complementary must be discovered. If they are substitutes, the question is whether transfer is most effectively carried out through local, wholly owned, foreign subsidiaries of multinational corporations; or through imports, licenses, joint ventures, collaboration agreements, sub-contracting, the hiring of experts; or whether it is not better to rely solely on indigenous scientific and technological capability by training students at home (or possibly sending them to be trained abroad), in order to expand indigenous institutions and know-how.

Actually, to some degree, indigenous capability and import of technology are complementary. Indigenous technological capability is necessary in order to use and maintain the transferred technology for adaptation to local conditions, to enlarge productive capacity in a growing market, and to get better terms for its purchase. In addition, indigenous capability may be desirable for innovation where the transfer or adaptation of imported technology is unsuitable. The real questions concern the best combination and most appropriate phasing of indigenous and imported technology.

In order to ascertain the best mode of acquiring the technology, preliminary questions about technical know-how of the following kind have to be answered:

1. Is the knowledge physically transferable or is it tied to a particular locality?
2. Is the knowledge freely available or do patents or other property rights impose a cost on those wishing to acquire it? If there are such costs, how can the bargaining power of the host country be strengthened so as to acquire the knowledge on the best terms?
3. Is the knowledge of the process or product fairly stable or is it rapidly changing?

4. Is the knowledge separable from other activities of the firm, such as using sources of supply or seeking market outlets, or is it inextricably bound through feedback and feed-forwards with knowledge or information drawn from these other activities? Is it, in other words, an integral part of the whole system or of parts of the system of the firm's organization and activities?

The answers to these questions will determine the most effective forms and institutions for acquiring the knowledge. Thus, if the knowledge is transferable, free, and separable, the solution is to ascertain it from books or articles. If property rights are attached to it, knowledge may have to be purchased. But the terms of the purchase will be partly determined by the extent of knowledge of the purchaser as to what he is purchasing, and to the extent that the transfer of technology and indigenous capacity are complementary. If the knowledge is rapidly advancing or integrally linked to other activities, inviting the multinational corporation may be the answer. The terms and conditions of this invitation are determined by many factors.

While a good deal of technology is freely available, "absorptive capacity" is required in the sense that there must be people willing and able to understand and apply the knowledge. Without a receptive, indigenous technology capability and a social structure adapted to receiving its fruits, even freely available and communicated knowledge remains unused or wasted.

There is no hard and fast line between knowledge that is freely available and knowledge that is tied to individuals or institutions. It is like the difference between a recipe for baking bread that anyone can find in any cookbook, and the experienced bread baker. "Knowing that" is different from "knowing how."

MULTINATIONAL CORPORATE CONSIDERATIONS

The multinational has three types of advantages over rival firms: ownership-specific advantages, location-specific advantages, and internalization advantages. The *ownership-specific advantages* must be sufficiently great to exceed the advantages of the indigenous firm in the form of knowledge, access, and command over the total environment. These advantages fall into two groups: those that can be separately sold (such as patents, trademarks, management skills, etc.) without diminishing the availability of these assets to the firm; and those that are inherent in the operations of the firm (such as economy of scale and integration, diversification of processes and products, division of labor and specialization, feed-backs and feed-forwards between markets and innovation, superior R & D capacity that yields a flow of innovations, economies of joint supply in purchasing, marketing, finance, organization, etc.). This second type of advantage is such that its yield to the firm is greater if it is part and parcel of the body of activities of the firm, and therefore it either cannot, or can only at a loss, be sold separately. Any specific advantage may change its nature over time, according to changes in the state of technology, competitive pressures, government regulations, etc.

Location-specific advantages determine where to produce. They are influenced by the prices, quality, and productivity of such inputs as labor, energy, materials, component parts, and semi-finished products, by tariffs and non-tariff barriers to trade, by transport and communication costs, by governmental interventions, by the investment climate, and by non-governmental sectors in the host country that influence the profitability of investment.

Internalization advantages determine whether it is best to establish a wholly owned subsidiary or to enter contractual arrangements by which the advantages enjoyed by the firm are transferred externally. Such contractual arrangements presuppose that the assets are marketable and transferable in space. It is largely changes in the assessment of the benefits and costs of this type of advantage that have determined the growing trend of alternative arrangements.

In deciding which kind of transfer to adopt, the firm will be influenced by three types of considerations. First, there are the differential costs of the transactions (searching for buyers and sellers, negotiating the contract, and monitoring the results). Second, there are the benefits from the different modes of transfer. A new and sophisticated technical process, subject to continual change and influenced by feed-backs from market reports and feed-forwards from the sources of supply, is likely to be more profitably exploited through internal than through external transfers. On the other hand, a fairly routine process likely to last a long time and fairly independent of information from marketing and production, is separable and marketable at a profit. Third, there are considerations of market failure, where uncertainty or ignorance prevail, that lead to the desire to internalize transactions.

In the light of these classifications, it is possible to explain these recent trends. Ownership advantages of dominant U.S. firms have been diffused as the result of the growth of rival firms in Europe, Japan, and increasingly in the more industrialized of the developing countries themselves. As one would expect, greater competition has reduced the rents to be earned from internalizing these advantages. In addition, indigenous firms have acquired increasing knowledge and skills in the process of learning by doing (and sometimes of learning by doing without) and through better education and training. It has also been argued that the main advantages of the more recent, smaller multinational corporations are of the marketable type rather than of that which is best internalized. Since the proportion of these new multinational corporations has increased, the new forms have increased with them.

The spread of technical knowledge and the spread of companies mean that the *relative* role of size and highly sophisticated technology has been reduced in favor of a greater proportion of assets that lend themselves to marketable transfers. The acquisition of these assets was helped by the growth of the international capital market, the resurgence of bond markets, and new sources of finance, such as the Arab capital surplus countries, whose financial surpluses have been channeled through private banks. There were also new and additional sources of technology (e.g. from the Soviet Union). Moreover, the bargaining power of developing countries has increased and, since they often have objections to wholly foreign-owned subsidiaries, they have been able to impose other forms and arrangements. Governments often prohibit wholly foreign-owned subsidiaries unless certain conditions are met, such as high technology or exports. At the same time, the foreign companies can reduce their risks, both political and economic, by reducing their equity participation.

There have also been changes in the locational advantages. The slower growth rates of the developed countries, the threat of protectionism, and the growing debt burden have led to a desire to save foreign exchange by substituting domestic production for imports. The new forms of contractual arrangements are then an alternative.

It is, therefore, the combination of governmental policies and the wider diffusion of ownership among many nations, together with the changing type of ownership-specific advantages, that has dominated over the opposite tendency of internalizing the advantages of advances in organization, communication, research, and transport brought about by the revolution in computers and electronics.

ANALYSIS OF NEW FORMS

The crucial question is: Who benefits from these "new" forms? Have they allowed host countries to steer multinational corporate activities in the desired direction? Or have multinational corporations been enabled to extract even higher monopoly rents while reducing their capital contribution and risk exposure?

In some cases, even though the multinational corporation loses from the host government-imposed solution, the host government itself gains little. Assume, for example, that the multinational corporation accepts the arrangement reluctantly as an alternative to the threat of expropriation. But the host government, objecting to excessively high profits earned and wishing to share in them, loses by reduced commitment on the part of the management of the firm to its activities. The firm not only shares profits but also control and management, and local decisions are less efficient as a result. In such a situation it would have been better for both parties to reduce the level of perceived risk. Less fear of expropriation or of restrictions on repatriation would reduce the required rate of return for the multinational corporations, and a lower rate of return would reduce the objections of the host government. Mutually agreed ways of risk reduction would yield positive benefits to both sides, whereas the "new" forms would, on these assumptions, lead to losses on both sides.

More specifically, it must be known whether there has been increased production and productivity or other contributions to policy objectives, what change there has been in the division of gains, and whether the transfer of ownership to host countries has been accompanied by a corresponding change in control. The new forms of resource transfer should be analyzed in four ways—the first implies positive sum games, the next two zero sum games, and the fourth negative sum games. These four interpretations have different implications for the answers of the questions.

The first interpretation is that before the new forms were widespread, the suspicion and the political fears of the multinational corporations led to high expected rates of return, so that the investment "paid for itself" within a short period. These high required rates of return, however, led to distrust on the part of the host developing country and to precisely those actions against which the high rates were intended as insurance. The host country felt that the company was "taking out of the country more than it was putting in" and expropriated the assets or restricted repatriation of capital and profits. In this atmosphere of mutual suspicion and fear, the net contribution to development of the multinational corporation was small, but average profits, taking high profits and losses together, were also relatively small and insecure. The new forms contributed to what amounts to mutual disarmament. Being given greater security, the multinational corporation lowered its requirements and took a longer time horizon; the host country reduced its hostile actions and was more welcoming to the multinational firm. More multinational corporate activity has now become possible, extending into new industries, sectors, and regimes which had previously not been open to multinational corporations. The result was mutually beneficial.

This mutual benefit is reinforced when the transfer of a degree of control from the multinational corporation to the host government benefits both sides. For example, the multinational corporation might maintain control over the variables of greatest interest to it, while the host government would take on labor relations and thereby reduce frictions.

Also if total returns on the assets are raised as a result of the new forms, the division of gains still remains to be determined. It is likely that this will not follow formal lines, such as the proportion of ownership, but will occur according to the distribution of knowledge and bargaining power.

An alternative interpretation is less optimistic. It maintains that the bargaining power of developing host countries has increased with improved knowledge, negotiating skills, and greater international competition among multinational corporations. As a result, a larger share of the gains from multinational corporate operations accrues to the host country. By "unbundling the package," the host country has learned to buy its ingredients on more favorable terms and reduce monopolistic exploitation. Increased competition among multinational corporations and the entry of new ones, to which the new forms are more congenial, has also eroded monopoly profits. Not only has ownership shifted to the developing host countries, but control has moved with it. The country's gain is the corporation's loss.

This interpretation would be strengthened if it could be shown not only that the number of firms submitting to the new forms has increased, but also that smaller-sized firms can benefit from them, thereby reducing the monopoly power of the large firms and raising the bargaining power of the host governments.

A third interpretation goes in the opposite direction. It argues that the share appropriated by the multinational corporations has not been reduced because they have learned to exploit their advantages in other ways than through 100 percent or majority ownership. What they cannot get in the form of profits, they now get through fees, contractual agreements, administered purchase and sales prices, etc. In the case of joint ventures, transfer pricing of imported inputs enables them to raise their share in the profits above their share in the equity. Their sacrifice of ownership, control, and profits is only apparent. Armand Hammer, chairman of Occidental Petroleum, claimed that after the required sale of 51 percent of its Mexican subsidiary, the profit on the remaining 49 percent was higher than the previous profit under full ownership.[3] Ownership had been sacrificed, but control and profits were maintained through transactions between affiliates.

Consider a chain of production, processing, and marketing from primary products to final sales. At each stage, a set of activities (know-how, capital, management, etc.) contributes to the process. Initially all stages and all activities are fully integrated into the wholly owned multinational corporation. When the host country then expropriates the production facilities, the firm retains control over those activities in which the barriers to entry are highest and its monopoly power is greatest. Thus the expropriation by the host country will have achieved little. Indeed, the host country may suffer if it now has to shoulder risks on the side of production or fluctuations in demands, while the multinational corporation reaps more stable, more secure, and higher profits from the retained activities such as marketing and management.

The following quote is testimony to this possibility.

> American policy should take unbundling one step further. It should abandon entirely the idea of direct ownership . . . and encourage the provision of production and marketing skills through service or management contracts. . . . Such contracts, because they offer a highly leveraged return on corporate assets, can be extraordinarily lucrative.[4]

The growth of small and medium-sized firms could be made consistent with this interpretation if it were thought that the large oligopolies raised unit costs by advertising, marketing efforts, and R & D to such an extent that it made possible, under the higher price floor, accommodation of smaller-sized firms.

Finally, the fourth possibility could be that the host government gains little while the corporation loses, or vice versa. If technology is highly complementary to managerial skills, it is more profitable to sell technology in combination with managerial skills rather than separately through licensing. If then the firm is forced to sell the two separately, it will either try to recoup itself or the transfer will be less efficient. Its interest and commitment will be reduced without any compensating benefit to the developing host country.

Each of these four possibilities may have been realized in different countries, under different conditions, at different times. In some cases, mutual accommodation has led to gains for both host country and company. In other cases, mutual suspicion has led to losses on both sides. In a third set of cases, host countries benefited at the expense of companies, and finally companies may have maintained or increased their gains at the expense of, or without benefit to, host countries. The outcome depends on the following factors.

1. The amount of genuine competition among corporations. The greater the competition, the more likely it is that gains accrue to host countries.
2. The indigenous technological capability and technological infrastructure of the host country.
3. The bargaining power and negotiating skill of the host country, which is partly a function of its indigenous technological capability and infrastructure.
4. The solidarity between potentially competing host countries for the purchase of multinational corporate assets.
5. The size and the rate of growth of the market. The larger the market or the faster it grows, the more useful it will be to the host country to develop its own technological investment capacity in expanding and erecting new plants.

An important conclusion of this discussion is that once host countries have become aware of the fact that the form the transfer takes is relatively irrelevant (i.e. 100 percent ownership or contractual arrangements), they will shift emphasis to the conditions attached to the transfer.

A word of caution should be added to this discussion. In these interpretations the player designated as the "host country" may prove to be one particular interest group within the host country. This group, although represented in the government, may have interests similar to those of the multinational corporations, but not identical with those of the masses.

> In a world where multinational corporations are global oligopolies exercising substantial discretion in the conduct of international activities, bargaining by an individual state to get these corporations to serve its goals may not involve any economic losses to the state; the result may simply be collusion, active or tacit, between host governments and firms, their disagreement limited to how to divide up the spoils.[5]

Although the authors do not say at whose expense the collusion takes place, it is possible that ownership, control, and profits are shared between a small power elite in the developing country and the multinational corporation, without any substantial contribution to greater equity, poverty eradication, or basic needs. At the same time, local power elites are hardly ever monolithic in their composition or interests, and the new forms may make these groups receptive to new pressures which make them more amenable to meeting domestic objectives.

Moreover, the collusion need not be between the official negotiators and the rest of the country. A private firm in the host country may purchase the asset (for example, the brand name) of a foreign monopoly at a substantial cost in order to exploit it in the home market. Foreign corporations and domestic monopoly are then the gainers, the consumers in the host country the losers.

BARGAINING AND INSTITUTIONS

As the multinational corporation has become one of the main vehicles for transferring modern, complex, and changing technology from developed to developing countries, an important aspect of policy is the terms on which the technology is transferred. In settling the bargain and in drafting the contract, a large number of items may be under negotiation. Some of these may refer to incentives such as protecting the market for the product or improving the attractiveness of imputs; others may formulate conditions for sharing the benefits with the host country; and still others will relate to policies such as conditions about repatriation of capital and profits, about raising local capital, etc. Through negotiation the consequences of the activities of the multinational corporation can be tilted in the direction of achieving the host country's policy objectives, such as growth with equity.

In order to achieve such gains, skilled and informed bargaining is necessary. Hitherto, multilateral technical assistance in negotiations of this type and in training negotiators has been on a relatively small scale, though often very effective. Through training courses, international organizations could render vital technical assistance in strengthening the bargaining power of less-developed countries in negotiating such contracts and could contribute to an informed dialogue between managers of multinational corporations and public officials. What is needed is both direct technical assistance in drafting contracts, possibly with the aid of a set of model contracts, and indirect aid through training, the provision of information, and encouragement of solidarity among developing countries in order to avoid competitive tax and other concessions.

Another important area of policy is the imaginative exploration of new legal and business institutions which combine the considerable merits of the multinational corporation with the maximum beneficial impact on national policy objectives. This area comprises joint ventures—both between private and public capital and between domestic and foreign capital— which go beyond window dressing to give the developing country access to information and decision making, and have various provisions for divestment and gradual, agreed transfer of ownership and management from foreigners to the host country. Thus, countries wishing to curb the power of large groups in their manufacturing sector may find investment reduced. This may make it advisable to institute a "joint sector" in which public capital is combined with private national management with or without an equity stake, or public capital with private international capital. Another possibility would be management contracts with national or international investors.

Thought and action in this area have suffered from a poverty of the institutional imagination which has lagged behind the advance of the scientific and technological imagination and the global vision of multinational firms. Too often discussions have turned on the ideological dispute between private and public enterprise, yet the real issues have little to do with ownership. Mixed companies can be devised that simultaneously harness private energy and initiative yet are accountable to the public and carry out a social mandate on the model of the British Commonwealth Development Corporation. Equally arid has been the dispute over the virtues and vices of private foreign investment. Here again, the task should be to identify both the positive contributions of foreign firms and the social costs they impose on the host country, to see how the former can be maximized or the latter minimized, and to provide for gradual, agreed transfer to national or regional ownership and management. There is a need for a legal and institutional framework in which social objectives which are not normally part of the firm's objectives can be achieved, while giving the firm an opportunity to earn profits by contributing efficient management, marketing, and technology.

An anti-poverty approach to development should explore the opportunities for a changed direction in the activities of multinational corporations. Such an approach would enlarge the scope for intra-Third World trade and investment. New types of multinational corporations located in developing countries have already emerged and should be encouraged. They are smaller and more competitive. They produce the simpler wage goods and services required by meeting basic needs, employ more labor-intensive technologies, and draw more on local materials. They make more use of local sub-contracting, thereby encouraging local powers of adaptation. They increasingly have accepted host country conditions in the form of joint ventures, greater participation of local personnel, and even minority share holdings. It might well be that their considerable flexibility will enable them to define a place for themselves in an anti-poverty approach to development.

AN ILLUSTRATION OF A NEW FORM OF PARTNERSHIP
FOR DEVELOPING COUNTRIES

The multinational corporation clearly has an important part to play in assisting the progress of the developing countries. At the same time a number of obstacles now stand in the way of its greater participation in the developmental process. New institutions and new procedures are needed to overcome these obstacles.

Some obstacles are practical, arising from the difficulties of operating in countries with shortages of skilled labor and basic utilities, others are political. The latter include the sometimes ambivalent attitudes of the governments of developing countries and the resulting political risks faced by the multinational corporation. The reluctance to welcome wholeheartedly multinational corporations has itself a number of causes. First, there is the fear, whether justified or not, that the multinational corporation may exploit its market power and deprive the country of valuable resources in general and, through remittance of profits abroad, aggravate balance-of-payments difficulties. Second, there is the fear that the enterprise will form a foreign enclave whose activities will not benefit and may harm the rest of the economy. Third, political fears of foreign domination or interference may add fuel to economic fears of exploitation.

But foreign enterprise has the capacity of bestowing great benefits on the economy of the host country. It can combine capital, skilled minds, and access to markets; it can transmit rapidly the latest products and technology to the host country; it can encourage the growth of a number of ancillary domestic enterprises; and it can reduce the economy's dependence on imports and increase its capacity to export.

The international community could help by investigating ways in which the fears of both overseas governments and private firms can be allayed and the advantages maximized. This could be done by devising a form of joint enterprise through which finance, skilled labor, and training are provided in a way that is both acceptable to the host government and carries sufficient profit to be attractive to the foreign firm.

One way of achieving this would be for a private firm to establish a joint enterprise with a local government or a government agency, such as a local development corporation. The foreign firm should advance not more than 49 percent of the capital, but enough to benefit when the enterprise succeeds, and of course suffer if it fails. It should have a substantial minority interest, while the local government has the dominant interest.

Such a holding would often be sufficient to secure a decisive role in management. However, it might be possible to arrange in special circumstances that, in the initial phase, the foreign investor should hold a higher percentage of the equity, as long as the arrangement for eventual transfer to local ownership is clearly stated. The foreign firm might also provide some of the money on a fixed interest basis or in the form of preference shares.

The equity interest of the foreign firm would be bought out by the local government at the end of a suitable prearranged period. For example, this period might be ten years, with provision each year after seven years to extend for a further five years up to fifteen years, or longer in the case of plantation enterprises. Various other forms of "rolling" continuation could be devised. Alternatively, the initial period could be longer, but with options at fixed points when either the local government could buy out or the firm sell out.

Managerial and technical staff would initially be provided almost exclusively by the foreign firm, perhaps under a management contract, but with the obligation to train local replacements within the specified period before the buy-out. The rate of replacement could not be specified contractually, but the local government would be able to use its representation on the board to ensure that it went forward at a satisfactory pace.

Housing and community services should be provided by the local government or some appropriate local statutory body established for the purpose. In view of the relatively short period of ownership participation, the foreign firm's capital should be concentrated on productive activities.

The scheme would operate through a tripartite agreement between the parent government of the firm, the local government, and the private firm. The parent government and the local government would provide a guarantee against expropriation. The parent government (or the World Bank) might also provide aid funds in appropriate cases to enable the local government to finance its participation, either directly or through one of the international financial institutions, or to help finance housing or community services required for the project.

Procedures for assessing an appropriate value at the time of buy-out would have to be agreed upon in advance, as well as procedures for arbitration should disputes arise.

Advantages

Most of the advantages of private enterprise are preserved. The foreign firm brings in capital, together with technology, market access, and a team, possibly with local experience. The overhead facilities and international experience which the firm can provide are thus made available. At the same time the fears which local governments or public opinion may feel are removed. The opportunity for indefinitely exploiting a monopoly or oligopoly position no longer exists. The fear of foreign ownership and domination is removed. The multinational corporation, on the other hand, acquires a guarantee against expropriation, combined with the incentive to enjoy a share in the profits. Clearly it would still carry the commercial risks of failure, but political risks would be eliminated.

The buy-out arrangement releases capital and know-how. These very scarce resources can thus be used on a revolving basis for initiating and pioneering new ventures and are freed from maintaining the going concern, which can more easily be transferred to local shoulders. The "spread effects" of enterprise on the rest of the economy are thus increased.

Fields of Application

The scheme would be particularly suitable for large-scale agricultural enterprises and for countries with a small entrepreneurial and managerial class. If new enterprises were successfully established, existing ones might also be converted into this type. Instead of expropriation, regimes committed to re-

placing foreign by domestic economic activity might be per-
suaded to work for the transformation of foreign-owned
enterprises into this new type of joint venture.

If such a scheme were to be accepted by the parent governments, it would be desirable to present it as a form of transfer which combines adaptability to different circumstances
with sufficient concreteness to have an appeal. It would need
to be announced with a good deal of publicity, after careful
preparation and consultation with selected host governments
and multinational corporations.

NOTES

1. See G. K. Helleiner, "Direct Foreign Investment and Manufacturing
for Exports: A Review of the Issues," Mimeo, (Toronto: University of Toronto, 1984).

2. A listing of "new" forms that have become more frequent since the
early 1970s would include:

- licensing agreements
- joint ventures
- turnkey projects
- sub-contracting (without equity participation)
- management contracts
- marketing contracts
- technical assistance contracts
- franchising
- capitalization of technology, giving equity participation to the
  owner of the technology
- phasing-out agreements
- trilateral cooperation or tripartite industrial cooperation
- counter-trade (various forms of barter-type arrangements between
  foreign trade organizations or private firms)
- durable links requiring that a firm market the production of another
  firm in a foreign country as in some buy-back arrangements
- leasing agreements

3. *New York Times,* January 5, 1981, quoted in Jan Svejnar and Stephen C. Smith, "The Economics of Joint Ventures in Less Developed Countries" *Quarterly Journal of Economics* 94 (February 1984): pp. 149–168.

4. C. Fred Bergsten, Thomas Horst, and Theodore H. Moran, *American Multinationals and American Interests* (Washington, D.C.: Brookings
Institution, 1978), p. 160.

5. Ibid., p. 332.

Technology: A Corporation's Major Asset

LOUIS H. WILKING*

Is the multinational corporate purpose to transfer its technology to Third World countries? Is it to fulfill business opportunities? Or, is it to do both? Until that issue is settled, academics and executives will be like ships passing in the night.

The main asset of a company is its technology. Chief executive officers will say that their major asset is their people, but if that is wrestled to the ground, a company's key asset is its technology. When they are asked to "give that away" or "sell it," they react negatively. For example, when Fiat went to Russia, Russia wanted a turnkey operation and got it. After being paid their fee, Fiat now finds the Russians taking a bit of their market away with the vehicles that they taught them to build.

As we move to realistic discussions of how best to transfer technology, the first requirement is to work on terminology. Academic papers can read like the *New York Times* or the *Washington Post* with phrases such as "monopolistic prices," "mutual suspicion," "high rates of return," "taking out more than is put in," "monopolistic exploitation," "if you can't get it out as profits, then get it through fees, contractual agreements, administered prices," and so on. As a businessperson, I do not like it when someone makes these accusations. What

---

*Louis H. Wilking is an executive assistant, group executive, of the overseas group for General Motors Corporation. Most of his career at General Motors has been spent in overseas management in Australia, South Africa, and Iran.

we should talk about is trust and how to best transfer technology. Remember this is not necessarily the intent of the multinational company, but it will happen.

Second, the interconnections and complexity of technology need to be recognized. It is too easy to oversimplify the notion of technology. Many observers view technology as coming in a bottle or a box, something that can be taken to the most remote area and given to users. In reality, a multinational corporation is a conglomerate of many technologies. My own business, transportation, starts with the technology of mineral extraction and develops those extracted materials into commodities such as steel, rubber, plastic, chemicals, and textiles in a raw or semiprocessed fashion. Each of those levels is a technology in itself. Then manufacturing technology is applied to those commodities, including metal-casting, metal-forming, and plastic molding. Again, each of these in itself is an extremely complex technology. On top of that, we machine it; we build tools; we have presses, forges, drills, dyes; and we have plants, each of which represent sophisticated technology. Further processing and assembly require more technology, as does marketing, distribution, design, and engineering. So, in a General Motor's sense, we have thousands of bottles and boxes of technology.

Even if it were assumed that the purpose of a multinational is to transfer its main asset, technology, another question remains. Would the Third World be in a position to absorb this technology? In many cases, they are not, certainly not in sufficient quantities. As in Father John Ridyard's experience in building a school, the first problem was how to get the cement to the school, 800 miles away, then how to make a brick, and on it went. If automobile technology is placed in a situation where people still cannot make a brick, it is a problem.

Education is probably the major ingredient required in this whole equation if Third World poverty is going to be tackled. Education will start at the very basic levels and will take years to develop a level that can absorb multinational technology in many places.

The attitude of Third World leaders must also be considered. In my experience across the Near East, Africa, and Asia, countries want high tech, which is capital intensive rather than labor intensive. The Shah of Iran spent $100 million building a sports stadium with a swimming pool, yet the Iranians do not swim. What they really need are docks, railroads, water, electricity, farming, and roads before they get into national airlines, engine manufacturing, sports stadiums, or, for that matter, Cadillacs.

As Streeten notes, there have been many new forms of investment and unbundling in the past fifteen years. Is it better for less-developed countries? Is it better for multinationals? It can be better for both. From a multinational viewpoint, it certainly minimizes the commercial risk involved in committing all of the capital at a high risk of loss. In the case of General Motors, before 1971 the company never had a joint venture of any kind. Our policy was, "If we cannot have 100 percent of the business, we will not come." World competition required us to say, "Let's approach that a little differently." If we are going to commit to Third World countries, we have to take a different approach. In 1971, when we wanted to be in the Japanese market, we eventually ended up buying 33 percent of Isuzu as a way of getting in. That seemed to work well. We now own 38 percent.

My time in Australia was spent setting up a venture in the Philippines. It took various forms and finally ended up being 60–30–10; the locals own 60, General Motors owns 30, and Isuzu in Japan owns only 10. We have the management contract and we control the business. In Korea, we started out with a 50–50 joint venture, again with a management contract in our name. We found out that it did not work and allowed the Koreans to take over management control. That has now become a very successful venture, producing the new Pontiac LaMans made in Korea with some German technology. Thailand was another kind of venture. We bought 49 percent interest in a manufacturing facility that made non-GM products. We owned 100 percent of the import and distribution company, but only 49 percent of the manufacturing company. That one failed but that was our fault. We picked the wrong products—the Japanese just ate us up with their cost base.

In Iran we were in a 45–45–10 agreement. General Motors had 45 percent, a local entrepreneur had 45 percent, and the Shah had 10 percent. Through three kinds of shares, we maintained control of the business. You already know the outcome of that one. The last word seemed to be that the Iraqis' bombs missed the airport and hit the plant.

In Kenya, the government owns 51 percent of the General Motors operation. We own 49 percent and we manage it. They control the board. That is a small but very successful operation. Zaire is another experience. We own 100 percent in Zaire. We could not find anyone who wanted to buy a piece of that action. To make Zaire go, we formed a Motors Trading Corporation. Its sole purpose was to generate barter trade. Our managers in Zaire spend most of their time trying to find coffee beans, copper, or other products that are put on the international market. If we can generate a million dollars in exports, we get 50 percent for imported automobile parts.

Egypt is our latest project. The fundamental ground rule in Egypt is to generate exports equal to the import goods deemed necessary. We accepted these conditions since we could build components in Egypt for the European market at about 10 to 20 percent less cost than producing them in Europe. We set up eleven different component companies there, but only took a 30 percent interest in the local company.

The Japanese multinationals are a different case. Initially they went abroad with licensing agreements. In most places they had no investment. Today, because of their tremendous trade surplus, the Japanese are investing in production facilities abroad. In the United States, they have joint ventures, wholly owned facilities, and Toyota has a so-so venture with General Motors.

Thus, we have many forms of ownership and control. Still, the initial question remains: Is the purpose of the multinational to transfer its technology or to fulfill business opportunities and, in the process, transfer technical capabilities to the host countries? It is the latter, not the first. This seems to generate suspicion, especially among academics, of the motives on the part of multinationals. Multinationals are looking for business opportunities. Then if they are willing to take high risk and enter, they will provide employment and help chronic imbalances in trade and foreign currency imbalances. Over time, they will provide skills and transfer that technology.

New Corporate Vision as a Prerequisite to New Directions

JOHN J. GILLIGAN *

The proposal for new arrangements that facilitate the transfer of resources, including technology and managerial skills, from multinational corporations to developing nations is interesting and provocative.[1] Streeten declares that thought and action in this area have suffered from a poverty of the institutional imagination that has lagged behind the advance of scientific and technological imagination and the global vision of multinational corporations.

Few of us would quarrel with the first half of that declaration. We do need more creativity in our institutional approaches to the problems of debt and development. But some, myself included, might want to know more about the content and character of the corporate global vision to which Streeten refers. He cites, for instance, the fear of expropriation as a primary deterrent to investment or expansion of multinational corporations in developing countries. That fear has been recognized and, by our government, met with such arrangements as the Overseas Private Investment Corporation. OPIC was chartered and funded by the Congress to protect American firms from the economic losses associated with expropriation. As the administrator for the Agency for International Development, I

---

*John J. Gilligan is the George N. Shuster Professor and director of the Institute for International Peace Studies at the University of Notre Dame. He has served as Governor of Ohio and as administrator of the Agency for International Development.

served on the OPIC board, *ex officio*. We reviewed many interesting case histories of American firms which had difficulties, and I quickly learned that "expropriation" became a sort of general shibboleth to cover a range of economic difficulties. One very large aluminum company, for example, which had opened facilities in Jamaica, with OPIC insurance written to cover it against expropriation, ran into substantial tax increases by the Manley government. They appealed for payment on the expropriation insurance coverage describing the tax increases as "creeping expropriation." I had heard of creeping socialism but that was the first time I had read of creeping expropriation. What happened in many instances was that almost any move undertaken by a host government was likely to be called expropriation in some form or another. I concluded that firms quite generally use the fear of expropriation, genuine or calculated, to justify very tough terms to the host country.

Streeten notes that foreign enterprise has the capacity of bestowing great benefits on the economy of the host country. He notes that it can combine the provision of capital with teams of skilled workers and access to markets. It can rapidly transmit the latest products and technology to the host country, encourage the growth of ancillary domestic enterprises, reduce the economy's dependence on imports, and increase its capacity to export.

Streeten goes on to indicate that the international community could help in the process of transferring resources by investigating ways through which the fears of both overseas governments and private firms can be allayed, and the advantages maximized. This could be accomplished by devising a form of joint enterprise to which finance, skill, manpower, and training are provided in a manner acceptable to the host government, and which carries sufficient profit to be attractive to the foreign firm.

The basic question, of course, is whether the multinational does in fact enhance development in the host environment. We can draw some evidence from the transfer of capital and corporate resources within the United States to the Sun Belt from what is now known as the Rust Belt. In this example, we remove the fear of expropriation and any distortions it might cause. Such moves, with their devastating impact on the communities where the older facilities were located, were encouraged by the host governments of the less-developed states in the Union. These Sun Belt states provided a combination of attractions: low wage rates guaranteed by right to work laws, property tax concessions running a decade or so (with, in some cases, wholly unforeseen consequences to the host government), provision of utilities, site improvements, even the issuance of government bonds to raise capital for entire factories to lure industries into the area, the relaxation of environmental regulations, or a lax enforcement of workmen's compensation and OSHA regulations. They provided a whole host of attractive offers.

There was very little evidence that the firms who moved south in the previous two decades in this country moved because of a global vision or a national vision. They went to make a buck.

A decade or so later, it is possible to gauge, in at least a preliminary way, some of the effects of what was, by all odds, a massive transfer of resources from one region of this country to another. We can look on the impact on the Rust Belt, which is easy enough to describe: abandoned cities, bankrupt school districts, rising unemployment especially for middle-aged workers who have no real opportunity of ever again moving into the workforce—the catalog is a long and dismal one. The curious thing is that there appears to have been remarkably little impact on the Sun Belt regions, which were supposed to be the beneficiaries of these moves. In relative terms, the increase in per capita income is hardly noticeable. The distribution patterns of income and wealth in the host states, or host regions, has changed almost not at all. Education and health indices and other social indicators have not moved significantly, at least in the preliminary estimates.

What has happened is the migration of the managerial class to the Sun Belt. But there has been no real change in the location of control, the management structure, or in the philosophies of the corporations making the move. This is evident not just in terms of how they have conducted themselves in the communities to which they moved, but in terms of the continued resistance of corporate management to legislation that has been promoted in some of the states of the Union, attempting to urge upon management the consideration of a participatory role for labor in such management decisions as reducing employment levels and transferring production facilities. In those communities which have been abandoned, where these corporations had operated, in some cases, for a century and had derived considerable benefit, many firms have not even given adequate notification of their intents to close facilities and move.

Streeten may be right on the point when he says that competition in the international arena may have changed the atmosphere to the point where managerial decisions are going to be modified by a different set of considerations than in the past. One would hope that would be true.

In summary, I certainly applaud Streeten's direct and careful description of alternative arrangements designed to benefit host countries as well as attract multinational corporations. In the process, however, I lay special emphasis on the need for change in what he refers to as a global corporate vision, to motivate the adoption of such new arrangements.

NOTE

1. Most of us are familiar with and grateful for Paul Streeten's quite insightful and lucid analyses of complex developmental problems. His paper is characteristically direct, modest, and thoughtful.

Entrepreneurs Go Where the Opportunity Is

*JOHN B. CARON**

What does all that we have discussed mean to corporate strategy? Entrepreneurs go where the opportunity is. There could be considerable opportunity in the Third World, and a role for the multinational that is beneficial to both the corporation and the less-developed country, but political and economic conditions of these countries certainly affect that opportunity. I see an analogy between the less-developed countries and the alcoholic. No matter who or what is to blame, an alcoholic's basic problem is drinking, and none of his problems can be solved unless he stops drinking. In the less-developed countries, the problem is governmental policies that lead to excessive borrowing and misallocation of resources; price controls that subsidize urbanization and discourage food production; inefficient industries which require huge government subsidies to keep them going; overvalued currencies; capital flight; and the incredible corruption. As long as these policies continue, there is little hope.

However, there are signs of change with the restructuring in Brazil and Argentina as examples, change that has been influenced by conditionality. Many people have pointed out that

---

*John B. Caron is the president of Caron International and a member of the University of Notre Dame Board of Trustees. He also serves as chairman of the board of the National Catholic Reporter and TECHNOSERVE, an organization devoted to assisting community-based enterprises through managerial and technical assistance.

conditionality has been counterproductive in many cases. A static environment is no solution, but in a growth environment there is hope. The International Monetary Fund is becoming more flexible, placing more emphasis on growth rather than austerity.

There are other factors that influence the opportunities available in less-developed countries. There is the question of equity and the importance of political stability. Food is a very practical reality. The political situation is important because nothing can get done without the support of the people. The less-developed countries are recognizing the needs for investment, for know-how, for export markets. Entrepreneurs go where the opportunity is, and filling these needs is a real opportunity.

Another factor is that there are more players eager to seize the opportunities. U.S. multinationals are being challenged by the Japanese and some of the newly emerging industrialized countries, and the atmosphere is very competitive. It is reminiscent of the great competition among banks for the OPEC dollar, which, of course, led to "loan mania." This new competition is an important part of the opportunity.

On the other hand, there are alternative opportunities. Deregulation of the banking industry is creating huge opportunities in this country for U.S. banks that could make them less interested in going to foreign countries, especially less-developed countries, because of the risk-reward ratios and opportunity cost.

A very interesting development could be converting debt to equity. This would involve very large sums of money, and I think it is going to happen in the United States. Consider the huge trade deficit the U.S. has, especially with Japan. The Japanese are not likely to stay in CDs and Treasury Bills forever, and it will be difficult for the U.S. to repay that debt. A major part of the solution could be shifting the debt to equity. I shocked some people when I voiced my concern about Japan buying the Bank of America. It could happen.

There are real windows of opportunity that the U.S. corporations are going to consider as part of their corporate strategy. The danger in the Third World is that not much will happen if less-developed countries take the attitude, "We are entitled to help. You got us into this mess and therefore you get us out of it." But with a willingness to correct problems, there could be considerable opportunity in less-developed countries and a role for the multinational that is beneficial to both the country and the corporation.

Discussion Summary

In spite of the desperate conditions in the developing debtor countries, most of the participants concluded that there would be renewed interest on the part of multinational corporations and more importantly, an enhanced contribution of multinationals to the rekindling of development.

As Chandra Hardy pointed out, multinationals need the Third World because of what is happening in the United States:

U.S. multinationals need the Third World. The trends in this country will force us there. The United States is restructuring from the smokestack industries, textiles, and shoes where we can no longer compete with foreign producers. These industries will have to go abroad.

Furthermore, I must dismally point out that the United States is now the world's largest debtor country. In a few years, this country will owe more to the outside world than the entire debt of the developing countries. Unless something dramatic happens to reduce our current account deficit, the United States debt to the outside world will exceed a trillion dollars in five years. That debt will have to be repaid.

Recognizing that U.S. private business and multinational corporations will have to go abroad, companies need to plan those activities and adjust their products and processes to meet the demands of the host markets.

INTERACTION BETWEEN MNCs AND LDCs

There was a rich discussion of the nature of the interaction between the multinational corporation and the host gov-

ernment. Some participants saw a promising future. Others believed that host country negotiations had lost sight of development.

Alejandro Foxley anticipates a more realistic investment environment as a result of host government experiences with the debt crisis:

The foreign investment issue is going to be much more qualitative than quantitative in the future, particularly for Latin America. What the countries will expect from foreign investment is some net contribution in terms of technology introduced and the opening of new markets. Latin American attitudes today are very different from what they were twenty years ago. Contrasted to the ideological bias against foreign investment of those years, today there is much more pragmatism. First, there is a realistic view that foreign investment is not going to solve the debt problem in terms of capital contributed. Second, Latin American countries now know that they must be selective. Foreign investment can be justified only if it contributes some of the very scarce factors that we face under the constrained developmental process.

Andy McCollough described the interaction in a market context:

The less-developed world is a heterogeneous mix of countries. Multinational corporations (MNCs) react primarily with the first or second economic tier of those countries.

It is difficult to generalize why less-developed countries (LDCs) in general are in the market for multinational corporations. The expectation on the part of the government (ignoring the political ramifications) must be that the results of the multinational location or relocation would be an improvement in the economic conditions for the citizens of the country. The LDC must envision that these economic conditions will be related to the capital, technology, and foreign exchange brought to the country and more recently, revenue contributions to the debt servicing process. LDCs will shop in the multinational market for a particular type of firm, depending on the needs of the particular country. Hence, it is a compartmentalized process where the country looks for those MNCs that meet its specific needs.

From the MNC side, the incentive for entry or expansion is the business potential. The MNC is not in the market to alleviate the economic conditions, or the poverty, of the country within which it might locate. It is conscious, or attentive, to the problems of the debt overhang of the particular host country only to the extent that these factors are related to the business dimension. The business environment can be articulated in terms of specific characteristics such as reliable labor, local supplies, governmental regulation, and political stability, or in terms of risk and return. However measured, the incentive set that is going to be offered by the LDC has to be responsive to those needs or desires of the MNC—that is, they have to offer something that impacts on the business measures of risk and return. Clearly, as indicated by Roy Crum, the incentive to be offered should be aligned with the country's objectives.

A dominant factor in this interaction is power. At the time of negotiation, the balance between the LDC and the MNC is typically one of unequal power. For the LDC, the usual opportunity cost statement is either the MNC with which they are negotiating, or none at all. Alternatively, for the MNC, it is "this LDC or some other." As the power balance shifts after entry, negotiating positions will change suggesting that it would probably be useful somewhere in the incentive set, if not in the negotiations, to subject the original set of incentives to review at some time in the future.

Paul Streeten argued that the interaction between the multinationals and host governments should be targeted toward "disarmament—a reduction of suspicion on both sides for mutual benefits."

Multinational corporations are always caught in a dilemma that comes from the high perceived risk associated with Third World investments. In addition to the standard economic risks, multinationals are concerned with the possibility of expropriation, the risk of not being able to repatriate profits, and a whole range of additional conditions imposed by the government on multinational corporate operations.

If the multinational perceives a high risk, they will demand a higher rate of return. If, *ex post,* the return is as high as expected, they will then either repatriate this profit or reinvest it in the local economy. If repatriated, the multinational will be accused of damaging the nation's balance of payments. If the profits are plowed back into the local economy, the multinational will be taking over a larger portion of the domestic economy through expansion, or through the purchase of local firms. This also alarms the host government. The answer is to reduce the suspicion and risk—to lower the required rate of return. This will eliminate the motives for expropriation and restrictions on the part of the host country, and produce benefits for both sides—like disarmament.

José Otaduy introduced the interaction between the multinationals and host governments with the legend of the fox which concludes "no more foxes with promises."

In the current Third World situation, facts are not very good and promises not much better. When a multinational enters or expands in a developing country, it promises employment, decentralization of the economy, regional development, taxes, the development of local suppliers, and on and on. It poses an ideal list that every government would accept.

How does a company negotiate this presence with the government? In most cases, these negotiations parallel a mutual kind of seduction. One side promises something and the other one grants a concession, then the other side offers a concession for the first side to promise something, and the result is an endless list of promises and concessions.

After the multinational makes the investment, all things come out very differently because neither side can possibly comply with the pyramided promises. The result is great disappointment on both sides and often a terrible divorce.

Take, for example, an agribusiness project brought to a small Third World town. The multinational becomes extremely important economically and therefore extremely important politically. Many stakeholders get into the picture. Unions are formed. Suppliers unite. The local government grows in importance. The federal government watches cautiously. As unions are formed, there is much greater local political leadership built upon added economic activity. The federal government does not want that local competition. All of the stakeholders' demands cannot be met.

This does not mean the central government or the multinational corporations were insincere in granting the concessions or making the promises. There is a political chain that is forged through the investment that puts the government in a difficult situation, finally forcing actions that it had not envisioned.

A concern was expressed that current negotiations between multinationals and host governments have lost sight of what development is all about. Denis Goulet stated:

The terms in which the question of the beneficence of multinational corporations in the developmental process are posed have been radically changed since the early 1970s. At that time the question was simple, "Do multinational corporations contribute to development?" Development was understood to be much more than just aggregate economic growth. It included social equity questions and a respect for sovereignty, at least normatively if not descriptively. The negotiations that I read about these days seem to be based on a mutual-gains model in which the host country negotiators have given up, or suspended, developmental goals. Their objective is now to seek income for debt servicing.

In the 1970s, there were four clear advantages that were putatively argued as coming from multinational investment. Multinationals brought capital, they created jobs, they provided technology transfer, and they opened up access to markets. I have often argued that these reputed contributions were overstated. Nevertheless, they were still central concerns on the part of host government negotiations. If one analyzes the contribution, multinationals do not bring much capital, they use the capital that is there. They create some jobs that were not there, but the issue is what alternative number of jobs might have been created and distributed with a more labor-intensive technology. As for technology transfer, the aspirations of the Andean Pact countries, even Mexico, Argentina, and India, in the late 1960s and 1970s, were for technology transfer beyond a geographical movement across their borders, to the eventual transfer of the capacity to generate new technology. That requires some research under the control of indigenous people.

At the present time, it appears that host countries are basically not negotiating with a view of using multinational potential contributions to promote development. Countries are focusing on the much narrower objectives of generating revenues or promoting exports for debt service. It is as though we are talking about rekindling development in a climate where nobody really wants to.

There was surprising agreement on the loss of developmental initiative on the part of host governments, but disagreement over the past multinational contributions to development, particularly as to the importance of jobs created and technology transferred. Ted Moran responded:

I believe you are largely correct in your observation that development is presently being defined fairly narrowly as a contribution to economic growth. Part of this narrow focus is a more realistic appraisal of what corporations can be expected to do. Multinationals employ about four million people across the world. Now, suppose that in a new international economic order, corporations were able to double their labor intensity by changing technology and hired half again as many people. That would be two million people across the Third World. That is just one good suburb of Mexico City, and will not make a significant difference in employment.

As for the transfer of technology, there is some truth in the statement that technology transfer is a contradiction in terms for multinational corporations. Multinationals will transfer some management skills because they need them, and they will train some people, many of whom will move to other firms or spinoff as competitors. As for technology itself, multinationals would be expected to keep control of their technology and would not attempt to spread it to others. It does no good to rail against these firms' attempts to control their own technology.

Ted Marks saw the host country objectives in a time frame.

The immediate problem is the tremendous debt overhang. The people who have the authority in government are not going to be there very long, and they must address the most critical issue—debt. Given its immediacy, we want to invite corporations who will assist in handling that debt.

For the longer term, employment and technology is important. Four million people is a very large number in itself. Beyond that, these are four million trained people in the working population. And, there are great ripple effects through the community.

Nicolas Barletta cautioned about expecting too much from a single corporation or a single policy.

We tend to expect too much from a single instrument. While an instrument may contribute to growth, we often want it to do all kinds of things for development. That is nonsense. With the present debt overhang, the first order of business is to obtain capital and exports (as supported by technology) to deal with the crisis.

Dennis McCann was concerned that the group had not thought through its basic paradigm.

The disturbing paradigm which gets in the way of our attempts to gain a thick description of the situation is that of strategic gamesmanship. It is clearly evidenced in the papers by both Ted Moran and Paul Streeten. Strategic gamesmanship is built around zero-sum games, win-win games, lose-lose games, and the tendency to see everything in strategic terms.

There is an implicit moral assumption in this kind of strategic thinking. The relationships within the game are fundamentally adversarial and the rewards of the game go to those who are most efficient and shrewd in maximizing their self-interest narrowly conceived. We must be cautious of this moral assumption regarding a set of relationships that are necessarily adversarial. We must realize that we live in a world of interdependence, and that we are all in this together.

Glade's metaphor of the rituals of reconciliation fit the notion of interdependence. In supporting this new paradigm, however, I would support maintaining the fiction of the debt. We know that for rituals really to work, the tokens of the ritual must be credible. This extension of the Glade discussion would lead us to greater flexibility regarding debt repayment, but it would involve some repayment.

A third paradigm was Caron's alcoholic metaphor. Extending that paradigm, credit must be identified as the source of the problem, not governmental policy. Following the metaphor, debtor countries must break all ties with the credit if they are to be cured, and step into the world of Richard Webb. Moderation simply will not solve the problem. If every country were to take this radical approach, the international credit system would be closed down.

PROTECTION VERSUS SUBSIDIES

Moran's statement that subsidies should be preferred to protection engendered a good deal of discussion. Howard Harris argued against both:

We focus on the economic situation and what we have to offer. We are not tempted by a governmental official who states, "If you'll do this for us, we'll give you a break." It is not special favors for multinationals, it is a good business climate that dominates.

McCollough described the governmental strategic choice between protection and subsidies in terms of minimizing market distortions:

I am concerned with the incentives being offered through the limitation of competition, as opposed to other, unspecified financial incentives.

We must recognize that multinationals have a population of alternative possibilities. For each location, the firm must perceive that there is an expected return in excess of the return required for the risk being assumed, in order for it to be a viable alternative. The host country, then, has to undertake some kind of strategy that will influence the multinational perception, or the reality.

The two basic governmental strategies are to limit competition, or to provide some other type of incentives. Both of these would, in an efficient market sense, be a distortion of the market, and thus disturb the optimal allocation of resources.

In analyzing these alternatives, then, Moran has suggested a preference not to limit competition because that distortion would be evident to the local populace and consequently could be politically unpopular. He seems to suggest that the other set of incentives might be chosen on the basis that part of the cost to the others could be shifted to a third party such as the World Bank or the International Monetary Fund.

Marks noted the movement toward greater market pressures.

There has been a shift over time from closely controlled, if not completely monopolistic or oligopolistic, multinational situations to a much more competitive situation in agribusiness, the chemical, and in particular, the pharmaceutical industries.

WHAT SHOULD BE ASKED OF THE MULTINATIONAL
CORPORATIONS?

Throughout the discussion, a concern was expressed that we might be asking too much of the multinational. Jean Wilkowski noted:

Multinational corporations invest in Third World countries to make profits, not necessarily because they are driven by do-gooder impulse, or to correct the debt situation.

Streeten argued:

It is dangerous to charge multinationals with social welfare objectives. Capitalists are not in the business of promoting common welfare or pursuing social purposes. Multinationals should be seeking the profits. The community, the state, and the laws should set the framework, the constraints within which these multinationals operate. Firms themselves should not be charged with promoting the common welfare. Macro policymakers should judge social welfare and set the rules. Companies should not place themselves in the position of judging that welfare. It could be counterproductive—encouraging inflation—or lead to a small labor aristocracy.

John Gilligan addressed the civic responsibility of business:

While I agree with the assertion that corporations are in business to make profits and not to conduct social welfare programs, they are still charged to have a sense of civic responsibility, whether they are operating in Akron or Addis Ababa. This is more than vocal support, they must attempt to implement policies and programs in regard to their employees, local community, and so forth.

Multinationals need to evidence a real concern for the well-being of the social structure, the entity into which they have moved and to which they are making a contribution. Far too frequently, multinationals perceive themselves to be victims in a situation where they are compelled by the bottom line, and by the shareholders, to make moves of one kind or another with little or no regard for the consequence to the community.

PART V

A Strategic Time for Change

LEE A. TAVIS *

The debt of Third World countries has imposed harsh conditions on the people and brings their economic and political
future into serious question. Given the interdependence among
countries, an interdependence heightened by the debt crisis,
the vulnerability of debtor developing countries becomes the
vulnerability of the developed world's financial system.

The deliberations presented in this volume show how a
diverse group of observers view what is going on in Africa,
Asia, and Latin America in light of the debt overhang and the
need to reactivate development. The complex intertwining of
issues and the constraints on the various actors—the debtor
nation governments, the various groups within each of the developing countries, the creditor banks, creditor governments
and societies, and the international financial institutions—have
been analyzed from different perspectives.

Throughout the crisis, the international financial system
has demonstrated surprising resilience, far more than many of
us would have imagined. It has survived with remarkably few
changes in the regulatory context and no changes in structure.
The key to the process has been the formation of banking consortia negotiating in close coordination with the International

*Lee A. Tavis is the C. R. Smith Professor of Business Administration
and director of the Program on Multinational Corporations and Third World
Development at the University of Notre Dame.

335

Monetary Fund (IMF). These groups brought order to what could have been a chaotic situation. Debtor countries have been willing to negotiate individually with these consortia and with the IMF as the lead creditor. The banks have essentially self-policed their own debt reserves, staying one step ahead of the regulators who, it must be said, have taken a remarkably lenient view of the quality of the loans in the banks' portfolios. In the process, the short-term interests of the banks have been well served.[1]

The present rescheduling process has been dubbed "muddling through." It is a test of power between debtors and creditors negotiated in a market environment, but a market that is neither competitive nor efficient. Debtor countries are acting alone, while creditor banks, at least initially, behaved as a cartel.

There is presently no motive for the individual banks to shift strategies. Indeed, individual bankers really have no alternative at this point but to continue their attempts to reduce exposure. Marks outlines the factors in the U.S. credit markets that draw bankers to concentrate at home. These pressures along with the push from the Third World encourage their strategy to reduce the developing country exposure:

> The environment in which banks operate in this country has not only presented opportunities for these banks, as John Caron noted, but much more intense competition than ever before. Foreign banks, such as the banks of Japan own, either entirely or substantially, many large banks in California and on the East Coast. Moreover, competition is no longer just among banks. Savings and loans have been given greater authority, and deregulation has allowed credit unions to invade what used to be the province—almost monopoly—of the banks. Investment bankers, by their dealing in commercial paper, can more efficiently transfer credit from a corporate provider to a corporate borrower. These other financial intermediaries have substantially reduced the role of commercial banks in normal consumer trade, and working-capital financing in this country. This has resulted in a major structural change for commercial banks.[2]

For U.S. bank regulators, Third World loans are problem loans, along with credits in the U.S. for energy and agriculture. With the low overall quality of loan portfolios in U.S. banks, the regulators have been pressing for a higher ratio of equity to debt.

Regulators have been hesitant to require that banks "write down" the value of Third World debt on their books in spite of the abundant evidence that it is not worth its face value. There are deep discounts in the secondary markets for this debt. Schemes such as the bond for bank debt swaps initiated by Mexico take place at significant discounts. Even though these markets are thin and discounts vary substantially over time, the depth of these discounts indicates real values well below book. Rescheduling itself is a recognition that these loans are not worth face value. Still the "writedown" of loan book values has not yet been required for a major debtor country. If the regulators were to require "writedowns" of major debtor loans to values approaching their present market values, most major creditor banks would be under severe capital adequacy constraints and others could be technically bankrupt.

The increase in loan loss reserves in the spring of 1987, initiated by Citicorp and followed by most other major banks, probably forestalled a regulatory requirement to decrease the book value of these loans. This was an insightful strategy for the banks since a potential loss reflected in a reserve does not technically impair a bank's capital adequacy as loan loss reserves are not deducted from capital when evaluating a bank's capital adequacy.

Debtor country governments have few strategic alternatives. They were initially subjected to classic IMF austerity, and then to the IMF's new conditions of structural reform. They have three options: to continue to act within the existent rescheduling arrangements and conditions, to attempt to cushion themselves from the international financial system, or to separate themselves completely from the system.

Most countries have opted to work through the rescheduling scenario, exerting whatever individual advantages they have. In the seminar, there was strong support for debtor strategies of focusing on the real productive dimension as opposed to the financial dimension of development, and on the mobilization of domestic savings to finance that development. Some concluded that this would necessarily mean partial withdrawal from the system. The Peruvian approach was viewed by some as the best alternative,[3] although it was noted that few countries had opted for that strategy.

There was no support among the participants for a debtors cartel, although we were surprised that there has not been more collaboration among the debtor countries. Foxley argued that a debtors cartel has not formed because until recently countries have believed that the cost would be too high.[4] He points out that a debtors cartel has been opposed politically by both the authoritarian regimes and by Latin America's new democracies, but for different reasons. Authoritarian governments want continuing contacts with the developed countries as their principal source of outside political and economic support. The new democracies maintain these contacts due to a political concern for the economic disruption that could be caused by a sudden break in the flow of credits. The latter argument has become much less persuasive, however, with the decrease in the flow of new credit since the end of 1984 and the general impression that banks will not voluntarily renew the flow for most borrowers before the end of this decade, if then.[5]

A TIME FOR CHANGE

There are two reasons to change the current rescheduling-based adjustment procedures operating in the structure of the international financial system. Indeed, they are the most convincing reasons to change any system: It *should not* continue; It *cannot* continue. The first is an issue of imbalance in the system; the second is an expression of fact. The present pace of debt service cannot continue because there are no more economic resources in the Third World to support it. The present vulnerability of the Third World will become the vulnerability of the First World international financial system.

The Adjustment Process Should Be *Changed*

As a result of the debt crisis, the gap in the standard of living between the developed and the developing world has widened, and there are implications in the present policies of debtor governments that will slow future social and economic development. Developing countries have lost ground and the burden of this has fallen most heavily on the disadvantaged. The wealthy and the upper middle class have access to mechanisms such as capital flight through which they can at least partially hedge the impact of austerity. Further, although the real incomes of many in the middle class have undoubtedly fallen, in some cases appreciably, a fair number have at least been able to hold on to their posts in the public bureaucracy or their positions in the professions as a means of riding out the storm, notwithstanding the economic hardship that has been visited on their peers who are proprietors and managers of local businesses.

The workers and the poor, however, do not have access to the kinds of hedging mechanisms available to others, nor the reserves, meager though they may be, with which the relatively more privileged have been able to cushion their fall. It is little comfort to the Mexican worker who has lost 40 percent of his real wages to point out that some of what he is losing was a benefit of the credit-induced growth. Unfortunately, the evidence, fragmentary as it is, suggests that the poor did not accumulate anything during the boom years, but that does not protect them from paying now.

Henriot and Jameson trace the impact of austerity on the poor, reporting criticism that austerity programs were imposed in a fashion that has special implications for the poor of the LDCs, as well as for a portion of the middle class.

> Currency devaluations increase the cost of imports, such as food, and of imports essential to developmental projects, such as oil. When combined with a reduction of subsidies and with wage controls, the resulting increase in the costs of food and transportation directly reduces the real income. . . . Imposition of wage controls and elimination of price controls cut workers' ability to meet basic human needs as prices rise and purchasing power is cut. Increased taxes, when levied on consumption or as value-added taxes, increase the cost of meeting basic human needs. Reduction of governmental spending lowers social services, food subsidies, and public employment—on all of which the poor and working classes are disproportionately dependent.[6]

That the poor should not bear the weight of correcting the debt imbalance has been a repeated theme in this volume. This requirement is based upon a well-established component of both secular and religious values. "When people are in need and cannot help themselves, others in a position to help incur the responsibility to do so."[7]

In addition to the immediate hardships imposed on the poor, many of the debtor country adjustments will prove counterproductive in the long term. This is not to say that the changes in governmental policy associated with austerity and the newer conditionality were not necessary—many were. Exchange rates had to be devalued, capital flight and corruption had to be addressed, parastatal assets had to be made more productive. But for other policies, a high price will eventually be paid.

The present debtor trade surpluses are more a result of reduced imports than enhanced exports.[8] Many of these imports are essential to industry and their reduction will lead to declining productivity over time. The drive to enhance exports may lead to the decrease of labor intensity in the export sector in order to compete on the international markets. This has long-term employment impacts. A shift from indigenous agriculture to cash crops for export leads to the displacement of indigenous farmers and a major change in the social fabric of rural areas, offsetting the potential for increased productivity and foreign exchange earnings.

Debt-for-equity swaps, while they may decrease the debt overhang in the short run, unduly reward nationals who have rushed their capital out of the country as they buy back in at a dual discount.[9] When these assets are purchased by foreign owners, countries will end up with foreign ownership of a much larger share of local industry. While this foreign ownership could well have a positive impact on productivity, it goes against most host governments' preferences.

The excessive emphasis on the short term has precluded a consideration of the long-term implications of present governmental policy. While short-term emphasis is a problem with most planning and control systems, in this case, the long-term implications of present governmental policies do not seem to enter the decision process at all.

There has also developed a fundamental imbalance in the role of the international financial system. The goal of economic activity is to enhance real output. The financial system is intended to service this goal by allocating resources to their most productive use. In the present adjustment process this hierarchy has been reversed. The requirements of the financial system are determining the possibilities for the production system. Glade wonders why we continue to subordinate real variables to financial variables in handling external debt.

> At the center of this approach is recognition of the dual, almost schizoid, character of modern economic organization, which, in capitalistic societies, derives its dynamics from the interplay between two quite different sets of phenomena: the pecuniary and the real. . . . One is almost tempted to reach back to the analogy of Plato's cave, with monetary variables serving as the shadows of the more substantive real variables of land, labor, capital, and entrepreneurship. Relations between the two sets of phenomena are, however, more complexly interactive than the Platonic metaphor suggests. As Keynes made clear in his analysis of the Great Depression, the monetary shadows that flit across the market wall of a capitalist economy are not merely projected images of the real but are quite capable, if left to their own devices, of exercising a devastating control over the realm of real resources—a relationship that would have seemed bizarre or even perverse to Plato.
>
> If the world learned anything from the experiences of the 1930s, the lesson might be summed up as the primacy of the real. That is, the participants in the national economy need not subordinate the organization of the real factors of production to the peculiarities of monetary dynamics. . . . The same lesson was brought home by the remarkable post-war recovery of Germany and Japan, where the financial systems—and a great deal else—lay in ruins, but where the primary policy targets were set on real variables and financial requisites were then mobilized accordingly. . . . we have not yet begun to apply the same insight, at the international level, to Third World debt.[10]

Webb describes the Peruvian efforts to separate the real from the financial in their attempts to stimulate development cushioned from the international financial system.[11]

"Muddling through" has led to an unjust allocation of the adjustment burden, to debtor strategies that will hamper development in the long run, and to a situation where the financial system has taken on an importance of its own. Muddling through *should not* be allowed to continue.

The Present Adjustment Process Cannot *Continue*

The international financial system has been tested since 1982 as it lurches from minicrisis to minicrisis with each renegotiation. It has demonstrated surprising resiliency. Terrell demonstrates how U.S. banks have dramatically reduced their exposure to non-OPEC developing country debt since 1982—a decrease in the ratio of total exposure to market valuation of capital from 330 percent at the end of 1982 to 129 percent in June 1986.[12] Still, progress within the system should not lull us into complacency. As one reads about the nature of the crisis, and the impact of present adjustment as outlined in this volume, one is stopped by Curtin's statement: "The debt crisis which erupted on the front pages of our newspapers in August 1982 was sudden in its appearance; however, its arrival was understood to be inevitable."[13] One wonders if we are missing the obvious signals of an impending second debt crisis.

Future challenges may be greater than those of the past. The Third World is against the wall, as Foxley bluntly portrays.

> Latin America has reached an impass. After five years of harsh adjustment programs, the prospects for economic growth in the major debtor countries are far from promising. Current projections, based on an oil price of $18 per barrel and interest rates around 8 percent, show a likely rate of GDP growth for the rest of the decade of not higher than 3.7 percent per year. At this growth rate, Latin America would be barely recuperating its pre-crisis levels of GDP by 1990. A full decade of growth would be lost. Moreover, given this growth rate and a labor force that grows at more than 2 percent per year, the employment prospectives for the rest of the decade do not look favorable. Total external debt would reach $480 billion by 1990. The debt-export ratio would still be, on average for the region, higher than 300 percent and, by some estimates, Latin America would still be needing something on the order of $30 billion a year in net capital in-flow.[14]

There is a link between austerity and political stability. While austerity policies have triggered riots in a number of countries,[15] there is a broader and more subtle erosion of political legitimacy:

> Recurring economic problems and stabilization programs may lead to a decline of what political scientists have called "diffuse support." Healthy and vibrant political systems rely on widespread acceptance of the basic institutions of the government and a prevailing belief in the general legitimacy of the political order. When this kind of diffuse support wanes, sectors of the society begin raising serious questions about the legitimate authority of the regime. Under these circumstances, the willingness of the citizenry to accept the institutions of the state—ranging from elections to law enforcement to tax collection—declines and the potential for sweeping political instability rises.
>
> Prolonged adherence to austerity planning, therefore, can undermine "diffuse support" and contribute to a deepening legitimacy crisis, at the same time that it weakens the state administrative apparatus and undercuts policy innovation. This combination of rising opposition and a weakening state can be quite combustible. Persistent political instability is a likely result.[16]

The present economic stagnation and the promise of persistent instability in debtor countries will surely lead to more serious challenges of the international financial system. Although there is no consensus as to the severity of such future challenges or to the system's ability to respond, there is acknowledgment that the international financial system is at serious risk.

NEEDED CHANGES IN THE SYSTEM

If the present rescheduling-based adjustment procedures should not and cannot continue, planned change is in order. There was strong uniformity among the participants as to what needs to be accomplished. Barletta said it well:

Adjustment is needed, but it can be achieved more effectively over a longer period of time through growth and human development. It would be self-beneficial as well as morally right for developed countries and the international financial community to now give the financial and the trade support required as a complement to the efforts of the indebted countries. The developed countries would gain in trade, financial stability, reduced immigration, and world stability. These are not insignificant gains. Developing countries should not be forced to choose between servicing external debt or providing for the welfare of their people.[17]

Given the complexity of the system, the many parties with opposing views, and the potential costs that must be part of any reformation, the key to the future lies in discussion and planning during a period of relative calm—not in the power-based relationships of isolated groups in an emergency.

There is a call for the provision of greater flexibility for debtor governments to apply individually what they have learned about development over the past decade. This must be spurred by policy changes in the International Monetary Fund (IMF) and the process must be supported by new funds flowing to those countries. There is also the need to deal with the present debt overhang through repayments, guarantees, or some form of forgiveness. The needed flexibility, the provision for new funds, and the reduction of the debt overhang must somehow be supported by an international financial system that can maintain confidence through the many different adjustments that will be required.

Experiences in attempting to impose the IMF conditionalities have provided valuable lessons to developing country governments which need to be applied in the future. Short- and medium-term adjustments have to be coordinated with long-term strategy.[18] Policies cannot be conceived as a purely macroeconomic process without due consideration of their effect at the micro level. Dramatic cuts in governmental budgets force the suspension of necessary investment projects and the reduction of social services needed to protect low-income groups from the worst effects of recession. The combination of tight domestic credit policies and the liberalization of the foreign exchange market are likely to induce capital flight.[19]

While the IMF played a valuable role during the crisis, preventing the collapse of the international financial system, the nature of the conditionalities it has imposed on debtor countries does not allow for the individuality of developmental needs for each country.[20] Typical austerity conditions are seen as contributing to political instability and having dire implications for the poor.[21] The specified periods of adjustment are too short and the IMF credits have been too small. IMF targets are in need of frequent revision due to the inability of most countries to meet them, and the interruption of the flow of external funds which accompanies these negotiations produces a climate of uncertainty.[22]

Although recent changes in the IMF programs suggest that it is reacting to the criticisms of its conditionalities, there is a serious question as to whether the underlying "market model" of these programs is suitable in the context of many of the debtor nations.[23]

Although the IMF has been broadly criticized for its role to date, the multilateral institutions are still seen as central to any real progress for the future.[24] However, the need for modification goes well beyond changes in the IMF to a broad reform of the international financial system. The criteria to be met by any systemic change include:

1. A more equitable sharing of the adjustment costs.
2. Reinitiation of the flow of credit and capital to developing countries.
3. Restructuring of local economies with a focus on long-term economic and social development.
4. An international financial system that can react in an orderly manner to more serious challenges than those posed so far.

In this kind of circumstance where costs must be allocated among stakeholders with such different worldviews and utility functions, there is a clear advantage to a comprehensive approach that embraces the widest possible range of issues. In these circumstances, agreement is much more likely when multiple rather than single issues are involved.[25] Moreover, if systemic change is called for, the full range of involved parties should participate in the discussion.

An approach to reforming the international financial system must thus be comprehensive—comprehensive in terms of the parties to be included, and comprehensive in terms of the issues addressed. Korth frames a solution which is "comprehensive, integrated, well-coordinated, and long-term." His solution would deal with the dual issues of relieving the present debt overhang and ensuring a flow of funds for future development.

As a means of easing the debt overhang, Korth outlines concessions that must be made by each actor and recommends that other private-sector resources be mobilized.[26] Debt rescheduling would form the heart of Korth's comprehensive package with rescheduling arrangements requiring a major sacrifice from the creditors through longer rescheduling periods, inclusion of all debts, the capitalization of past-due interest, reduction of lending spreads (perhaps retroactively), and the elimination of rescheduling or refinancing fees. Guarantees and judiciously applied subsidies would be provided by international agencies and First World governments. As the banks cooperate with the comprehensive solutions negotiated by their governments, auditors and commercial bank regulators must ensure that the banks are not penalized. A private-sector program for guaranteeing new loans modeled after the Foreign Credit Insurance Association would bring additional resources to bear. The securitization of loans would reduce risk for individual banks as loans are packaged as portfolios and sold on the secondary markets. Adjustment programs such as those required by the IMF should be continued but not in a way to hinder the creative steps taken by debtor governments.

Against these program components directed to the relief of the debt burden, Korth recommends three steps to ensure the flow of new funds for development. World Bank resources would be increased so that the Bank can expand its programs of funding developmental projects for commercial as well as non-commercial countries. The IMF should receive additional capital and begin to borrow on the private markets. Both the IMF and the World Bank should issue guarantees of new loans to provide developing countries access to the private financial markets.

Korth's recommendations would deal with the first two criteria (equitable sharing and reinitiation of flows). The long-term developmental impact would depend on the enlightenment of the participants to the negotiations—flexibility provided to Third World governments and the ability of these governments to apply the lessons learned in the past decade. In total, the Korth package should reduce the risk to the international financial system.

Some proposals are more modest than Korth's, others more dramatic.[27] A number of suggestions include an explicit cap on debt service, perhaps tying the cap to exports. Webb outlined the Peruvian unilateral adoption of this approach.[28] Sachs has established a formula for debt relief, tied to debtor country declines in per capita income.[29] Other proposals would extend the Korth recommendations by calling for new international institutions. Foxley, for example, would create a Latin American Development Fund.[30] Meissner would create an International Reserve Bank to provide balance-of-payments loans in conjunction with the IMF and the World Bank.[31]

Each of these proposals could be set against our four criteria, with some serving more effectively than others. The real issue at this juncture, however, is not which change in the system will be the "best." The real issue is: How will the "best" solution be decided? How will the tradeoffs as to whom will bear what costs be worked out? How will the preferred option be selected and where will existing or new institutions fit? We need now a mechanism for discussions and negotiations to decide these issues.

There have been numerous requests for dialogue on the issue forthcoming from groups in the Third World, proposals that have received a cool reception in the developed countries.[32] The ministers of the intergovernmental group of 24 on international monetary affairs, for example, have repeatedly called for such a dialogue. In a meeting on September 26, 1987 they stated:

> An effective solution to the debt problem transcends the financial sphere itself and can be found only through increased concerted actions by, and cooperation among, the parties involved.

The group of 24 has already insisted on the need for an expanded dialogue among industrial and developing countries and has proposed different sorts of initiatives. This dialogue is needed now more than ever. A real concerted effort is required to remove the prospect of a deadlock and to pave the way for a cooperative solution to the debt problem.[33]

Webb notes how difficult a task it will be. He sees an ideological block on the part of bankers to a comprehensive solution:

A general or comprehensive solution runs counter to a practical rule that is close to ideology: Problem borrowers must be dealt with on a case-by-case or ad hoc basis. With general rules, a bank gets swamped. With an across-the-board solution, banks give up much more than they would by dealing with difficult debtors one by one.[34]

The task is momentous[35] and must be undertaken in a period of relative calm rather than in the midst of the next crisis. We need a moving force to draw the key parties (debtor and creditor governments, multilateral financial institutions, and the commercial banks) into a dialogue. That force should come from the banks.

IMPLICATIONS FOR MULTINATIONAL BANK AND CORPORATE STRATEGIES

The debt situation in the Third World has wreaked havoc for U.S. multinational manufacturers, agribusiness, resource firms, and service companies, as well as for the banks. At this point, however, multinational banks and multinational corporations are in very different positions relative to alternative courses of action. Individual banks are seriously constrained in their debtor country activities—individual bankers have no alternative but to reduce their exposure of developing country debt. As an organized group, however, bankers have significant power to create change in the international financial system.

On the other hand, multinational corporations, although caught up in the financial and economic effects of the debt crisis, are not in much of a position to bring about change in the system but are individually much less constrained in their Third World activities. Multinational corporations do have a near-term future in the developing world and are in a much better position to respond boldly to the opportunities and needs of those countries.

Banker Strategies

In the rescheduling negotiations, banks have been successfully pursuing a power-based strategy. In a power-based strategy the institution pursues its own best interests, relying on its position of power relative to the negotiating opponent.[36] This power-based strategy has proven to be financially advantageous for the commercial bankers in the bilateral monopoly relationships of the rescheduling environment.

From the bankers' point of view, however, power-based strategies may have run their course. While there may still be some short-term gains, debt servicing, at best, will be slow. At worst, there will be a threat to the system, leading to massive losses borne unevenly by individual banks and revolutionary changes made in the midst of crisis. Decisions made in the time of panic will undoubtedly be tilted away from the banks with a demand that they share a greater burden than would be the case in an ordered restructuring of the debt, negotiated in a planning rather than survival mode.

Now is the time for banks as a group to shift to a participative strategy and as a group, bring pressure to change the system. Systemic changes are surely the most difficult to bring about.[37] Modifications in the international financial system require not only the balancing of the interests of various groups within a national regulatory context, but the balancing of interests for groups in one country with those in another when there is no international regulatory structure. It takes a great deal of conflict resolution and coordinated effort within each group, and a concentration of power to bring about change under these conditions. For the banks the coordination within the group has peaked. Cartels have a tendency to fall apart. For some time, the regional banks have chafed under the pressure of those at the money center to extend new credit. When Citicorp increased its loan loss reserves, it demonstrated its willingness to act alone. J. P. Morgan made arrangements to securitize Mexican debt without consulting other banks. These are not the joint actions of a cartel.

On the debtor's side, the less-developed countries have not yet formed a cartel. If Foxley is correct, the reasons for a debtor country to "go it alone" have diminished.[38] When debtor countries form a consortium, they will be combining sovereign power with their cartelized economic strength.

Individually, banks cannot implement a participative strategy. Managers of individual multinational banks have no alternative but to continue to reduce the exposure of their banks. With the pressures from the United States stakeholders on the commercial banks, the feasible region of decisions is very small. The pressures pulling them to opportunities and to counter-threats in the United States as well as those pushing them out of developing countries are strong.

As a group, however, banks are still in a power position to pressure for comprehensive change in the system. A key lever for the U.S. banks could be the United States government. Although our government has supported increases in funding for multilateral institutions and exerted its influence on rescheduling negotiations, it has been hesitant to assume a position of leadership relative to the debt crisis—perhaps because of the tie to our own budget deficits. Secretary Baker's "Program for Sustained Growth" presented at the 1985 IMF–World Bank meeting reflected a shift in the U.S. recognition of the problem, but not a major change in strategy.[39] The most positive specific step has been the Treasury's agreement to issue bonds for the collateralization of Mexican debt.[40] This is the first time that the U.S. government has directly participated in the financial arrangements. Still, it is leadership, not participation, which is needed.

At this time the practical response is also the ethical response. The ethical requirement to ease the burden of developing countries is also the one that would optimize the long-run returns for the banking group. However, this synchronization is transitory. In the next severe test, the banks will have far less power to influence the outcome, whether motivated by ethical considerations or by survival.

Multinational Corporations

The role of multinational corporations in rekindling Third World development is more through enhancing productivity in those countries than through the capital to be contributed. Even in the boom years, the private foreign-directed investment flow to the Third World was only around $4 million. During the credit-spurred growth of the late 1970s and early 1980s, foreign direct investment was dwarfed by private credit.

In a free market, technology and managerial skills will flow, along with capital, to those locations with the most favorable investment climates in terms of long-term risk/return characteristics.[41] Two factors affect these opportunities: the economic realities of the marketplace and government regulation. The political legitimacy of the government, its stability and continuity, influence both.

Multinational corporate economic opportunities begin with business conditions within the countries. The debt crisis has stifled economic growth for Third World debtor countries, casting a pall over their future. Foxley grimly outlines the present circumstances for indigenous business in Latin America:

> Adjustment policies during and after the debt crisis were characterized by reductions in investments of up to 30 percent and by the persistence of a recessive trend in the economy. For firms, this meant low sales levels and chronically idle capacity. Stagnation in sales weakens the ability of the companies to pay off debt. Recessive adjustment with restricted credit pushes interest rates up and sales down. This, in turn, sets off an *internal* debt crisis: Firms cannot pay back their credit and the proportion of banks' nonperforming loans goes up sharply, resulting in bankruptcy among some banks and financial institutions, and governmental intervention to stave off bankruptcy in others. Efforts to save productive firms from bankruptcy lead either to liquifying the debt through inflation, as in the case of Brazil and Argentina, or to repeated renegotiation of the debt with the banks,

as in Chile. In the latter case, the governments, through their central banks, subsidize the renegotiated interest rates and assume the exchange risk if, for any reason, the private debt is "dedollarized."[42]

Multinational corporate investment has reflected these local economic circumstances. As Moran notes, it has been cut by 25 percent. There is, however, the strong possibility that multinationals will respond positively to signs of recovery.[43]

For multinationals that strategically want to expand in developing countries, there is an unusual, perhaps fleeting, opportunity to share in Third World recovery through debt-equity swaps. The possibility of debt-equity swaps provides good financial buys of indigenous firms at prices significantly below initial asset cost and well below their replacement value. The economic value of these assets, however, is based on their ability to generate cash. In the case of the multinational corporations, the cash flow is in repatriated dollars.

In pricing the local equity the multinational must value the asset as it will earn after the multinational makes its contribution—capital for expansion, new products, productivity to the manufacturing process, and access to foreign markets—contributions not available to local firms, particularly in their present depressed circumstances. Where local assets can be synergistically combined with the multinational corporate contributions, asset values can be dramatically enhanced.

The multinational corporate interest in debt-equity swaps is different from that of the banks. Corporations are interested in productive investments and control—foreign direct investment. Banks are looking for enhanced market value of the swapped equity and will accomplish that through portfolio values.

Banks can now hold securities for five, and perhaps ten years.[44] The diversification of these portfolios, by industry as well as country, will increase the value of individual securities in more active secondary markets as banks liquidate their debt through debt-equity swaps. We can expect the shares of various indigenous companies to be traded separately and become components of numerous portfolios. Added marketability will aid in solving the banks' debt liquidity problem and in easing the debt overhang for the developing countries. For the multinational corporation, however, it means that the cost of buying-in will increase and the blocks of shares necessary for control will be less available.

In addition to the movement of equity into portfolios, another limit on the availability of indigenous equity for direct foreign investment will come from the debtor governments. While governments would not be alarmed at these equities held as portfolio investment, they may intervene to halt the denationalization of their economies through direct foreign investment.[45] Debtor countries are already demonstrating their concern such as the Mexican moratorium on swaps declared while the program is under "review" or Brazil's tight restrictions.[46]

At issue is whether the future of developing country economies will be different. The slow response of the international financial system to the obvious need for change in the adjustment process for Third World debtor societies is a major hindrance to the recovery of their private sectors. All the evidence presented in this volume points to the economic and ethical misallocations of resources associated with the IMF traditional adjustment programs, and the rigidity of the uniform structural adjustments required by the new conditionality.

A positive factor is that debtor governments have learned a great deal about how to manage their own economies over the past decade.[47] In the future, it is to be hoped that with less rigid conditions associated with servicing the debt, these governments can be expected to apply their own insight. Two dimensions of this new future are the move toward market-dominated developmental planning and the enhanced understanding of the potential contributions of multinational firms reflected in more enlightened regulation.

Developing country governments have learned to rely more on market mechanisms. Reliance on free market forces is seen as a means of preventing government from misjudging global demand and supply.[48] However, this does not mean a hands-off policy and the absence of governmental planning and regulation.[49] The reality of mixed economies in Latin America requires an active regulatory role for the government as well as the necessity of governmental intervention for the protection of the poor through vigorous social programs.[50] Chapman summarized the extensive seminar discussion on the role of the market in host government planning as "governmental planning with the market, not against it."[51] In the poor countries of Africa, market-oriented developmental strategy must be approached with great caution. The peasants and urban poor are much less integrated in the cash economy in Africa than they are in Latin America or East Asia.[52]

As governments move toward a greater reliance on markets in their economic planning, they will reduce the use of market exclusivity as a means of enhancing the "investment climate" for multinational corporations. While this may decrease excess local profits for these firms and, in a sense, lead to a less favorable investment climate, as Moran points out, it will surely enhance the firm's contribution to economic development.[53]

The nature of regulation could well change. Host countries have realized that foreign investment will not solve the debt problem in terms of capital contributed. As Streeten points out, they will become more selective and will expect from foreign investment sure net contributions in terms of technology introduction and the opening of new markets. They will be less concerned with the form a transfer takes and will place more emphasis on the conditions attached to the transfer. New and creative joint ventures—combining private and public capital and domestic and foreign capital—should be explored as host countries seek to channel the energy of multinational corporations in directions that will simultaneously achieve the host country's objectives.[54]

While host country regulation of multinational corporations is becoming more sophisticated, it is also becoming more realistic. The debt crisis has contributed to a less idealistic approach to the regulation of foreign investment, especially among Latin American governments. As those countries struggle with the opening of their product markets in competition with the international export markets, they understand more completely the risk/return characteristics of the marketplace.[55]

While the learning gained over the past decade is and will be reflected in realistic but sophisticated demands on multinational corporations by host governments, the multinationals are now in a much stronger bargaining position than they were a decade ago. Host governments need the contributions that multinationals can bring. Even though they are not a major source for new capital, the ability of multinationals to channel funds directly to productive uses in the developing countries was a contribution sorely missed as Third World debt accumulated, and would serve well the rekindling of development. In terms of our earlier distinction between the real productive system and the financial system, the contribution of the multinational reflects the correct hierarchy—its primary contribution is to real production with the flow of capital supporting this production. This productivity focus is the key to possible multinational corporate participation in rekindling development.[56]

Beyond the ability to enhance local productivity, multinationals provide access to hard currency markets for those locally produced goods.[57] Host government officials are presently pushing products through these channels by political strength, as a component of direct investment negotiations. As productivity increases, economic pressures will join the political push of goods through these multinational channels.[58]

The more realistic as opposed to idealistic recognition of potential multinational contributions will enhance the strength of the multinational at the bargaining table. How should multinationals wield this power? They can pursue power-based strategies that have been effective for some corporations in the past and are momentarily serving the bankers well, or they can pursue a more cooperative strategy by participating with host government officials to work out a role for multinationals that would optimize the long-term financial interests of the firm while contributing to host country development.

The nature of the negotiation interface between multinationals and host government officials is not encouraging.

Goulet argues that these negotiations have lost sight of development:

> The negotiations that I read about these days seem to be based on a mutual-gains model in which the host country negotiators have given up, or suspended, developmental goals. Their objective is now to seek income for debt servicing. . . . It is as though we are talking about rekindling development in a climate where nobody really wants to.[59]

Observing the interaction between multinationals and host governments, Otaduy notes:

> In most cases, these negotiations parallel a mutual kind of seduction. One side promises something and the other one grants a concession, then the other side offers a concession for the first side to promise something, and the result is an endless list of promises and concessions.
>
> After the multinational makes the investment, all things come out very differently because neither side can possibly comply with the pyramided promises.[60]

In spite of problems with objectives and promises in the negotiations between multinationals and host governments, participative strategies can serve the needs of both the multinational corporation and the nation state during the debt recovery. Interactions at this critical time for both parties are analyzed in the second volume of this series of "Multinational Managers and Developing Country Concerns."[61] The conclusions were that multinational power-based strategies were ill-advised in spite of the present power balance in favor of the multinational corporation.

Just as in the case of multinational banks, power-based strategies must rely on the continuing ability of the multinational to deliver effective rewards or penalties. Continued penalties tend to trigger disengagement, they would exacerbate the risk for the firm in what is already a tenuous economic and political environment. On the reward side, multinational power will diminish over time unless a continuous flow of valued new technology is introduced. And we know from experience that excess returns negotiated as a result of today's power will be renegotiated later.

Beyond the corporate inability to maintain the level of threats and rewards necessary for a power-based strategy to work, host governments, as emphasized throughout this volume, are far more sophisticated than they were during the earlier decades when many multinationals relied on power.

While individual multinational banks are caught up in a system where they have no alternative but to pursue power strategies, multinational corporations are not. Multinational corporations are closely tied to the future of the Third World by existing facilities and by the future need for resources and markets. These firms are in a position to explore new ways of participating in host economies and of interacting with host governments. They can take a longer-term view and a bolder stance—strategies that can gain through participation.

While there are gains to be achieved through participation, there are also costs and risks. Tavis and Glade conclude:

> Participative strategies are demanding of the firm. Proactive risks must be taken, information needs to be shared on a continuing basis with weak guarantees (especially in the law) that it will not be used against the firm.[62]

In this participative future, managers must be cognizant of the Goulet and Otaduy caveats. The multinational contribution is best valued as a component of long-term development, not short-term artificial growth, and unfilled performance promises will lead to renegotiation and cancellation.

Concluding Comments

Any analysis of developing country debt must begin with the poor people in these countries. They are paying a high price to service a debt they had little to do with, and from which they gained little. They should not and will not continue to bear this burden. The persistence of economic pressures on these people is unjust and is bound to cause political upheaval. The vulnerability of the Third World will become ours as their inability to repay becomes a determination not to repay.

This volume, reporting on a Third World debt seminar held at the University of Notre Dame, has traced the linkages from the debtor-country poor to the international financial system. Views expressed by the seminar participants are surprisingly uniform. There is full agreement about the severity of the impact on the lower- and middle-income classes of people in the developing debtor countries. The only real dissent centered on whether the poor would have lost ground even without the debt crisis.

It is clear what must be done to relieve the causes: Debtor countries now know what they must do; banks know they are pressing debtor countries to the breaking point but are not individually in a position to let up; the international financial system has demonstrated remarkable resilience but remains at risk; the IMF has moved beyond austerity in its imposed conditions but continues to be quite inflexible; the U.S. government needs to assume a strong leadership role.

The present process of dealing with Third World debt should not, and cannot, continue. Some movement must be initiated toward an ethically based structural solution where each individual recognizes the full extent of his or her responsibility and that of the institutions each represents. Banks and bankers should take the ethical lead in modifying the structure which, at this point, is also serving their enlightened self-interest of their institutions.

We have not offered a single best technical solution to the debt crisis. Indeed, whatever the solution, it will be a compromise arising from discussions among all the involved parties. It is argued that we need to get our objectives straight—an equitable balance in dealing with the debt overhang in the short term and the rekindling of development in the long term. Of immediate importance is to initiate a dialogue among governments, international institutions, and the banks.

NOTES

A number of participants critiqued this manuscript. Particularly helpful comments were made by Ken Jameson, Bill Glade, and Chris Korth.

1. Terrell demonstrates how banks have dramatically reduced their exposure to Third World debt since 1982 in spite of the deferral of payments. Henry S. Terrell, "Vulnerability of Multinational Banks," this volume.

2. Leonard Marks Jr., "The Retrenchment of Multinational Banks," this volume.

3. Richard Webb, "The Problem Is Adjustment, Not Debt," this volume.

4. Alejandro Foxley, "Latin American Development After the Debt Crisis," this volume.

5. Feinberg attributes this lack of a uniform approach to the fact that Latin American countries do not have a history of close cooperation and that major debtors such as Brazil, Mexico, and Venezuela want to take advantage of their own geopolitical positions. Feinberg also makes the interesting point that it is not only the central bankers and finance ministers of the debtor countries who would be expected to work cooperatively with creditors, but that many middle-class Latin Americans as well as the elite have participated in the flight of capital, giving them a "stake" in the strength of the dollar and the stability of the international financial system. Richard E. Feinberg, "Latin American Debt: Renegotiating the Adjustment Burden" in Richard E. Feinberg and Ricardo Ffrench-Davis, editors, *Development and External Debt in Latin America* (Notre Dame, Ind.: University of Notre Dame Press, forthcoming).

6. Peter J. Henriot, S. J., and Kenneth P. Jameson, "International Debt, Austerity, and the Poor," this volume.

7. This principle is well established in secular moral philosophy as well as in religious traditions across the world. Regardless of religious belief, we are all mandated to meet our obligations to society and particularly to the disadvantaged. Beyond that, the principle to aid the marginalized who cannot help themselves is a cornerstone of Judeo-Christian tradition and of other major religious traditions across the world. For an extended discussion of these notions, see Lee A. Tavis and William P. Glade, "Implications for Corporate Strategies," in Lee A. Tavis, editor, *Multinational Managers and Host Government Interactions* (Notre Dame, Ind.: University of Notre Dame Press, 1988). In pre-crisis times, this principle was at work between the affluent northern hemisphere and the poverty-stricken south. Since 1982, the imbalance has become more severe and the principle even more violated. See Lee A. Tavis, "Stewardship Across Natural Borders" in T. R. Martin, editor, *Stewardship: The Corporation and the Individual* (New York: K. C. G. Publications, Inc., 1983), pp. 74–88.

8. Jeffrey D. Sachs, "A New Approach to Managing the Debt Crisis," *Columbia Journal of World Business* 21 (Fall 1986): pp. 41–49.

9. See Foxley's comments in the discussion summary for Part 2, this volume.

10. William P. Glade, "Rescheduling as Ritual," this volume.

11. Webb, "The Problem Is Adjustment, Not Debt."

12. See Terrell, "Vulnerability of Multinational Banks." Friscia notes, "The lenders—commercial banks, the International Monetary Fund, the World Bank, international agencies—have greatly refashioned themselves for a new world of structural change and limited debt growth." See A. Blake Friscia, "The System is Resilient," this volume. Korth agrees with the process of the system but warns that there are still serious threats. See Christopher M. Korth, "Vulnerability in the International Financial System," this volume.

13. Michael E. Curtin, "The Role of International Institutions in the Debt Crisis," this volume.

14. Foxley, "Latin American Development After the Debt Crisis."

15. Henriot-Jameson, "International Debt, Austerity, and the Poor."

16. Rose J. Spalding, "The Political Implications of Austerity," this volume. Although Spalding shares the Henriot-Jameson concern that the threat of losing "diffuse support" might give pause to the new democracies of Latin America, she notes that it has been effective in bringing down some technocratic military regimes.

17. Nicolas A. Barletta, "A Time for Adjustment With Growth," this volume.

18. Guillermo O. Chapman, Jr., "Interlocking Time Frames: Adjustment, Structural Change, and Strategies," this volume.

19. Foxley, "Latin American Development After the Debt Crisis."

20. Ibid.

21. Henriot-Jameson, "International Debt, Austerity, and the Poor."

22. See Foxley, "Latin American Development After the Debt Crisis," and Kwan S. Kim, "East Asian Coping Strategies: The South Korean Case," this volume.

23. Henriot-Jameson, "International Debt, Austerity, and the Poor."

24. Summarizing a recent conference sponsored by the Interamerican Dialogue, Feinberg and Ffrench-Davis noted that some authors and commentators paint a picture of the IMF as rigid, ideological, dominated by the North—and as inducing unnecessarily costly stabilization programs. Others note that national governments house economists at least as competent—and more grounded in local realities—as those employed by the IMF. Still, Feinberg and Ffrench-Davis concluded:

> Even the more critical authors have not given up on the Bretton-Woods agencies. On the contrary, they would generally advocate increasing the agency's resources while altering their programs to make them more sensitive to the policy preferences of national authorities.

Richard E. Feinberg and Ricardo Ffrench-Davis, "Overview" in Richard E. Feinberg and Ricardo Ffrench-Davis, editors, *Development and External Debt in Latin America.*

25. This notion is developed in a previous volume of this series. Through the inclusion of multiple issues, zero-sum games can be converted to positive-sum games (Lee A. Tavis and William P. Glade, "Implications for

Corporate Strategies," in *Multinational Managers and Host Government Interactions*.) We employ this concept, recognizing that it reflects a "gamesmanship" strategy to which Dennis McCann has objected. (See Dennis McCann's comments in the discussion summary of Part 4.) Still, early in the negotiations, little more than a self-interest based approach can be expected. Perhaps, later, after the initial tensions subside, and interrelationships are fully recognized, we could move to another paradigm.

26. Korth, "Vulnerability in the International Financial System."

27. Bergsten, Cline, and Williamson analyzed twenty-four specific options for modifying bank lending practices. For each alternative, they (1) summarized the impact on debtor countries and on commercial banks, (2) analyzed the accounting and regulatory implications, and (3) evaluated the effects on the international financial system. Their categories include: restructuring policies already in use (9 options), a set of alternatives for the smoothing of payments for the capitalization of interest (7 options), options that link payments to a country's capacity to pay (4 options), and options for debt relief (4 options).

Their analysis provides a clear indication of what is involved with each of these alternatives. The analysis of the accounting and regulatory impact is especially useful. They posed the adoption of a rather modest set of their options to enhance rescheduling. In anticipation of a deterioration in the system, however, they proposed a set of contingency plans. C. Fred Bergsten, William R. Cline, and John Williamson, *Bank Lending to Developing Countries,* Special Report 10, April 1985 (Washington, D.C.: Institute for International Economics).

28. Webb, "The Problem Is Adjustment, Not Debt."

29. Sachs, "A New Approach to Managing the Debt Crisis."

30. Foxley, "Latin American Development After the Debt Crisis."

31. C. F. Meissner, "Debt: Reform without Governments," *Foreign Policy* 56 (Fall 1984): pp. 81–93.

32. For an excellent review of the case for an intergovernmental dialogue, indeed, for a review of the full debt problem, see Sidney Dell, "The World Debt Problem: A Diagnosis. Report to the Group of 24," *Studies on International Monetary and Financial Issues for the Developing Countries,* United Nations, UNDP/UNCTAD Project INT/84/021, January 15, 1986.

33. "Ministers Press for Rise in Financial Flows, Policy Coordination," *IMF Survey,* International Monetary Fund, November 2, 1987, p. 331.

34. Richard Webb, "Comprehensive Solutions: Needed But Not Likely," this volume.

35. Some authors have observed that the national limits on regulatory authorities, the technology of the international financial system, and the existence of lax regulatory environments make it virtually impossible to regulate international banks. See Donald D. Hester, "Time, Jurisdiction, and Sovereign Risks," paper presented April 10, 1987 at College of Business Administration Research Seminar, University of Notre Dame, Notre Dame, Indiana.

36. The implications of power-based strategies are outlined in Tavis and Glade, "Implications for Corporate Strategies."

37. The first volume of this series discusses the difficulties of analysis, agreement, and change at the systemic levels. See Peter J. Henriot, S. J., "Restructuring the International Economic Order," pp. 34–54; William P. Glade, "A Role for Multinationals: Multinational Firms and National Economies," pp. 102–111; Donald McNeill, C.S.C., and Lee A. Tavis, "The Nature of the Debate," pp. 254–264 in Lee A. Tavis, editor, *Multinational Managers and Poverty in the Third World* (Notre Dame, Ind.: University of Notre Dame Press, 1982).

38. Foxley, "Latin American Development After the Debt Crisis."

39. Curtin, "Role of International Institutions in the Debt Crisis."

40. Cf. "Morgan Bank Outlines Its Mexican Debt Plan," *New York Times,* December 31, 1987.

41. John B. Caron, "Entrepreneurs Go Where the Opportunity Is," and comments by Andrew McCollough in the discussion summary of Part 4, this volume.

42. Foxley, "Latin American Development After the Debt Crisis."

43. Theodore H. Moran, "Multinational Corporations and North-South Relations: Old Threats and New Opportunities in the Coming Decade," this volume.

44. *Wall Street Journal,* August 14, 1987.

45. Foxley was strongly critical of debt-equity swaps from the development viewpoint. See Foxley's comments in the discussion summary for Part 3, this volume.

46. Cf. Albert Andrew, "Mexican Debt Prices Fall on Secondary Market," *American Banker,* November 13, 1987, or Martin Schubert, "Trading Debt for Equity," *The Banker,* February 1987.

47. Foxley, "Latin American Development After the Debt Crisis."

48. See Barletta, "A Time for Adjustment With Growth," and Kim, "East Asian Coping Strategies: The South Korean Case."

49. Foxley, "Latin American Development After the Debt Crisis."

50. See Foxley's comments in the discussion summary for Part 2, this volume.

51. See Chapman's comments in the discussion summary for Part 2, this volume.

52. Kim, "Continuing Crisis in Sub-Saharan Africa," this volume.

53. Moran, "Multinational Corporations and North-South Relations."

54. Paul P. Streeten, " 'New' Directions for Private Resource Transfers," this volume.

55. Foxley, "Latin American Development After the Debt Crisis."

56. The capability of multinational corporations to enhance the productivity within debtor countries through the infusion of technology and managerial skills has been broadly, but not uniformly, acknowledged in this volume. Gilligan, for example, might agree with the possibility of contribution, but argues that a new global vision is necessary on the part of the

multinational corporation if that contribution is to be realized. See John J. Gilligan, "New Corporate Vision as a Prerequisite to New Directions," this volume.

57. The first two volumes in this series present the many nuanced views of multinational corporate contributions to economic and social development in the Third World. See *Multinational Managers and Poverty in the Third World* and *Multinational Managers and Host Government Interactions.*

58. See, for example, the negotiations between IBM and the Mexican government in Kenneth P. Jameson and Juan M. Rivera, "The Mexican Case: Communications under State Capitalism" in *Multinational Managers and Host Government Interactions.*

59. See Goulet's comments in the discussion summary for Part 4, this volume.

60. See Otaduy's comments in the discussion summary for Part 4, this volume.

61. Tavis-Glade, "Implications for Corporate Strategies," *Multinational Managers and Host Government Interactions.*

62. Ibid.

Participants

"Rekindling Development: Multinational Firms and Third World Debt," NOTRE DAME

Nicolas Ardito-Barletta

General Director
International Center for Economic
    Growth
Panama, Republic of Panama

Ernest J. Bartell, C.S.C.

Executive Director
Helen Kellogg Institute for
    International Studies
University of Notre Dame

Cesar A. Batres

Senior Partner
Batres y Asociados
Tegucigalpa, Honduras

Thomas A. Bausch

Dean
College of Business Administration
Marquette University

Jeffrey H. Bergstrand

Finance Department
University of Notre Dame

John B. Caron

President
Caron International

Guillermo O. Chapman,
    Jr.

Presidente
Investigación y Desarrollo, S.A.
Panama, Republic of Panama

Roy L. Crum	Director Center for International Economic & Business Studies University of Florida
Michael E. Curtin	Executive Vice President Inter–American Development Bank
Manuel Martínez Domínguez	Presidente Searle de Mexico, S.A. de C.V. Mexico, D.F., Mexico
Earl W. Doubet	President Caterpillar Americas Caterpillar Tractor Company

Alejandro Foxley	Helen Kellogg Chair in International
	    Development at Notre Dame
	President, Corporation for Latin
	    American Economic Research
	Santiago, Chile

Michael J. Francis	Chairman Government and International Studies University of Notre Dame
A. Blake Friscia	Vice President, Economics Group The Chase Manhattan Bank, N.A.
Yusaku Furuhashi	Dean College of Business Administration University of Notre Dame
Animesh Ghoshal	Economics Department College of Commerce DePaul University

John J. Gilligan	Director Institute for International Peace Studies University of Notre Dame
William P. Glade	Economics Department The University of Texas
Denis A. Goulet	O'Neill Professor in Education for Justice University of Notre Dame
Bernard J. Hamilton	President and General Manager Latin America & Caribbean Division American Express T.R.S. Company
William J. Hank	Chairman and Chief Executive Officer Moore Financial Corporation
Chandra Hardy	Senior Economist The World Bank
Howard F. Harris	Vice President, Corporate Affairs CPC International Inc.
Peter J. Henriot, S.J.	Director Center of Concern Washington, D.C.
Theodore M. Hesburgh, C.S.C.	President Emeritus University of Notre Dame
John W. Houck	Management Department University of Notre Dame
Kenneth P. Jameson	Helen Kellogg Institute for International Studies Economics Department University of Notre Dame

Maryann O. Keating	Economics Department Indiana University South Bend
Gerard M. Keeley	Executive Vice President American Security Bank, N.A.
Kwan S. Kim	Helen Kellogg Institute for International Studies Economics Department University of Notre Dame
Robert F. Kohm	Manager Environmental Planning & Analysis Aluminum Company of America
Christopher M. Korth	International Business Department University of South Carolina
Tang Thanh Trai Le	Law School University of Notre Dame
David C. Leege	Government & International Studies University of Notre Dame
Leonard Marks Jr.	Independent Director and Consultant
Dennis P. McCann	Director Center for the Study of Values DePaul University
W. Andrew McCollough	Professor and Chairman Finance, Insurance, and Real Estate Department University of Florida
Donald P. McNeill, C.S.C.	Director Center for Social Concerns University of Notre Dame

Theodore H. Moran   Karl F. Landegger Professor and
                                Director
                             Program in International Business
                                Diplomacy
                             School of Foreign Service
                             Georgetown University

José Otaduy   Senior Vice President
                             Coca-Cola Latin America
                             The Coca-Cola Export Corporation
                             Mexico, D.F. Mexico

Frank K. Reilly   Bernard J. Hank Professor
                             College of Business Administration
                             University of Notre Dame

Tony G. de la Reza   Presidente
                             Texaco Panama Inc.
                             Panama, Republic of Panama

John J. Ridyard, M.M.   Executive Director
                             INTERAID

Juan M. Rivera   Accountancy Department
                             University of Notre Dame

David F. Ruccio   Director of Latin American Studies
                             University of Notre Dame

John T. Ryan, III   Executive Vice President
                             Mine Safety Appliances
                                International

Roger B. Skurski   Director
                             Center for the Study of
                                Contemporary Society
                             University of Notre Dame

Rose J. Spalding Political Science Department
DePaul University

Paul P. Streeten World Development Institute
Boston University

Lee A. Tavis C. R. Smith Professor of Business
Administration
Finance Department
University of Notre Dame

Henry S. Terrell Division of International Finance
Board of Governors
Federal Reserve System

Edward R. Trubac Director
Center for Research and Banking
University of Notre Dame

Richard Webb Economics Department
Catholic University of Lima
Lima, Peru

Charles K. Wilber Economics Department
University of Notre Dame

Louis H. Wilking Executive Assistant, Group
Executive
Overseas Group
General Motors Corporation

Jean Wilkowski Chairman of the Board
Volunteers in Technical Assistance

Oliver F. Williams,
C.S.C. Associate Provost and Management
Department
University of Notre Dame